AF477679

Philosophy and the Return of Violence

Philosophy and the Return of Violence

Studies from this Widening Gyre

Edited By
Nathan Eckstrand
and
Christopher Yates

continuum

The Continuum International Publishing Group
80 Maiden Lane, New York, NY 10038
The Tower Building, 11 York Road, London SE1 7NX

www.continuumbooks.com

Library of Congress Cataloging-in-Publication Data
A catalog record for this book is available from the Library of Congress.

ISBN: HB: 978-1-4411-5272-5

Typeset by Newgen Imaging Systems Pvt Ltd, Chennai, India
Printed and bound in the United States of America

CONTENTS

Introduction

Christopher Yates

Turning and turning in the widening gyre
The falcon cannot hear the falconer;
Things fall apart; the centre cannot hold . . .
        —William Butler Yeats, "The Second Coming" (1919)

War is the father of all, king of all.
        —Heraclitus (ca. 500 BC)

Philosophy, like poetry, is sometimes occasioned by its time. Both consist in an inner drive to affirm and delineate the contours of higher, perhaps transcendent, truths. And yet there are moments in which the distress of a given age or the force of given events situate the muse of the poet and the task of the thinker in the ache and strain of his or her historical horizon. Yeats penned his verse in the grim aftermath of the Great War. Heraclitus, it is fair to surmise, conceived his metaphysical aspirations amid the strife of Asia Minor. Though occasioned by the concrete, such works are also tethered to their respective traditions (even at a point of origins), and lay an inevitable accent on the larger registers of the poetic and the philosophical. Yeats will ghost the verse of Auden; Heraclitus will worry the minds of Plato, Nietzsche, and Heidegger. In this way, the occasioned reflection bears both an outward and inward focus—there is an action on and in a historical moment, as well as an action upon and within one's community of discourse.

This volume is organized around the subject of "violence" at a time when the scope of violence threatens to widen beyond the reach of definition or deliberate philosophical concentration. Today one feels the reverberations of violence tumbling in and through the specters of genocide, racism, oppression, terror, poverty, sexual trafficking, abuse, addiction, and war. The term "violence," moreover, has been put to such extensive predicative use in the media, the humanities, the social sciences, and the ideologies of state rhetoric that it is difficult to fully identify or comprehend the manifold subjects that play host to its careening course. With the fleet of analytical tools available to us in this age of media and information, we are able to make empirical estimations that nearly overwhelm our capacity for moral reckoning and remedy. We can learn, for example, that 27 million persons are enslaved today, and that owing to the prevalence of debt–bondage arrangements, nearly 50 percent of forced labor victims are under the age of 18.[1] We learn that human trafficking is the fastest growing criminal industry in the world, that nearly 2 million children are trapped in the commercial sex trade, and that the market value of illicit human trafficking comes to no less than $32 billion.[2] We learn that an estimated one in every three women in the world, according to the United Nations, "has been raped, beaten, coerced into sex or otherwise violently abused in her lifetime," and that approximately one in five women "will be a victim of rape or attempted rape in her lifetime."[3] Fact sheets and rights reports inform us that illegal property seizure is rampant in Kenya, for example, and that 70 percent of India's prisoners, according to the British Broadcasting Corporation, "have never been convicted of anything."[4] American journalists, criminologists, and policy-makers consider the perplexing specter of a United States prison population that leaped from 319,000 in 1980 to 1.3 million in 2000, and a balance of federal corrections expenditures that rose from $541 million in 1982 to more than $6.9 billion in 2006.[5]

Alongside evidence of global injustices and astonishing domestic criminal data, there are pointed calls to address extraterritorial matters of torture and other human rights abuses. A 2005 U.S. Department of State report on torture ranges more than 160 numbered paragraphs, many of which are devoted to parsing the definition of torture as conduct "specifically intended to inflict severe physical or mental pain or suffering."[6] And the sentiment conveyed by U.S. President George W. Bush's 2003 statement that "[t]orture anywhere is an affront to human dignity everywhere" reflects a moral touchstone that Secretary of State Hillary Rodham Clinton echoes in her prefatory remarks to the *2009 Country Reports on Human Rights Practices*: "The principle that each person possesses equal moral value is a simple, self-evident truth; but securing a world in which all can exercise the rights that are naturally theirs is an immense practical challenge."[7] Compiling analyses of 194 nations, the report continues: "As we survey the world, there still are an alarming number of reports of torture, extrajudicial killings, and other violations of universal human rights. Often these violations relating to the integrity of the person are in countries where conflicts are occurring . . . In many countries, human rights defenders are singled out for particularly harsh treatment and, in the most egregious cases, they are imprisoned or even attacked or killed in reaction to their advocacy."[8] There is, we are told, "a larger pattern of governmental efforts to control dissenting or critical voices" that amounts to "a chilling effect on freedom of expression," and serves to mask the "escalating discrimination and persecution of members of vulnerable groups—often racial, religious, or ethnic minorities, but also women, members of indigenous communities, children, persons with disabilities, and other vulnerable groups that lack the political power in their societies to defend their own interests."[9] Such a diagnosis today is a rather even-toned way of recalling what Plutarch observed of Antiquity when, reporting on the Roman conspiracies of Anthony, Lepidus, and the young Caesar, he remarked that "they let their anger and fury take from them the sense of humanity, and demonstrated that no beast is more savage than man, when possessed with power answerable to his rage."[10]

By no means comprehensive, the above examples serve to illustrate not only the range of violence in our world, but also the manner in which a moral framework for critique and confrontation is readily assumed, indeed insisted upon, in the very reporting. What kind of entities, communities, or nations would we be did we not respond to savagery with abhorrence? But do we have appropriate and resilient intellectual and juridical bases for response? What are the discourses and traditions by which we understand, critique, and seek to redress manifestations of violence?

Sometimes a frank appeal to moral conscience and responsibility does provide traction for remedying the default preponderance of a violent state of affairs. Anthropologist David Kennedy, for example, has formulated an urban crime prevention strategy motivated in part by Immanuel Kant's conception of moral autonomy and committed to measures of what Kennedy calls "focused deterrence."[11] Working in conjunction with police departments and social-services agencies in cities as diverse as Cincinnati, Boston, Providence, Rhode Island, and High Point, North Carolina, his *Ceasefire* program centers on events called "call–ins"—local meetings in which known gang members are invited to a face-to-face gathering with police personnel and community leaders (often in a courthouse), are asked respectfully to "stop" committing crimes, and are offered various community service and job placement resources to ease their transition from the gang lifestyle. The strategy is by many counts successful. In Cincinnati, the local *Ceasefire* team saw a 50 percent reduction in gang-related homicides between 2007 and 2008.[12] Though urban areas are obviously diverse in both criminal challenges and social capital, the simple effectiveness of direct moral appeal, combined with the mobilization of available resources, has also won attention as a model for groups focused on redirecting the paths of potential young jihadists overseas.[13]

One could say that a similar deployment of moral appeal underwrites the larger discourse of "human rights" reflected above. The delineation of, and adherence to, an authoritative code of rights subsisting domestically and between nations is not only the living premise assumed by the U.S. Bureau of Democracy, Human Rights, and Labor in its annual human rights report, but is, of course, vital to the ongoing adjudication of the 1949 Geneva Convention accord concerning the treatment of prisoners of war. In recent years, however, matters of global security, enemy combatants, and the affiliated United States "war on terror" have laid a cumbersome and contentious stress on the strength of these and related moral appeals. How much violence is justifiable in preventing violence? Are so-called unlawful enemy combatants entitled to the same rights as conventional prisoners of war? Are the democratic nations of the West and the policy-makers of Washington, D.C., reliable spokespersons for the global interests in "freedom" and "security"?

As early as 2002, Judith Butler observes that the detention practices of the United States at Guantanamo Bay, Cuba, together with then–Defense Secretary Donald Rumsfeld's distinction between "prisoners of war" and "battlefield detainees," illustrate a troubling "manipulation" of Geneva Convention precedents and a cynical dichotomization of "the perspective of the civilized" and that of the so-called "barbaric other."[14] Butler contends that the Geneva accord has proven to be "based on an outmoded notion of war and soaked in bias toward the nation–state," which "makes it difficult for POWs who do not belong to recognized states with conventional armies to lay claim to protection under international law."[15] Her interest is by no means in defending programs or acts of terrorism, but rather in highlighting the escalating assumption that "[l]egitimate violence is waged by nation–states," that only "'[h]igh [p]arties' can legally go to war and deserve the human rights protections guaranteed by the Geneva Conventions," and that applying the category of "de facto, illegal combatants" to detainees likewise consists in a convenient division of the "inside" and "outside" under the guise of permissible protocols.[16] Guantanamo detainees, Butler notes, were rendered "outside the law, outside the framework of countries at war imagined by the law, and, so, outside the protocols governing civilized conflict." The abhorrence of "terrorism" notwithstanding, Butler holds that, by equating the term with "illegitimate" warfare, the Bush administration propagated the assumption that only those forms of violence committed by established states could be sanctioned, and that "the extraordinary character of terror justifies the suspension of law in the very act of responding to terror."[17] Beneath the rhetoric of freedom and security, and alongside a discourse of "human rights" susceptible to narrow interpretation, is the question of "who does and does not count as a human" and the authority of the nation–state to determine this matter, even in wartime.[18] Coincidentally, Butler's critique is to some extent echoed in the State Department's aforementioned *2009 Country Reports on Human Rights Practices*, which concedes: "[D]uring the past year, many governments applied overly broad interpretations of terrorism and emergency powers as a basis for limiting the rights of detainees and curtailing other basic human rights and humanitarian law protections."[19]

Though we cannot do justice in these pages to the complexities surrounding questions of human rights, terror, and crime prevention, their mention does impress upon us the range of social, political, and philosophical issues attached to the diagnosis of violence in our day. At the same time, they begin to illustrate the manner in which the analysis of violence, the strategies for mitigating it, and the viability of critiquing those discourses and their attending policies necessarily press us—as individuals, citizens, and scholars—back upon the terrain of philosophical reflection. Empirical data, anecdotal evidence, and social-political argumentation present us with pathways into the theme, but the fact remains that violence is not a subject matter reducible to a single medium of interpretation or a single academic discipline. It goes by many names, ghosts manifold discourses, and is manifest in numerous phenomena. Phenomenologist Bernhard Waldenfels observes that violence, in fact, "has many faces" and "seems to be something strange." That it is irreducible to a singular essence or nature only enhances the aporetic manner in which its appearance resists direct theoretical or practical confrontation. Waldenfels describes how such violence preys on vulnerabilities in orders ranging from law, morals, and politics, to technology, religion, and language itself. Its character, cruelty, and subtlety are cultural and symbolic, bodily and mental, private and collective, even anonymous.[20] Attuned to such modalities, it is not the assumption of this volume that there is some great malice or apocalyptic madness gathering into a global storm, or that a basic, discernable contrast between violence and nonviolence affords us with a ready grid for interpreting global events or ideas. Violence is as much at issue in the basic events of otherness between strangers as it is in the extraordinary hostilities of war and genocide. At times partner to rank evil, at times legitimated as necessary, the spectrum encompassing militance and just reprisal does not lend itself to ready measure.

Few thinkers have had understood the aporetic nature and force of this topic as acutely, or with as much influence, as Walter Benjamin. Written in 1921, his *Critique of Violence* contains an incisive prolegomena to breaching the ends–means cycle in which violence is traditionally understood and justified under the paradigms of law and justice.[21] Benjamin identifies the place of violence in natural law and positive law theories (as a "raw material" or as a "product of history," respectively), and highlights their shared assumption that "just ends can be attained by justified means, justified means used for just ends."[22] To critique violence, then, one must remove it from this cycle of justification by way of assuming the standpoint of a "historico–philosophical view of law."[23] By so doing, one learns that on the side of positive law, the difference between legitimate and illegitimate violent means is determined on the basis of their purported ends, and the chief end is "the law's interest in a monopoly of violence." Cases of individual violence, even potentially in the case of labor strikes, are, thus, treated as threats to the law, in which case, agents must be divested of their violent means by the sanctioned violence of the state.[24] No institution understands the "lawmaking character" of violence better than the state, and where the positive interests of nations are concerned militarism and policing claim a monopoly on violence, at least as an implicit threat, in order to protect the lawmaking and law–preserving functions.[25] This cycle is evident in the treatment of capital crimes, for, as Benjamin explains, "in the exercise of violence over life and death more than in any other legal act, law reaffirms itself." And yet, he continues, "in this very violence something rotten in law is revealed."[26] We have already glimpsed a recent formulation of this same concern in Butler's account of the Geneva accord and the "justified" violence toward Guantanamo detainees. The use of violence in the preservation of positive law, says Benjamin, reveals how law stands in an "ambiguous moral light." The regulation of conflicting human interests appears to operate intrinsically according to violent means.[27] Legal contracts, he admits, require a right to violence in their parties; parliamentary achievements, for example, are always already "in their origin and outcome are attended by violence."[28]

Such statements are indicative of the way in which Benjamin drives up the price of a genuine critique of violence, compelling us to appreciate how embedded the use or threat of violence actually is in the exercise of statecraft. Non-violence, accordingly, cannot be simply asserted, but must be advocated as an "unalloyed means of agreement" that obtains "in a sphere different from direct, legal means." To illustrate this change of standpoint, he refers to the function of agreement and resolution in the sphere of human understanding and language— where objects and goods, not lawful legitimacy, are the intended outcome.[29]

Returning to the political paradigm, however, it is evident that violence cannot be excluded in principle, since the security of the law depends on the option for a violent legal means. Moreover, beyond its appearance under the paradigm of legal theory and practice, violence also enjoys a *mythical* aspect at the very foundations of law.[30] For the ancients, for example, violence did not subsist so much in the realm of means to legal ends, but issued from the agency of divine justice and attached itself directly to "all divine end making . . . all mythical lawmaking."[31] What mythical and legal violence share in common, from the standpoint of a philosophical history of the theme, is that there is a deployment of violence (as threat, punishment, or both) on behalf of the law that effectively renders the law dependent on cycles of violence, and is, therefore, fragile or "alloyed" in its very constitution. If violence alone guarantees law, then the law is indirectly dependent on the very thing it fears. Consequently, perhaps the endgame of Benjamin's study is a break in the cycle of dependency—a break instantiated by the immediacy of "revolutionary violence" and/or a break anticipated in the coming of divine justice in the shape of a Messianic God.[32]

Points of contention notwithstanding, Benjamin's ground-breaking work set the stage for ensuing philosophical approaches to violence much in the same way as his historical moment stood not only on the heels of the First World War but also on the cusp of tremendous industrial, social, and military upheavals that continue to this day. The result is a continued period of overlaid oscillation between concrete occasions of violence and concerted efforts toward understanding and critique. It is in this sense that philosophy faces the return of violence, time and again. When, in 1934 for example, Simone Weil ascribed a state of "dizziness" and "disequilibrium" to a state of affairs she termed the "social machine," it was as though she beheld a situation in which the announcement of the "weeping philosopher" had solidified the predicament of the Irish poet.[33] A violent gyre was widening before her. For Emmanuel Levinas, the occasion of the Second World War and the totalitarian forces lingering in its wake rendered the twentieth century a time in which suffering and evil were "inflicted deliberately . . . in the exasperation of a reason become political and detached from all ethics."[34] For Hannah Arendt, this dizziness, disequilibrium, and detachment of a tumultuous age signaled, moreover, a force of debilitation against which philosophy must hasten to the call of "action," or suffer a world "doomed beyond salvation."[35] Alarming words uttered in alarming times. The Socratic conception of "justice" as a harmony of parts may well be true, but when a state of disharmony or discord arises violently, willfully, or even blindly—when, as Martin Luther King Jr. remarked, "Injustice anywhere is a threat to justice everywhere"[36]—philosophers such as these feel the burden of their age and are moved by an elusive yet unwavering necessity to forge a counterweight.

One recent thinker whose work is caught up in this movement in a pivotal way is Iris Young. Her "Five Faces of Oppression", for example, includes a rigorous clarification of the terms of critique that recalls the spirit of Benjamin's study.[37] Where Benjamin exposed the cycle of violence under patterns of law–making and law–preserving, Young positions a critique of oppression by exploring the manifestations of injustice in contemporary liberal society. The clarification of "oppression," like that of violence, entails the recognition that there is not one set of criteria for delimiting the matter. Accordingly, Young tracks the modalities of oppression in five categories—exploitation, marginalization, powerlessness, cultural imperialism, and violence—in each case citing oppression as a "condition" for the identification of certain social groups. Distinct from the traditional understanding of oppression as "the exercise of tyranny by a ruling group" or malicious "Other," this conception is alert to the more systematic, and at times subtle, constraints felt by groups that emerged as self-conscious social movements amid the developments of the "new left" in the 1960s and 1970s—activist movements among groups such as radical feminists, American Indians, African Americans, and gay and lesbian liberationists.[38] "In its new usage," she explains, "oppression designates the disadvantage and injustice some people suffer not because a tyrannical power coerces them, but because of the everyday practices of a well-intentioned liberal society."[39] Insofar as social groups are "forms of social relations" as opposed to substantial entities, they are vulnerable to the subtle yet insidious forms of oppression that emerge from within the "unquestioned norms, habits, and symbols" which constitute the "institutional rules" by which society abides.[40] Each of Young's categories qualifies as violence in the general sense we have employed, and each case also reflects on shortcomings in our contemporary understanding of justice. Much like Butler's alertness to the "bias" the Geneva accord shows to nation–states and conventional warfare, Young shows that the "social ontology underlying many contemporary theories of *justice* is methodologically individualist or atomist. It assumes that the individual is ontologically prior to the social."[41] The bias Young has in mind, then, is the tendency to focus on individual moral wrongs and, thus, overlook violence as "a phenomenon of social injustice," its "systemic character, its existence as a social practice." Oppression, in this way, must be understood as an offshoot of an overly subjective liberal ontology, and as bound up with the project of cultural and social self-interpretation. The systemic shape of the forms of violence Young has in mind, moreover, is not reducible to a manifest injustice that a "distributive" understanding of justice alone could remedy.[42] The confluence of what others call material and normative forms of violence poses a turbulence of oppression that static economies of justice and morality cannot abate nor explain.

Young's voice is one that reminds us of both the urgency of our subject matter and the depth of consideration required if one is to wager a critical interpretation of violence at its intersection with social life and political order. To set philosophy to the task of understanding and confronting violence is to engage an occasion confronting this age, and to simultaneously engage a tradition of reflection and critical methodology for which questions of peace, justice, and personhood are already vital. This task is obviously limited on both fronts. The philosopher, with important exceptions, is seldom a reformer, peacemaker, or advocate in any practical sense. Scholarship is usually not mistaken for social activism, nor typically credited with concrete gains in the economy of social–political utility. It does not pretend to mimic or attain the clarifying work of socio–cultural analysis, good journalism, daring humanitarianism, or legal legwork. But what the philosopher knows is that the distress of an age has very much to do with the ideas of that age—with the assumptions and terms that give rise to potentially scandalous ideology and rigid dogmatism. Citing the difficulties inherent in the relation between justice and violence at the end of the twentieth century, Jacques Derrida spoke of the necessity "to *change* things and to intervene in an efficient and responsible (though always, of course, in a mediated way), not only in the profession but in what one calls the city, the *pólis*, and more generally the world. Not, doubtless, to change things in the rather naïve sense of calculated, deliberate and strategically controlled intervention, but in the sense of maximum intensification of a transformation in progress . . . In an industrial and hypertechnologized society, academic space is less than ever the monadic or monastic ivory tower that, in any case, it never was."[43] Such change is necessary, but not easy. At times, it may well be an enterprise in freedom that is itself vulnerable. Arendt similarly indicated in her own moment of "intensification": "Unfortunately, and contrary to what is currently assumed about the proverbial ivory–tower independence of thinkers, no other human capacity is so vulnerable, and it is, in fact, far easier to act under conditions of tyranny than it is to think."[44] Whether philosophical thought is in fact imperiled by the same conditions that occasion it is a question only certain thinkers and their communities may answer. What is clear for the situation in which this volume finds itself, and the freedom its contributors no doubt embrace, is the basic notion that to work amid ideas, even to work selectively amid a tradition that formulates and wrestles with these same ideas and the discourses surrounding them, is in the very least to set a necessary work of reflection in motion. When the concrete "gyre" widens, as Derrida, Arendt, and others well know, so, too, do the assertions and responses of other thinkers of other times; and these questions attain a new vitality which the heirs of the philosophical "tradition" are equipped to meet and measure out.

Accordingly, the goal of this volume is to offer a compilation of some of the finest recent scholarship on matters provoked by questions of violence and nonviolence—philosophical work that is occasioned at once by the hard realities of our day, and by the sharpest implements of our tradition and its methods. The aim is, thus, a critique in a broad and two-fold sense of the term: (1) a critique that looks *outward* upon violent structures, events, and practices; and (2) a critical appraisal of those elements and ideas *in* the philosophical tradition itself that raise the thematic question of violence, or even enact a violent displacement of wisdom's proper course. Readers may expect to find in these chapters careful and insightful discussions of violence in the following modes: at the foundations of the political order, in the ambitions of war and peace, in recent and historical structures of power and discourse, amid the cultural and ethical tensions brought to the fore by globalization, and the scene of violence that arises in and through the basic phenomena of otherness and enmity at the ground of human identity. Common to each of the essays contained herein is, thus, a labor of reflection occasioned by the question of violence and conceived as a work of vital clarification that, in varying ways, means to stave off the entropy of thought in the widening gyre.

The discussion is organized into three sections. We begin with a group of papers exploring the intersection of philosophical vigilance, political necessity, and the precarious course of peace and justice. John McCumber's "Philosophy after 9/11" issues a resounding call for philosophy as a discipline, discourse, and community to feel the force of 9/11 not only as an historic event, but as a crushing blow to the illusions of philosophical autonomy. For all its horror, says McCumber, 9/11 compels philosophy to shift from the cultural and academic margins toward its more central vocation as a public, living discipline. If the Enlightenment devotion to freedom is now imperiled by charging fundamentalisms and lingering metaphysical dogmatism, it is for philosophers, precisely, to join together and take up what McCumber calls a *vindication of life*. In "Who Counts? On Democracy, Power, and the Incalculable," Dennis Schmidt begins to answer this very charge. His aim is twofold: to reckon with the present paradigms of "globalization" and "technologization" that pose novel problems of magnitude for democracy, and to delineate the crux of the historical-political problems that obtain under these paradigms. Schmidt asks: Can democracy today adapt its power and escape its totalizing tendencies such that the *singularity of the individual* is recovered and meaningfully sustained? A similar question could be asked of the tendency of modern republics, such as the United States, to trust themselves as the authors and arbiters of *peace*. Robert Bernasconi uncovers a historical and textual route to the heart of this dilemma. In "Perpetual Peace and the Invention of Total War," he captures the precise, if overlooked, place that universal history and cosmopolitanism occupy in Immanuel Kant's conception of perpetual peace, and indeed mark it with a troubling, and perhaps unintended, deferral of ethics in the face of necessary war. The result, Bernasconi explains, is a posture bent on enduring war fought for perpetual peace, letting loose the agony and horrors of war by couching them within a historical framework. Proximate to the appraisals of democracy and peace stands, for Simon Critchley, the abiding question of meaningful political engagement in an era of deep-seated antagonism. In his "Violent Thoughts about Slavoj Žižek," Critchley makes good on a sporting title by elaborating his analyses of authoritarianism and anarchism alongside Žižek's interpretations of objective violence and ideology. It is Critchley's view that the possibility of nonviolence on the subjective level and in anarchist politics can counter the deadlocked drift toward passivity in the face of systematic violence and political antagonism.

The second group of essays concerns the roots and events of violence at what we call the borders of enmity, otherness, and identity. Appearing for the first time in English translation, Paul Ricoeur's "Respect for the Other and Cultural Identity" is a an address given at the October 2000 Congress of the International Federation of Actions by Christians for Abolishing Torture. As a defense of *human dignity*, Ricoeur's discussion is not only "occasioned" in the terms we have alluded to, but takes as its theme the core tensions of personal and collective identity, and the violence inherent in the collision of ideology with personhood, otherness, and memory. It ends with a call for protest and action to oppose the inheritance of foundational violence. Echoing concerns similar to those of Ricoeur, in "Strangeness, Hospitality, and Enmity" Bernhard Waldenfels sets forth a provocative phenomenology of the violent tensions inherent in the experience of the *stranger*, both on a personal and collective level. He traces manifold figures, including the integration and neutralization of the strange in Modernity, radical strangeness, the ambiguity of the strange, iterative strangeness, as well as the issues of hostility and hospitality caught up in the cultural and emotional topography of otherness. Waldenfels' insights also raise for us associated questions of identity and personhood in this matrix of enmity and otherness. These questions comprise the starting point for Richard Kearney's insightful and personal summons to a pilgrimage of alterity and auto-critique in "Beyond Conflict: Radical Hospitality and Religious Identity." Situated against the assimilating tendencies of Jürgen Habermas's call for a discourse of public secular norms, Kearney highlights the constitutive role of alterity within (and not just between) religious traditions. So doing, he emphasizes the need to retrieve a work of translation within confessional self-reflection and interreligious dialogue—a form of *kenosis* that not only opposes factionalism and violence, but emerges "already" from the depths of religious belief. For Jeffrey Bloechl, the roots of normative order may also be exhibited in the underlying existential border–country that marks the very encounter of *otherness*. In "Towards an Anthropology of Violence: Existential Analyses of Levinas, Girard, and Freud" Bloechl asks: If the political order's effectiveness in surmounting the problem of violence can never itself escape the possibility of violence, then what basis remains for the urgent conceptual and practical work of peace? Framed by recent scholarly interests in the possibility for an eschatological ground for pitting peace against violence, he trains his phenomenological focus on the root relationship between excessive violence and humanity in the thought of three figures for whom the event of otherness captures the precise and volatile tension between the capacity for violence and the possibility of nonviolence. In view of the distinctly modern tendency to globalize concerns about violence under the auspices of "human rights," Peg Birmingham's "Agamben on Violence, Language, and Human Rights" invites us to consider, with Giorgio Agamben, whether such a discourse is not already prejudicial and, therefore, tenuous. Birmingham distinguishes the question of rights per se from the "declaration" of modern rights in order to underscore the problematic *logos* driving the political shape of the latter formulation.

By distinguishing, with Agamben, voice from speech, she charts the possibilities for a redistribution of "rights" discourse from its attachment to the central figure of the citizen to the limit figure of the refugee. This displacement toward the material dimension of language and the bareness of human experience enacts an exposure, as opposed to a declaration, of the ontological roots and communicability of human rights at the birthplace of the political and the origin of the contemporary subject.

The role of the political and the violence of *logos* in the question of rights make for a fitting point of departure for the four focused studies that comprise our final section on power, nonviolence, and discourse. In his "Violence and Nonviolence," James Dodd initiates an innovative approach to a question already lingering in many of the above discussions: What is the precise relationship between violence and nonviolence? Beyond a dualistic or basic dialectic configuration, Dodd demonstrates how the interplay between violence and nonviolence (indeed, the intrinsic if overlooked "force" of the latter) compels us overcome an over-reliance on "instrumental" distinctions, to explore the constitutive shape of violence itself, and ultimately to consider the underlying meaning of "world," within which conceptions of violence are framed. The complexity characterizing modes of violence, of course, begs the question of the basis and practicability of any "critique" of violence. It is with this question in mind that Johanna Oksala considers what the parameters of "A Foucaultian Critique of Violence" would entail. In a remarkable and judicious assessment of the thinker of archives and genealogy, discourse and power, Oksala distills the relevance of Michel Foucault's reading of historical and social–political practices to renewed methodologies of critique along two primary considerations: first, that violence must be analyzed in its historical and contingent modes rather than clouded by anthropological or essentialist assumptions; second, that violence is in fact associated with the ascendant modes of "rationality" and social "improvement" disclosed by Foucault, and thereby open to critique and change—if not to absolute renunciation. It is this second possibility for a Foucaultian critique of violence that is central to Peter DeAngelis's parallel study: "The Logic of Violence: Foucault on How Power Kills." DeAngelis tracks the Foucaultian analysis of power through its political rationalities, disciplinary power, and biopolitics in order to clarify not only Foucault's methodological developments, but also the emergent "logic" of violence interwoven with the intentions and exercises of biopower. In so doing, DeAngelis skillfully maneuvers us into the diagnostic core of Foucault's later work on strategies of rationality and power, such that we are introduced to the very work of critiquing mechanisms of violence enabled by Foucault's insights. It is with this renewed sensitivity to the concrete and discursive modalities of violence operative in modern rationality and power that we turn to the urgent question of social norms and human vulnerability. Finally, in her "The Remainder: Between Symbolic and Material Violence," Ann Murphy brings acute sensitivity and deft reflection not only to the facts of "material" violence and symbolic or "normative" violence, but to the contemporary problem of understanding their exact relation, without assigning temporal or ontological priority to either the normative or material realms. Drawing upon the analytic tools of Kant and Foucault to track this relationship in the work of Judith Butler's (as well as in the context of recent phenomenology), Murphy highlights the co-constitutive, though irreducible, nature of material and normative violence (and the symbolic complexity of their affiliate discourses). She contends that Butler's work, though varied, signals a crucial "remainder" within this intersection—a clear resistance to attributing outright inaugural or causal status to social norms in relation to discrete or ethical violence, and, moreover, a still deeper level of reflection on the relationship between normativity and ontology, violence and power.

It is by virtue of the singular merits of each of these essays that we are able to offer in this volume a contribution to the larger task of posing and treating the questions of violence. Our hope is that the reader will find this to be done in a manner equal to the restless resourcefulness felt by philosophy in an age that occasions concerted discernment.

In addition to this collection's generous cast of contributors, special thanks are in order for the advice and support given by John Sallis, Richard Kearney, Phillip Braunstein, and the philosophy departments of Boston College and Duquesne University. Mark Gedney of Gordon College, as well, deserves high praise for pulling translation duty on two of our texts, in two different languages; without his skill and discipline this volume would lack the pivotal contributions of Paul Ricoeur and Bernhard Waldenfels. The authors and publishers gratefully acknowledge the following for permission to reproduce and/or translate copyright material: Dennis Schmidt's "Who Counts? On Democracy, Power, and the Incalculable" appeared in *Research in Phenomenology*, Volume 38, Number 2, 2008 (Brill); Paul Ricoeur's "Respect for the Other and Cultural Identity" is used with permission from the International Federation of Actions by Christians for Abolishing Torture; the original French version of this lecture, "Fragile Identite: Respect de L'autre et Identite Culturelle," may be found at http://www.fondsricoeur.fr

Notes

1. International Justice Mission (IJM), *Fact Sheet on Forced Labor Slavery*, citing Kevin Bales, *Disposable People: New Slavery in the Global Economy*, and International Labour Organization, http://www.ilo.org/global.
2. IJM, *Fact Sheet on Sex Trafficking*, citing U.S. Department of Health and Human Services and citing UNICEF and United Nations.
3. IJM, *Fact Sheet on Sexual Violence*, citing U.N. Development Fund for Women and U.N. Millennium Project.
4. IJM, *Fact Sheet on Illegal Detention*, citing the *British Broadcasting Corporation*.
5. Seabrook, "Don't Shoot," 4.
6. U.S. Dept. of State, *Second Periodic Report of the United States of America to the Committee Against Torture*.

7. *Ibid.*, at note [1], from *President's Statement on the United Nations International Day in Support of Victims of Torture*, 39, U.S. Bureau of Democracy, Human Rights, and Labor, Preface, *2009 Country Reports on Human Rights Practices*.
8. *2009 Country Reports on Human Rights Practices*, Introduction.
9. *Ibid.*
10. Plutarch, *Plutarch's Lives, vol. 4*, 439.
11. Seabrook, "Don't Shoot," 5. See also Kennedy, *Deterrence and Crime Prevention*.
12. Seabrook, "Don't Shoot," 6. It is interesting to note that Cincinnati Police Department Lieutenant Colonel James Whalen, originally a skeptic, remarked in 2008: "We will never engage in this kind of gang work again without academic support . . . No police department should" (*Ibid.*, 9).
13. Seabrook, "Don't Shoot," 9.
14. Butler, "Guantanamo Limbo," 1–2, 3.
15. *Ibid.*, 1.
16. *Ibid.*, 3.
17. *Ibid.*, 4.
18. *Ibid.*, 5.
19. *2009 Country Reports on Human Rights Practices*, Introduction.
20. See Waldenfels, "Violence as Violation," 87–105.
21. Benjamin, "Critique of Violence," 277–300.
22. *Ibid.*, 278.
23. *Ibid.*, 279.
24. *Ibid.*, 281–282.
25. *Ibid.*, 283–284.
26. *Ibid.*, 286.
27. *Ibid.*, 287.
28. *Ibid.*, 288–289.
29. *Ibid.*, 289.
30. *Ibid.*, 293–294.
31. *Ibid.*, 295.
32. *Ibid.*, 300.
33. Weil, "Sketch of Contemporary Social Life," 29. The text is extracted from her 1934 *Reflections Concerning the Causes of Liberty and Social Oppression*.
34. Levinas, "Useless Suffering" in *Entre Nous*, 97.
35. Arendt, "Labor, Work, Action," 42.
36. King Jr., "Letter from a Birmingham Jail."
37. Young, "Five Faces of Oppression."
38. Young understands "groups" to be "an expression of social relations" and, thus, distinct from "aggregates and associations." A social group is defined "by a sense of identity" (*Ibid.*, 40–41).
39. *Ibid.*, 39.
40. *Ibid.*, 42, 39.
41. *Ibid.*, 42, my emphasis.
42. *Ibid.*, 57–58.
43. Derrida, "Force of Law," 237.
44. Arendt, *The Human Condition*, 324.

Chapter 1

Philosophy after 9/11

John McCumber

What Does it Mean to Philosophize after a Historic Event?

We philosophize today "after" many things: *after* the election of 2008, which began a new era in American history but came after the election of 2004, which pushed the United States and the world to a very dark place; *after* the collapse of communism in Eastern Europe in 1989; *after* the intellectual and other depredations of the McCarthy era; *after* the Civil War, the French Revolution, the Peace of Westphalia, the Council of Nicea, the crossing of the Rubicon, the Melian Deed. . . . Does any other discipline come *after* so many historic events?

What it means, in general terms, to philosophize after a historic event is a question I can hardly hope to answer here. For one thing, none of the task's terms has been defined. What is "philosophizing"? What does "after" mean here? What is a "historic event"?

I will begin with this last term. What makes an event historic? Was the impact of the meteorite that seems to have destroyed many dinosaur species 65 million years ago a "historic" event? Was the LeBron James trade to Orlando a "historic" event? Before an event can be historic it must first be historical, and the James example shows us that historical events never stand alone: an event gains "historicality" through its position in a meaningful sequence of events—a "history." However we specify what makes a sequence "meaningful," I claim James's trade does not stand in such a meaningful sequence and so is not historical, let alone historic.

We can say that an event is historic as well as historical if it affects the later history in which it is embedded, and does so in important ways. Not all historic events matter to philosophy. Though coming up with an example of one that does not matter is surprisingly difficult, I think it can be done. Lindbergh's crossing of the Atlantic, for example, changed the world in many ways, but not in ways that mattered much to philosophy. We can put this as follows: While we philosophize today *subsequent* to Lindbergh's flight, in the sense that it comes before us on the universal timeline, it does not affect philosophy in any immediate way and is not something philosophers must necessarily take account of.

Let us say that we philosophize "after" a historic event when that event changes philosophy itself. This means that it comes before us, not merely on the universal timeline but in a particular history—the history of philosophy. Since that history is longer than that of any other discipline (except poetry), we can say that philosophy (in its cumulative sweep) indeed comes after more events than any other discipline—though all disciplines are equal in the number of events to which they are subsequent on the universal timeline. The very fact that that there are historic events affecting philosophy makes some people uncomfortable. Individuals who believe that philosophy is an "autonomous" discipline, for example, often mean by this that it is, or should be, changed only by *philosophical* events—by the discoveries and innovations of philosophers themselves. Yet it seems obvious that historical events do affect philosophy: the death of Socrates, for one, inspired his young friend Plato to abandon tragic poetry and devote himself to philosophy. And who can say that Plato did not change philosophy?

This leads us to the final term that was undefined in my original question, "philosophizing." What does this involve? What, for that matter, is philosophy (other than just the results of philosophizing)? There are good reasons not to answer this question, as very serious damage has been done to philosophy in the last 150 years, and continues to be done, by people who think they know what it is well enough to exclude those who work on its margins. Philosophy is a type of discourse, and, as such, it has, like all discourse, various objects or themes. It follows that there are two ways in which historical events can affect philosophy: *indirectly*, through its objects or themes, or *directly*, by changing its very nature as a discourse which seeks wisdom about matters such as truth, meaning, and morality.

To philosophize after an historic event thus means that the event in question was historical, that is, it stood in a sequence of events; it affected the subsequent components of that sequence in important ways and, thus, was historic; and among the things it affected was philosophy itself, either directly or indirectly.

Indirect Effects of 9/11 on American Philosophy

Changes in philosophy can also be brought about by historical events, either freely or necessarily. If it means anything to say that philosophy is an autonomous discipline, it means that philosophers are free to determine what they will discuss. Historical events become philosophical objects or themes, affecting philosophy indirectly, only when philosophers choose to start talking and thinking about them. This does not mean that philosophers always eagerly seek out those objects or themes—often they discuss matters they would rather avoid. The most important recent case of this is the Holocaust. It is a painful and degrading topic, but philosophers were called upon to take it up by Emil Fackenheim after the Six Day War,[1] and to some extent they have.

Any indirect change in philosophy brought about by a historical event is then a free one in the sense that it comes about because philosophers choose to respond to that event by changing the topics of their discourse. Changes in philosophy itself—what I am calling direct changes—may be freely chosen by philosophers; but they can also be necessary, in which case the change comes about independently of the choices or the wishes of philosophers.

Several prominent philosophers, if not many, have indeed chosen to take 9/11 up as an object of reflection. The main examples known to me are Jacques Derrida's and Jürgen Habermas's interviews with Giovanna Borradori that were published as *Philosophy in a Time of Terror*, Judith Butler's *Precarious Life*, and the essays in Marsoobian's, Rockmore's, and Margolis's, *The Philosophical Challenge of September 11*.[2]

These are all important examples of how 9/11 changed philosophy indirectly by becoming a topic of philosophical reflection itself. They show philosophers choosing to respond to what could be called a historical imperative, one that can be articulated as follows: 9/11 began a national struggle with terrorism that is chiefly, as Richard Clarke has argued, a "war of ideas."[3] Whether we want to call it a war or not (another topic on which philosophers should be heard), philosophy has much to contribute to this struggle. Contemporary Islamic fundamentalism, for example, is hardly an ancient thing—or even, at bottom, a Muslim thing. As Paul Berman shows in *Terror and Liberalism*,[4] it appeals to ideas about nationality and religion that were first articulated by Fichte. In order to be effectively refuted, those ideas must be attacked where they first sprang up, that is, in philosophy.

One of the fronts in this struggle concerns a problem Socrates presented to the Athenians: that of the role of authority in human life. Should I simply do what the leaders of my family, nation, tribe, or religion tell me to do? Or should I consult my own critical reason, in what Kant called Enlightenment? This question, like other philosophical questions, is never definitively settled. if only because new forms and justifications for authority continually arise and must be continually defended against.

This kind of historically occasioned defending is, I take it, what the philosophers mentioned above are all doing in their responses to 9/11, in very different ways, of course. Their efforts contrast with what I am undertaking here in two ways.

First, 9/11 will only affect philosophy in this "indirect" way if philosophers want it to. The books I have mentioned show a small minority of philosophers *choosing* to make 9/11 a central theme of their reflections, and if we subtract the non-Americans the minority is smaller still. They could have done otherwise as many of their colleagues have done, turning a blind eye to history and to crises in the surrounding society and culture, which is nothing new in American philosophy. Where were American philosophers during the McCarthy era? Where were they when the Johnson and Nixon administrations consciously misused such concepts as "nation," "freedom," and "victory" to manipulate the United States in Vietnam? When Martin Luther King challenged America to "rise up and live out the meaning of its creed,"[5] where were the philosophers who undertook to explain what that creed entailed and why a creed needs to be lived out? The facts are that time after time, when their country has faced crisis, American philosophers have been missing in action. This is an important matter, and I will come back to it. For the moment, I am using it to illustrate what I take to be a *good* thing about American philosophy: that philosophers are free not to reflect on history if they do not wish to do so.

Second, none of the philosophers I have mentioned take 9/11 to require direct changes in philosophy; they all apply philosophical tools developed elsewhere to this new topic. What I want to argue here, by contrast, is that 9/11 is not merely an appropriate object for philosophical reflection, but that it also requires new philosophical tools, or new deployments of old tools. Moreover, 9/11 does this *necessarily*: the changes I have in mind will come whether philosophers want them, or choose them, or not. After that terrible day, the very nature of philosophy *had* to change, *will* change, and *has* changed.

First Direct Transformation in American Philosophy: A New Kind of Community

I will discuss the direct changes brought about in philosophy by 9/11 on two levels: that of the philosophical community (the group of people that does philosophy) and that of philosophy itself as a discipline with a particular set of goals and methods. This distinction, to be sure, is a tendentious one. It is traditional to claim that philosophical methods and the truths they arrive at do not depend on who is using them but are valid independently of culture and history. On this view, history cannot change the nature of philosophy itself, and the kind of reflection in which I am engaged here is misguided at best. It is also fashionable in many settings today to say that the goals, methods, and procedures of philosophy are nothing more than abstract ways of referring to the concrete discursive practices of a specific group of people, i.e. "philosophers." In that case, philosophy is bound to the cultures and societies in which it is practiced, and no part of it is ever unaffected by history. I am not going to worry about this very large issue because my present use of this distinction will be merely tactical; whether the distinction between philosophy itself and the community of people who do it is valid or not, I think it is appropriate for organizing my reflections. Ultimately the distinction will prove irrelevant. Even the most traditionalist reading of the nature of philosophy, one which seeks to exempt it utterly from the throes of history, cannot spare it from 9/11.

My claim at this point is simple: The philosophical community in which we have all grown up, and in which some of us have grown old, *no longer exists*.

An essential feature of that community was that it was isolated and marginalized within America. The degree of this was captured by reporter Michael Hill, writing in *The Baltimore Sun* on January 12, 1999, two and a half years before 9/11:

> In the last week of December, some of the top names in philosophy gathered here for the annual meeting of the Eastern Division of the American Philosophical Association. Were such a gathering to have taken place in a city in Europe . . . the

media would have trained their attention on the affair, eager to learn the thoughts of the educated elite.

But this convention passed, as it does most every year, with hardly anyone outside the prescribed limits of professional philosophy paying any attention. . . . Whatever these philosophers are saying, they are saying it only to one another. [6]

Hill was kinder than his *New York Times* colleague Taylor Branch, who in 1977 had compared the American Philosophical Association's Eastern Division meeting—the preeminent annual gathering of American philosophers—to the back lot of the zoo, where they keep the animals no one wants to see—kookaburras, emus, giant sloths, and the like.[7] Such isolation, though I have decried it elsewhere, was by no means wholly regrettable, for the autonomy of philosophy largely depended on it. It afforded philosophers a private sphere—what Richard Rorty calls an "enclave of freedom" within which they could do, or omit doing, whatever they wanted. A philosopher could spend a year, or even a career, on the finer points of some argument or text, worrying over it again and again with no worries that anyone would ever ask her what she was doing or why on earth she was doing it.

Halcyon days indeed, but they are over. 9/11 ended them. The events of that horrible day taught everyone anew ancient lessons about how precarious life and civilization are. In so doing it awakened many people to the need for careful, informed thinking about just those things—to the need for philosophy. The signs are growing that philosophy, often against the wills of its more prominent academic practitioners, is making a return into the public realm. Books of popular philosophy are selling well, "Socrates cafes" are burgeoning,[8] and as the *New York Times Magazine* documented in its issue of March 21, 2004, philosophical counseling is coming to be recognized as an important form of psychotherapy.

Philosophy is even more front and center since the election of 2004, for what is the red-blue split in America if not a *philosophical* split? It is not religious, as it is so often painted, because religion is found on both sides. It is about philosophical issues such as the role of religion in society, when life begins and how it should end, when war is justified, what degrees and kinds of freedom really matter to society, what marriage is or should be. Did not Barack Obama, himself a Blue Christian, repeat continually in the 2008 presidential campaign that the economic crisis in the United States is the result of a "failed economic *philosophy*"?[9]

What recent American politics has shown—I will talk in a moment about how the red-blue split relates to 9/11 itself—is that we are now coming close to Senator Daniel Patrick Moynihan's so-called nightmare: the specter evoked of a Congress debating philosophical rather than economic questions. It caused Moynihan great concern, as it should us. Do American philosophers want to stand by while Congress hashes out—and makes hash of—philosophy? Or do they want their voices and arguments to be heard? And what will they do when, as seems inevitable, they are consulted by various congresspeople trying to come up with the national answers to philosophical questions?

American philosophers remain free, of course, to avoid responding to this challenge; and, as I have noted, they have done so before. What is different this time is that ignoring the problems of the surrounding society will not enable philosophy to remain at the margins of American culture and society, for it will itself be a *public* decision. If philosophers shirk the challenge this time, the surrounding society will notice.

The other crises I mentioned—the McCarthy era, Vietnam, the civil rights struggle—were not overtly philosophical. Philosophers could have contributed to their resolution, but nobody asked them to and their absence was not noticed. The present construal of the red-blue split as religious in nature shows that philosophy's absence from American debates has still not been noticed. But it can remain unnoticed only as long as people see the split as between a religious red side and an irreligious blue side. Now that religious people on the blue side are beginning to make their existence known, that is already changing. Whether philosophers choose to enter public debates in response to Moynihan's nightmare, or prefer to continue pursuing their traditional kinds of issues, is thus irrelevant to the point at hand, which is that philosophy's "enclave of freedom" has *already* been definitively breached. Even if philosophers remain in their traditional seclusion, they will do so in a public way: they will have to build barricades around their comfortable "backwater." Philosophy's days on the margins of American culture have ended. Philosophers will be either central participants in American debates or central nonparticipants.

As a result of 9/11 American philosophers must not merely address topics they have largely avoided before, but become a different sort of community: one near the center, not at the margins, of the surrounding society. This amounts to a transformation in the philosophical community, but—to return to my tendentious distinction—not in philosophy itself. There is no demand that philosophy's tools and goals be changed. What has changed, radically, is the kind of community that makes use of them. But there is an even more disturbing pull for philosophy to transform itself. It is a pull that cannot be resisted and that imposes basic changes on the way philosophy itself is done by causing a second transformation in the nature of the American philosophical community.

Second Transformation in the Philosophical Community after 9/11

To understand this, we must first note that an event can be historic without making any great rupture with the past. Many (if not most or all) historic events are important not because they begin new things, the way a Kantian moral act does, but because they force into the open things that are already there—beneath the surface, so to speak, of the time. Historic events often *cause* changes in the behavior of individuals and groups, then, by *showing* underlying realities. This is the case with 9/11: it forced us to recognize the increasing disaffection of religious terrorists from the modernized portion of the human race. It did not cause that disaffection, but much of what it *has* caused—the curtailing of American civil liberties, Guantanamo, Abu Ghraib, the increasing disaffection of the United States from the rest of the human race—has come about because 9/11 made that other disaffection visible.

Many different things have been advanced as to those causes for terrorists' hatred of Americans; a hatred which runs so deep that individuals would rather die than allow the United States to continue on. They include sexual and political freedom, modern versions of Christianity and/or Judaism, wealth, Middle East policy, science, democracy, and capitalism. The list is strenuously debated. What is not debatable is that its components all have one important thing in common: each is largely a product of philosophy. Where would political and sexual freedom be without Locke and Nietzsche? Modern religion without Feuerbach? Wealth without Smith? Recent Middle East policy without Strauss? Science without Descartes? Democracy without Rousseau? Or, to be sure, capitalism without Marx? Where would any of these things be without Kant? And those are just a few examples! It would be very foolish to assume that religious terrorists the world over do not know this, or that they will not figure it out. Philosophy is not only a component in the struggle with terrorism; it is, or deserves to be, the number 1 target of the terrorists. This means that our part in the so-called struggle of ideas is not an option. The struggle is for self-preservation—"necessity" of the very rawest, and most stringent, kind.

What am I talking about here? Metal detectors at philosophical meetings? Conferences held on military bases? Police guards in front of philosophy departments? Philosophers with unlisted phone numbers, who constantly vary their route to work and dare not eat their lunch in the Quad? I don't *think* any of these things will happen. But, frankly, I cannot quite rule them out. Philosophers must therefore join the struggle of ideas; they cannot, this time, sit by and let history take shape around them, which would amount to collective, and maybe individual, suicide. In a life-or-death struggle, it is important to get a clear view of the enemy. I said that the red-blue split in America was a result of 9/11. Garry Wills made the connection clear in an op-ed piece in the *New York Times*:

Where [besides America] do we find fundamentalist zeal, a rage at secularity, religious intolerance, fear of and hatred for modernity? Not in France or Britain or Germany or Italy or Spain. We find it in the Muslim world, in Al Qaeda, in Saddam Hussein's Sunni loyalists. . . . It is often observed that enemies come to resemble each other. We torture the torturers, we call our God better than theirs—as one American general put it, in words that the President has not repudiated.[10]

Wills is arguing two things here. One is that what the terrorists hate is Enlightenment itself—the commitment to reason in private and public affairs which, since Kant's essay "What is Enlightenment?" has defined philosophy itself with fewer exceptions than we think, as I argue later. Wills's other point is that when we see 9/11 as an attack on Enlightenment values, we see that those values are threatened here at home as well as in the Muslim world.

What 9/11 forced into the open is a global backlash against the Enlightenment, one with different branches and essentially stretches from the Pakistan-Afghan border right into our own Bible Belt and beyond. When Jerry Falwell and Pat Robertson claimed that God allowed 9/11 to happen because America had given itself over to abortionists, feminists, gays, lesbians, and the ACLU,[11] they were merely showing their true affinities, for Falwell and Robertson have more in common with Al Qaeda than they do with the moderate members of their own Christian communion—just as Al Qaeda has more in common with the 700 Club than with standard Islam.

The Direct Transformation of American Philosophy after 9/11: The New Enlightenment

If I am right, 9/11 forced into the open a global war on the Enlightenment, which may come to include attacks on philosophy itself. A struggle for self-preservation has thus been imposed on philosophers by history. What must they do to win it? Here is where 9/11 forces changes in the nature of philosophy.

First, philosophers must articulate and defend the Enlightenment, in the traditional Kantian sense. What does it mean to say that we humans are free? Why is freedom a good thing? What are its proper limits? What happens if it leads to injustice or social disturbance? These questions have been long debated by philosophers, but today they need new formulations, for the terrorists pose them in a new way: why, they ask, is freedom—or anything else—*better than death*? If terrorists love death as much as we love life, as the Madrid bombers claimed, why should they not bring it to the rest of us? Aren't they doing us a favor?

Prior to any traditional defense of the Enlightenment we need what I will call a "vindication of life". This vindication is presupposed by the Enlightenment in the sense that someone who does not value life is not going to go on and subscribe to Enlightenment norms. It cannot, therefore, be carried out in a discourse that justifies itself solely by its conformity to such norms—the kind of norms exemplified in Habermasian claims of truth, social appropriateness, and personal sincerity.[12] Those norms themselves, as Habermas argues, must be validated prior to the discourse that explicitly operates in terms of them. Habermas seeks such validation in everyday language, claiming that those norms are implicitly appealed to by our every utterance in the life-world. But even that argumentation would not suffice here, for we are dealing with people who reject language itself, on the grounds that in order to talk you must be alive—and they don't want to be alive. They value not speech but instant communion with their God. Appeals to the life-world make no sense to those who seek only a death-world.

I frankly do not know what this philosophical vindication of life is going to look like. I do suspect that two of our main instructors in it will be Plato, who in the *Phaedrus* and elsewhere examines rhetoric as a necessary *supplement* to philosophical argumentation, and Nietzsche, who seeks to vindicate life not by supplementing Enlightenment (Habermasian) norms but by *countering* them with insults, jokes, fables, and other untrue, inappropriate, and ironical comments—all in the service of the revised version of Kantian critique Nietzsche called genealogy.

Defending the Enlightenment in the familiar sense of the capacity to make use of free and rational argument in public and private life only begins the struggle, for Enlightenment so defined does not stand alone. In order to flourish, it requires the services of two ways of thinking that are nonargumentative, and thus unfamiliar to many philosophers. These other ways of thinking can themselves be seen as forms of Enlightenment, but have often been viewed as its enemies. I have discussed them in detail in a number of places.[13] What I offer here is a highly compressed summary.

One of these ways of thinking is what I will call the Dialectical Enlightenment, originally instigated by Hegel. Dialectic, as I see it, is not a silly exercise in self-contradiction or historical mythology but a kind of thinking that reconstructs the unique histories of specific groups, and does so in a rational way. The rationality here consists in meeting two criteria, which can be roughly stated as follows:

1. No relevant facts pertaining to the history of the group are omitted from its story.
2. Those facts are arranged to tell the unified and coherent story of an ongoing development.

Since the transition from one stage of a story to the next can be called, in Hegelian parlance, a "negation" of that stage, such a narrative is structured by negations and so is dialectical. Why is such thinking needed? What is its point? The answer lies in a weakness of the Kantian view of Enlightenment (some would call it a crippling weakness). Kant's model for how judgments relate to experience is one of subsumption, in which an intuition—a representation of empirical reality—is "brought under" a concept. An engineer's judgment that a bridge can be built across a river at a certain point is a complex case of this. It brings the givens of riverbed and current, presumably as conveyed in a geological report, under the concept of bridge site. The aim of Enlightenment, as Kant understands it, is to make sure, by free and rational debate, that some given subsumption is correct: to determine whether a particular sentence is true or false.

In order to subsume something under a concept, we must assume that thing is static. For it is going to furnish the subject of our judgment, and if it is unstable then the subject of our judgment will be equivocal. If the riverbed is constantly changing, for example, then the engineer's judgment that this part of the riverbed is a good place for a bridge could refer either to the riverbed as described in the geological report (assuming the report described it correctly), or to the riverbed as it actually exists now, which may be very different.

This kind of thing causes trouble enough when we are talking about rivers and bridges; when we are talking about human beings the problem is exacerbated, often to an unbearable degree. For human reality is never—except perhaps under highly exceptional circumstances—merely a static set of states of affairs that passively await subsumption. Any human individual or group has its own ongoing dynamics and processes already underway. Any project, enlightened or not, is going to intervene in these processes: it is going to carry some of them forward and curtail or stymie others. In order to see, in a given case, whether this can or should be done, we must reconstruct the history of the group of people affected by the project. If, for example, the history of the people living near a proposed bridge can be reconstructed as a history of increasing commerce, building the bridge is probably a good idea. But if a more comprehensive reconstruction also reveals a history of increasing sensitivity to the natural beauty of the river, on the part of the local population, the bridge becomes more problematic.[14]

Human beings are always caught up in various and manifold developments, or histories. Any rational plan—no matter how "enlightened" the debates that produced it—must connect with those histories in certain ways if it is to be successfully introduced. A plan that results from free and rational discussion may still be the "wrong" plan if it does not intersect in the right ways with the ongoing developments taking place among the people who will be affected by it.

But how can we tell whether it does or not? We must reconstruct the history of the group, not merely by trotting out a lot of random facts about the group's past but in such a way that we can identify the processes underway in the group, and among those processes can further identify those that have historical staying power; those that are the most comprehensive and unified. It is with these processes that our plan must intersect rightly if it is to have a chance to succeed. A dialectical reconstruction of the kind I have sketched enables us to think clearly about that intersection. Enlightenment in the traditional sense— the free use of reason to decide upon action—thus requires Dialectical Enlightenment if it is to succeed. Otherwise it will produce plans that, however rational and otherwise meritorious they may be, do not connect with the people for whom they are made, and so will be rejected by them. We don't need much philosophizing to see why such thinking is needed; the United States itself has traditionally been rather unenlightened in this regard. Enormous national efforts, from welfare and urban renewal to Vietnamese and Iraqi democracy, have run into enormous trouble simply because the people involved in those efforts did not recognize the unique histories of the groups they were seeking to transform. Only the Hegel-based Dialectical Enlightenment, I suggest, can save us from further chapters in that sorry saga.[15] The Dialectical Enlightenment is thus a necessary part of Enlightenment itself. And it must be defended along with Enlightenment in the usual sense, for people who reject the results of enlightened discourse are unlikely to accept such discourse itself.

The third kind of Enlightenment that philosophers need to articulate and develop as part of the struggle with terror is what I will call the Meta-Enlightenment. Just as Dialectical Enlightenment seeks to connect us to history and the rational past, so Meta-Enlightenment seeks to open us up to the future. Under such guises as deconstruction, it is neither a silly exercise in global skepticism nor an anti-Enlightenment effort to undermine the basic norms of discourse. Rather, it is a relentless preparation for the possibility that all our certainties may be undone. It seeks to replace easy answers with tough questions, superficial clarity with profound puzzlement. Such puzzlement is not an intellectual game but necessarily accompanies every single proposition or sentence that is ever decided upon, argued for, or even entertained. No matter how well formed such a sentence is, no matter how clearly its terms are defined, there is something about it that we cannot understand except within very narrow limits, and that is its future: what will happen, or not happen, as a result of its being entertained, argued for, or decided upon. How could Plato know, when he articulated his theory of forms, that one obscurity in it—the precise nature of the relation between forms and sensibles, the meaning of the word "participation"—would be filled in by Aristotle's denial of the separation between forms and sensibles, thus launching philosophy, and indeed the entire Occident, onto endless new adventures?[16]

The possibility that one's thinking is defective is easily recognized in the abstract; various kinds of lip service to one's own uncertainties are practically de rigeur among today's enlightened thinkers. It is much less easy to track down, in a specific case, just *where* one's own views are most likely to be overturned or filled out in surprising ways. For that, we must develop an eye for the lacunae, the intractable obscurities, and the latent contradictions that haunt our discourse and which we ourselves cannot, or cannot as yet, remedy. As Derrida puts it, we must "aim at a certain relation . . . between what [the thinker] commands and what she does not command among those schemas of her language, of which she makes use. This relation is . . . a signifying structure which critical reading should *produce*."[17] Derrida's writings in general, along with the later works of Heidegger, can virtually serve as textbooks for how to go about this—for how to open thought up to the radical uncertainty of the future.

This third kind of Enlightenment thinking is painful if only because it requires us to locate the irremediable deficiencies in our own thinking. The difficulty of this is attested when Derrida, in words I elided from the quote I just gave, specifies that the relation between what an author controls and what she does not control in her text is "unperceived by the writer" herself. Derridean deconstruction is difficult enough; but it must be made even more difficult, for it must become self-deconstruction—or, as I call it, demarcation.

Meta-Enlightenment is necessary to the other two forms of Enlightenment. For to dispense with it is, intellectually, to deny the future. If we do that, then we are claiming either that things must always be as they are now, which is foundationalism, or that they must always be as they have been before, which is fundamentalism. Fundamentalism, of course, is not limited to radical Islam.[18] Fundamentalist approaches to Christianity, as I suggested earlier, differ from fundamentalist Islam only in details; both approaches seek to deny the future by carrying us back to the past. But the same basic mind-set, in the guise of foundationalism—the claim that some doctrine or other has been established definitively and so for all time—finds its way even into science, as the view that what science presently tells us about reality is the final word. As such, it is virtually endemic in philosophy itself. Even Kant, the founder of "critique," fell into it in his 1799 repudiation of Fichte: "The critical philosophy must remain . . . confident that no change of opinion, no touching up or reconstruction into some other form, is in store for it; the system of the Critique rests on fully secured foundation, established forever; it will be indispensable too for the noblest ends of mankind in all future ages."[19] Such foundationalism guides the many readings of Hegel that reify Hegelian "Spirit" into an absolute foundation of all things, or those of Heidegger, which similarly reify "Being" and "Appropriation."

The three Enlightenments belong together then, and must be articulated and defended together. They are all parts of America's new struggle of ideas, of the defense of the Enlightenment, and of philosophy's own battle for self-preservation. Formulating, updating, and defending all of them together is a tall order, and American philosophers may long for the days when they passed quiet lives in academic backwaters. But those lives are a bygone luxury. In the new professional lives imposed on them by history, philosophers must not only defend those three ways of thinking, they must *practice* them. Philosophical issues are bequeathed us by history, usually the history of philosophy itself. In order to understand them we must understand the history that has bequeathed them. If we are philosophers, we must understand that history rationally. A philosophy that is dialectically unenlightened has no disciplined way to choose its problems, with the result that it will be caught unaware by the significant events in its own history—as so much American philosophy was by 9/11. Enlightenment and Dialectical Enlightenment pursued without regard to Meta-Enlightenment yield philosophies that all too easily lapse into reawakened dogmatism. This only concedes victory to the enemy, for it makes the struggle of ideas into what so many would like it to be—one set of dogmas fighting one another. And when it comes to the foundationalist metaphysics of true sentences, or of Being or of the World Spirit (which of course is really the Western Spirit), against fundamentalist metaphysics based on Allah and Christ, guess who is going to win?

Meeting the challenge of 9/11, in the form of the worldwide backlash against the Enlightenment that 9/11 forced into the open, thus requires a new way of doing philosophy itself: it is a direct alteration in philosophy. Old philosophical tools need not be abandoned, but must be used in new ways. Each and every philosopher must expand her repertoire of such tools to include, not merely the standard arsenal of argument forms, of which our Analytical colleagues make excellent though wrongly exclusive use, but also the Hegelian techniques of dialectical reconstruction and the Heideggerean/Derridean techniques of deconstructive questioning. Philosophy, in other words, must become a very different kind of discourse than it has been recently.

This has implications on the level of the philosophical community—for the American philosophical community must become very different from what it has recently been, not only in its relations to the larger world but within itself. One way to sum up much of what has to happen is to say that the time for taking sides is over. Philosophers can *no longer afford* to define themselves as Analytical but not Continental; Continentals can no longer divide themselves into modernists and postmodernists. The Age of Pluralism—do what you want, but don't expect us to read you or support you for tenure—is over. Philosophers, of all stripes, must join together, move forward together, hang together.

Otherwise, they will all hang separately.

Notes

1. See Emil Fackenheim, *Quest for Past and Future: Essays in Jewish Theology*, Boston: Beacon Press, 1970.
2. Giovanna Borradori, Jacques Derrida, and Jürgen Habermas, *Philosophy in a Time of Terror: Dialogues with Jürgen Habermas and Jacques Derrida*. Chicago: University of Chicago Press, 2003; Judith Butler, *Precarious Life: The Power of Mourning and Violence*, London: Verso, 2006; Joseph Margolis, Armen T. Marsoobian, and Tom Rockmore, *The Philosophical Challenge of September 11*, London: Wiley-Blackwell, 2005.
3. Richard A. Clarke, "The Wrong Debate on Terrorism," *The New York Times*, April 25, 2004.
4. Paul Berman, *Terror and Liberalism*, New York: W. W. Norton, 2003.
5. Martin Luther King, "I Have a Dream." Washington D.C. August 28, 1963.
6. Michael Hill, "U. S. Pays Little Heed to Philosophy," *The Baltimore Sun*, January 12, 1999, p. 2A.
7. Taylor Branch, "New Directions in American Philosophy," *The New York Times Magazine*, August 14, 1977, p. 180ff. It helps here to see that Americans have always had a conflicted relationship with philosophy. Where most nations are founded on ethnicity, religion, or history (not to mention sheer force), ours is founded on a set of ideas—on a political philosophy. Though this makes philosophy uniquely important to Americans, it also pushes us to view philosophy as something finished and over with, rather than a living discipline. New philosophical discoveries, especially in the areas of social and political thought, could imperil the very foundations of the Republic. In America, philosophy is dangerous—far more so than in other countries. Because of this, philosophy tends to get pushed to the far margins of American intellectual enterprise, and in recent decades philosophers have been content to remain there, well off the radar of the larger culture.
8. A friend of mine, working for the Obama presidential campaign in far southern Indiana, found no decent bookstores or eating places but plenty of churches and some racists—and one brave little coffeehouse, with a vibrant Socrates café every Sunday evening.
9. For two examples of this, see Barack Obama. Golden, CO. September 16, 2008, and Barack Obama, "Remarks of Senator Barack Obama: Renewing the American Economy." New York, NY. March 27, 2008.
10. Garry Wills, "The Day the Enlightenment Went Out," *The New York Times*, November 4, 2004.

11. For details see Gustav Niebuhr, "A Nation Challenged: Placing Blame; Falwell Apologizes for Saying an Angry God Allowed Attacks," *The New York Times*, September 18, 2001.

12. Habermas, Jürgen, *Theorie des kommunikativen Handelns*, Frankfurt: Suhrkamp, 1982, I 25–151.

13. See my *Time in the Ditch*, Evanston: Northwestern University Press, 2000, pp. 127–67, and *Reshaping Reason*, Bloomington: Indiana University Press, 2005, *passim*.

14. Kant himself masks this kind of consideration with his requirement that the people must be able to consent to an enlightened proposal—for this is precisely the kind of thinking that is required in giving one's consent to a project.

15. In the case of Islamic terrorism, this means presenting a variety of plausible pathways from where Islamic societies are now to a freer and more "enlightened" state, rather than the single course of having enlightened ideas imposed upon them by America.

16. See on this my *Metaphysics and Oppression*, passim.

17. Jacques Derrida, "L'exorbitant," at *De la Grammatologie* (Les Editions de Minuit: 1967) p. 227; see *Of Grammatology*, trans. Gayari Chakravorty Spivak. Baltimore and London: The Johns Hopkins University Press, 1997, p. 158.

18. In the case of Islam, such a meta-Enlightenment would involve "deconstructing" the Koran, rendering it less easily usable—or mis-usable—as a guide to politics but, I suspect, enriching it in many other ways.

19. Kant, "Open Letter on Fichte's *Wissenschaftslehre*, August 7, 1799, cited after the translation in Kant, *Philosophical Correspondence 1759–99* (Arnulf Zweig, trans. and ed.), Chicago: University of Chicago Press, 1967, p. 254. This contrasts sadly with Kant's generalized recognition of fallibility when, in "What is Enlightenment?" he says that no generation can bind future generations to any dogma. On this cf. my "Unearthing the Wonder: A 'Post-Kantian' Paradigm in Kant's *Critique of Judgment*," forthcoming.

CHAPTER 2

WHO COUNTS? ON DEMOCRACY, POWER, AND THE INCALCULABLE

Dennis J. Schmidt

"*Oute archein oute archesthai ethelo*"[1]

Otanes

The distance between the historical realities of the time and place from which I write these words and the historical realities which gave birth to the word and idea of "democracy" is so great that one must wonder if the idea of democracy is still up to the task of negotiating the space of public life in our times. There are two ways, two differences, in which one can immediately see this distance. The first is a matter simply of magnitude: the population of Athens in the fifth century BCE was about 250,000 people, but of those only about 30,000 counted as citizens; on the other hand, the population of the world today—and today one must speak of the world if one is to speak of democracy—is about 6.75 billion. Number has always been central to the idea of democracy as majority rule, but the numbers one must tally today seem to outstrip any possible meaning. There is a link between democracy and demographics, and the difference in this regard between today and ancient Greece is so great that one must wonder if the term "democracy" must become just as different to match the needs of our age. But even if one were inclined to characterize these demographic differences as only an increase of the same, the second set of differences would still make evident how removed our world is from the Greek political situation in which democracy emerged as an idea. These differences are visible in the terms that are enlisted to speak of political life in the Greek world in contrast to those that we use in our times: place, war, sovereignty, identity, and law have given way to terrorism, cyberspace, globalization, and mass destruction. One sees clearly that the nature of political life has changed, not simply its magnitude. One might even argue that, until rather recently, the traditional terms of political discourse did indeed remain effective and appropriate, so that until recent times the Greek world was still able to speak to other times. But it seems reasonable today to ask whether this notion, which emerged as central to the self-conception of ancient Athens, can still have a meaning in an age that conceives of itself as the age of globalization (or as what Heidegger called variously *Machenschaft* and *Gestell*). Has the space of political life changed so dramatically that this idea of democracy might not find a place any longer in the realm of the political? Do we still preserve this idea as something of an ideal because it does offer something to be desired, or simply by virtue of a failure of our imaginations to match the challenge of our times?

Is there something about the character of the present historical juncture that poses a special, perhaps utterly new, problem for democracy? While a careful and extended analysis of the present historical realities might indeed expose several such new challenges to the life of democracy in these times, there is one aspect—one hesitates to call this only an aspect—of our times that I would single out, namely the convergence of "globalization" and "technologization." In order to make this point, this chapter is divided into two parts. In the first part, I discuss the word "democracy," in order to give some indications of just how the word itself opens the idea of democracy in all of its complexity. Here, I turn mostly to the Greek sensibility that gave birth to this word. In the second part, I take up the question of setting this Greek notion in the context of transformations that we are witnessing today.

Democracy

The word "democracy" and the ideals we take it to represent has an undeniable charm and, as a consequence, it has long held a grip on our political imaginations. It seems so adaptable, so flexible to the needs of that imagination, that one sees that it has been taken up by both the right and the left, and even as the self-description of governments that are anything but democratic. It is—and indeed always has been—used cynically as much as it is used idealistically. It is cynically used as a rationale for war—consider George W. Bush's efforts to validate the Iraq war—just as it is used idealistically and as a genuine call for a better world. What makes this possible, what gives the word its charm and its chameleon character seems to be its invocation of "the people," this capacity to say "we." The word itself points to this elemental aim of political life: this fundament that is announced when we say "we, the people." Lincoln expressed this eloquently and simply when he said that "[Democracy marks] a new birth of freedom . . . government *of* the people, *by* the people, *for* the people."[2] There are, of course, many questions that such a remark raises, but among all of these questions about "the people," the *demos*, one seems to stand out as primary, namely, "*who counts?*" Who are "the" people? Who counts as a citizen and not simply as a subject in the democracy? From the outset, counting has always been as much a matter of "mattering" as of simple "numbering." Even if democracy is majority rule, it has never been simply a numbers game.[3] The most important and decisive questions for any democracy come long before any tally takes place.

Not surprisingly, the first uses of the word "democracy" in ancient Greece pose this question "who counts?" with an increasing awareness of its complexity. One of the first appearances of the word "democracy" is found in a tragedy, where one reads in Aeschylus' *The Suppliant Maidens* (463 BCE) the following line describing democracy as a matter of majority rule: "*demou kratousa cheir hope plethynetai*"[4] ["the law of the ballot in which the majority of the people prevails"]. Thirty years later, in 431 BCE, Pericles (who was among the first sponsors of Aeschylus) will deliver his celebrated "Funeral Oration" in which he will say of Athens, at least according to the reports of Thucydides, that "as for the name of our political arrangement, we are a democracy, since the many, not just the few, participate in governing."[5] Again, the reference is to number, to the majority. However, here it should be noted that the speech in which this is said commemorates the (re-)burial of the dead and that there was a question prior to this commemoration that had to be answered first, namely, who counted, that is, who mattered enough to count among those to be commemorated by such burial?[6] The Periclean age marks a turning point in the understanding of what it means to "count" in a democracy. So, for instance, Pericles significantly restricted the conditions of who could count as a citizen when he issued a decree that made it necessary for both parents to be Athenians in order for a child to count as a future citizen (previously, having one Athenian parent sufficed). Some 30 years after Pericles, in 403 BCE, Theozotides issued a decree concerning war orphans in which the word *demokratia* is found for the first time in a public decree.[7] Theozotides's concern is to limit the responsibility of the state for the support of the sons of those non-citizens who died fighting on behalf of the democracy. Once again, the question is: who counts and who does not? In this decree, the sense of the democracy as having an "inside" and an "outside" becomes far more evident. So, one sees that from its very early appearance in Aeschylus to its more formulated expression in Theozotides—a period of only 60 years—the notion of democracy moves from being simply a matter of counting, of numbers, to understanding the question "who counts?" as "who matters?" to finally defining an inside and an outside of democracy itself.

The fifth century BCE was the time of the formation of the first democratic governments and the three appearances of the word during that time noted above are among the earliest references to the idea of democracy. Initially defined as the rule of the many, the question of democracy begins to unfold as the question of who counts: who is inside the democracy. But this question of the "inside" of democracy is actually twofold. First, there is the simple question of who belongs to the process, who, in other words, is a citizen. Second, there is the subtler and more interior question of who belongs to the majority. From the beginning, and for its every future, democracy always has these two kinds of others that it confronts: the other of the outside and the other of the inside, the other to the democracy itself and the other to the majority that rules. In both cases, those who are the others of any democracy experience the democracy first of all as a power held by others. While the usual emphasis of any account of the word "democracy" falls upon the role of the people—of the *demos* named in the word—the challenge of every democracy is named in the accent brought to it by the second root of the word: *kratos*: "victory," "superiority," "power," and "force."[8] The question that democracy faces, if it is to distinguish itself from other forms of rule, is how this *kratos* is to be brought into the *polis* without it becoming, or being experienced, as simple violence and coercion, as, in other words, the closure of the free space requisite for democracy.[9] Consensus precedes the entry into a democracy—the consensus of free individuals to abide by the outcome of counting up numbers. One enters into this consensus, this pact, in order to evade the possible violence that could otherwise attend the struggle for and transfer of power in a *polis*. This on-going consensus requires the maintenance of such a free space.[10] Nonetheless, to become the outside—whether it is the outside to the democracy, or the outside of the majority—is to submit oneself to the superiority, even if only the superiority of number, of the victor. In the end, every democracy will eventually produce its own outside—even one that is within that same democracy—such that the rule of the people will be the rule of victory, even of power. The Greeks were sensitive to this double sense of democracy's outsides and so in Greek, there are different words to describe how the two different forms of the "outside" proper to every democracy confront the "inside" of that democracy: *stasis* is the name of an internal discord, ultimately of the possibility of a civil war, that emerges from the internal othering of democracy; *polemos* is the name of the war upon the other of the outside of democracy.[11] *Stasis* names the conflict in the middle of the city itself, the conflict internal to the *polis*; *polemos*, on the other hand, names the conflict with that which is simply outside of the city. In light of this sense that *kratos*, power, is at the heart of the very possibility of democracy it is no surprise that one tradition of tracing the production of the word *demokratia* in ancient Greece argues that the word was originally coined by the enemies of the democrats: the threat of force, something that democracy would most of all like to avoid, haunts the very word itself—both the inside and the outside of what it names. This tension of the inside and outside and this specter of force are embodied in every democracy.

One sees that this logic of inside/outside is neither simple nor static. That, for instance, is why the question of immigration goes to the heart of the very notion of democracy. Those who ask to enter the inside of the democratic process challenge this essential distinction and promise to move it in new directions. Consequently, immigration, which one would expect to be a welcome factor in the growth and health of any democracy, is nonetheless felt as a threat by those who define not only the inside, but the majority that rules from within. Yet another way in which one can see the strangeness and danger of these notions of inside and outside is in the case of what Derrida refers to as a certain "suicide" of democracy.[12] Such suicide would be found in the case of a democratic process that yielded power to a majority that abolished the democracy under which that same majority came to power. This "autoimmune pervertibility of democracy"[13] is indicative of the potential of the power that democracy sets free. Thus, while the word "democracy" speaks of the "power of the people"—the *kratos* of the *demos*—it is clear that power belongs to the very idea of democracy in a complex manner. The circulation of power operates according to the logic of inside and outside, a logic that is not necessarily binary or dialectical, but, so long as the democracy has not calcified in its own institutions, marks an antinomy at the heart of every possible democracy. This absence of any fixity of the power at the basis of a democracy, the fact that the people belong to history (which will forever shift the logics of inside–outside), is the reason Derrida can say that "democracy is defined, as is the very ideal of democracy, by this lack of the proper and the selfsame . . . there is no absolute paradigm, whether constitutive or constitutional, no absolutely intelligible idea, no *eidos*, no *idea* of democracy."[14]

In a different way, Plato, too, will hint at the chameleon-like nature of democracy. It is, says Socrates, "just like a many-colored cloak decorated in all hues, this regime, decorated with all dispositions . . . it's a convenient place to look for a regime . . . because, thanks to its license, it contains all species of regimes, and it is probably necessary for the man who wishes to organize a city, as we were just doing, to go to a city under a democracy."[15] To speak of democracy as a decorative fabric is an expression of its best possibilities. However, in fact, it might be more appropriate, more in tune with its realities, to speak of democracy as having a chameleon-like nature: it can change, power can turnover, it will produce new insides and new outsides, and it will still remain itself.

Derrida will take this point about the lack of any firm idea of democracy further and suggest that there is "in the final analysis, no democratic ideal."[16] However, such a claim might go a bit too far. As some of the greatest speeches, eulogies in the best sense of the word, on behalf of democracy—one thinks of both Pericles and of Lincoln, among others—have reminded us, the majority might well rule but that does not mean that the majority should ever conceive of itself as the *totality* of the people.[17] The greatest number might well win the power, but if properly understood, the people who constitute a democracy will always be a greater number still and, in every democracy that lives up to its name, those who hold power should know themselves to be accountable to the greatest possible number, not simply to the majority. The *demos* is always greater in number than the number of those who hold the *kratos*. Ideally, those who constitute a majority grasp this and do not arm themselves with power, but recognize the minority, the weak, and those without power equally as full citizens of the *demos*, that is, as equals if not in number, then in worth. There is something of an infinite extension of the very notion of the *demos* that is needed here, an extension that is not only for the present, but for every future, as well. In short, an impossible extension of what is named by the *demos* is the only way in which *kratos* will not be at the heart of every possible democracy. Everyone must count and, indeed, everyone must count equally.

But even if such an extension were possible, a new problem soon becomes visible: such an absolute equalization of every citizen would equally be the absolute erasure of the singularity of each citizen. Of course, this is the problem for democracy long before any such absolute equalization. As soon as we begin to count votes, the singular individual is reduced to an abstract number, a cipher of singularity, and thereby suffers an alienation that is quite peculiar to democracy.[18] "This antinomy at the heart of the democratic has long been recognized . . . it is the one between freedom and equality—that constitutive and diabolical couple of democracy . . . . equality tends to introduce measure and calculation . . . whereas freedom is by essence . . . heterogeneous to calculation and to measure."[19] This is the double obligation of the democracy: to the freedom of the singular individual and to the equality of the people, in which every individual counts equally with every other individual. Derrida puts this point well when he says that "these two laws are irreconcilable one to the other. Tragically irreconcilable and forever wounding."[20] Caught between these demands—to count and to equalize, to struggle against the production of an outside, and to recognize the singularity of each citizen—democracies can only ever mitigate the conflict produced by demands that belong to its own flexible nature.

But power contracts by nature and consolidates itself. Handing power over to the greatest number counted will always set in motion these sets of irreconcilable claims which are collateral to the very nature of counting to find a majority: the production of the outside and the presence of the strange figure of the singular individual who, as such, *as singular*, does not count. Of course, the aporia of democracy is lodged in the dual character of every individual: as singular—one might say, as *jemeinig* or as an end unto oneself—the individual is non-reducible, free, and incalculable; as one of the people, the individual is equal to all others and bound by and to this equality. *Kratos*, this victory of the greatest number, this power granted by the individual, who has entered into the pact of democratic counting, to the *demos*, is the beginning of the enigma of democracy. It is also the locus of the truth and the risk of democracy, namely, that in a democracy, power is always contested.

Democracy is founded on this chameleon nature, this lack of a singular, static ground. It is founded on process and the purpose of that process is to determine the seat—or even the source—of power. As such, power is the site of disputes and the only guarantee it promises is the turnover of power when necessary. No one holds the position of power in a democracy—it is always an open question—consequently, the place of power is an empty one, an open place. At the heart of every democracy, one finds this empty place. Because its only stable task, the only given for democracy, is this turnover, one needs to say that democracy, regarded from any present moment, is always incomplete, always en route to something else. If democracy must be understood as always incomplete, then it must also always be understood as a question of what must come next, that is, as a matter of the future.

This lack of foundation stands in sharp contrast with the traditional philosophical project of providing a foundation for the just *polis*. Plato is the first, but certainly not the last, to argue that the proper foundation of the just *polis* is truth and that, as the one who can distinguish truth from opinion, the philosopher should be king.[21] Such a belief, however, evidences how philosophers who regard themselves as the monarchs of truth tend to set themselves in opposition to the very notion of democracy. Arendt refers to this philosophical tendency to found political life upon a conception of truth as "the tyranny of truth." This tendency to link the foundations of political life with truth is also the reason that philosophers often regard the task of government as educating its citizens. One sees this clearly in Plato's remarks that "a polity is a thing which nurtures men, good men when it is noble, bad men when it is base."[22] So long as philosophy is conceived as a matter of foundations, one might say that so long as philosophy remains metaphysically invested in grounds—in knowing them, producing them, identifying them—it will only find it difficult to grasp the nature of democracy.[23]

In Greece, democracy emerged as a form of consensus prior to any struggle—the consensus to negotiate the movements of power in the *polis* by the simple process of counting. It was designed to preserve the movement of power and the freedom of those who participated in the *polis* to try to influence that movement. But one sees, then, that the word "democracy" is itself full of consequence; counting may be a simple exercise, but belies what is in fact a rather complicated matter. Democracy is, in the end, a rather messy idea: never complete, always the site of contested claims, of self-critique as well as self-assertion. It is the refusal of a single vision. Plato was right to describe it as "a many-colored cloak decorated in all hues."[24] The Greek world that coined this word soon learned that this was the case. The questions that follow as soon as one reflects upon its elements—upon the idea of the people and the idea of power—open the notion of democracy as a complex one, indeed as one necessarily incomplete and, in some sense, impossible. This means that in every reality, every form it assumes in any present, democracy will always remain as much a matter of promise as of that existing reality.

Machenschaft *and* Gestell

Of the ideas that were to fashion the twentieth century in ways for the most part pernicious, one that stands out above the others, so far-reaching and indeed immense were its consequences, is the idea of the good community . . . the evidence before us should at least prompt us to inquire: might there not be something pernicious in the very idea of community, at least when it manifests itself, as has frequently been the case, in a world where technology has extended its grip over the whole planet? This is the crux of the matter: are community and technology somehow incompatible?[25]

Incomplete and impossible though it may be, the richness and openness spoken of in the word "democracy" has given it a long life and has let it serve as an inspiration in many political movements. As a promise, it points easily to a new future and, so, readily lends itself to reform and even to revolutionary movements. As always incomplete, democracy requires its own persistent reinvention. And yet, despite its enduring charm, despite its constant promise, it is also the case that one finds arguments today that democracy is inadequate to the needs of our times, that the nature of the public realm has so fundamentally changed that something new is needed to match the challenges of that world. One sees such a claim for instance in Heidegger's remark that "for me, it is a decisive question just how a political system—and which system—can be accommodated to the contemporary technical era. I do not know an answer to this question. I am not convinced that it is democracy."[26] Is such a remark simply the reflection of an undemocratic prejudice—whether that prejudice is rooted in Heidegger's own personal views or in the tendency of philosophy to resist the notion of democracy (or both)—or does it raise an important question about the sufficiency or capacity of democracy to measure up to the task of today?

The contention driving such a claim is not that a democratic state cannot exist in a technologically advanced state. Such a claim would simply be false and without any basis. Rather, the contention is that the space of political life, the realm of the common, has been changed in such a way that we now find ourselves confronting power in new forms, forms that are not flexible and that do not submit themselves to anything like the turnover of power that is so basic to the democratic process in which "inside" and "outside" must be able to trade places. The argument is that in the present globalized age, technological reason, and its structures and institutions, has imposed a new logic of power, one that has no outside. It is this totalization of power, this totalitarian condition, which leads Heidegger to refer to our age as a time of "extreme distress" and as the "beginning of the lack of history,"[27] that is, as the inauguration of a time in which power will not take different forms. One might say that ours is an age in which power will not turn over, that is, it will not submit itself to the transfer at the heart of the democratic process. Rather, this is a time in which power empowers and preserves itself and that signals the closure of the space of political life, the closure of the space of decision.

Heidegger's argument is that in the age determined by technological reason and its global expansion everything is encased in the security of a path that is planned and exact and steerable, and which masters everything."[28] This then is the time of the triumph of calculation and an equalization of all things. This means as well that this is equally the time of the disappearance of the other of what can be counted and calculated, namely the singularity of the individual who cannot be reduced to an abstract number, the singularity in which freedom resides. Heidegger gives two names to the character of that which defines our epoch. The first name is *Machenschaft*; the second name is *Gestell*. Both of these designations of the essential character of our times are attempts to give a name to the force that has colonized the space of all appearances, including the space called the *polis*, that space in which alone we can appear as both subjects and as citizens, the space of the common and the struggle for it. To speak of *Machenschaft* and *Gestell* is to suggest that these forces now define the conditions of appearance—above all as a matter of calculability—and equally the shape of power as that which we cannot control, but which controls and defines us. "What does *Machenschaft* mean? That which is set free into its own chains. Which chains? The schema of thoroughly calculable explainability through which everything draws closer to everything else and becomes thoroughly alien to itself, indeed becomes completely other than what is simply alien."[29]

Of course, the arrival of such forces does not happen as a *coup*, but is a long and slow arrival. Indeed, for Heidegger, these forces are simply the end station of the history of philosophy, which has taken itself to be metaphysics. That is why Heidegger says that "the essencing of power is the most extreme form of metaphysics."[30] Power increasingly becomes its own rationale and, as this happens, it begins to sever its connection with a people. I have suggested that democracy begins as an effort to avoid the violence that can accompany shifts in power. It begins as a way of providing for the peaceful turnover of power. This means that power must belong to history, to the process of the *polis* becoming different, even new. But, if Heidegger is right about the conditions of power in the reign of *Machenschaft* and *Gestell* and we are indeed entering a period that lacks history, then one can perhaps begin to understand why he expresses doubts about the capacity of democracy to respond to the challenge of our age, namely, the challenge of piercing the increasing uniformity and reduction of life to what is calculable. Once the roots of power cease to belong to the people, and once such power globalizes itself, democracy does indeed seem to lose its capacity to be a force of history. No sovereign power seems able to confront the power of the globalized organization of life under the regime of technology.

In place of any possible sovereign power, today we find the final possible alternative to the present shape of power. What is left as such an alternative is the power of individuals who stand completely apart from sovereignty and the turnover of power. We call such individuals "terrorists"—those whose power is terrible, terrifying, and monstrous—simply because the form of the power they express is outside that which has no outside. What is left, what is expressed by such power, is the assertion of unreason and real powerlessness in the form of the individual.[31] What is left is irrational, incalculable, inefficient, nonsense. Such is the only remaining outside of power and so long as there are no alternatives, such explosive expressions of powerlessness will not cease. Efforts to step outside the static tyranny of the new form of power as it is figured by globalized technology will always have something of desperation about them, something of nihilism, since it is a form of power that will not turn over itself. When the locus of power can no longer be contested, when power has calcified and become total, leaving no alternative political power, then simple violence, naked brutality, is all that remains as a means of contesting the established power. There has always been political brutality and unspeakable violence; our age did not invent terror and horror. But our age has witnessed an intensification of certain dimensions of violence, an intensification changing the landscape of every exercise of power and turning the attempt to contest power into violence of a new order: open, public spaces can now be dangerous, no one is considered innocent, children have become weapons as well as targets, strangers are threatening, the material shapes of everyday life—airplanes, envelopes, shoes—are turned back upon individuals as weapons. Sovereign nations are not attacked; individuals are attacked. In short, the old forms by which those in power were confronted and power was contested have taken a new form, namely the form of raw violence, and the reason for this is that the power in power is itself a fundamentally new form. Or, so Heidegger would argue.

Preserving Democracy

In the Greek world of its beginnings, democracy rested upon two sets of necessary conditions. The first of these conditions took the form of a prior agreement, the consent of all who would be citizens, to abide by the rule of the majority. This condition is met by individuals prior to any sense that there is a *demos*. It is something of a pledge, in which each person agrees to abide by a count, by numbers, that has yet to be tabulated. The second of the conditions requisite for democracy is, as Aristotle argued, the *freedom* of every individual, the absence of any coercion in matters of the democratic process, in the voice one has, and equally, the *equality* of all individuals when it comes to the matter of counting.[32] These conditions are, of course, at odds: the first requires that each citizen be recognized as a singular being, an end unto oneself; the second requires a reduction of each citizen to an abstract equality in which no one is different. If Heidegger's claims about the present historical juncture are right, if we do indeed live in an age in which a sort of reduction to what is calculable is definitive, an age in which singularity is effaced, if not erased, then one can see how it is that the conditions of democratic life are in jeopardy. Despite the glaring inequities in the world, a curious equalization of everyone as an abstraction, as a simple number, is being achieved today and, at the same time, the singularity that is the locus of freedom seems more than ever to be alienated. Facing a form of power that will not turn over, the source of which will not change, any people, all peoples, seem to be in the strange condition of being outsiders.

If Heidegger's argument about the nature of technological reason, the *Gestell* and *Machenschaft*, is right, then the possibilities of democracy in our time must indeed be considered in the light of the challenges of technological reason and the globalization that such rationality makes possible. Above all, one must ask how it is that we can preserve—or perhaps recover—an openness that permits the appearance of individuals in their singularity, that is, in their difference from others. One must also ask, just as urgently, how it is that power can transfer itself and not be calcified into one form. In other words, how it might be possible for history to begin again. Heidegger expressed a sense of helplessness before this question: "only a god can save us," he said.[33] That comment is not a declaration of faith; it is rather a statement of despair and hopelessness: we are powerless; only an outside, something beyond our understanding, can introduce change and set history into motion anew. It is not difficult to see the reasons for such a claim: globalization has, by virtue of the technologies that drive it and render it possible, shown itself to be a homogenization of the world and a shrinking of the spaces of political life, the spaces, that is, of differences. Nonetheless, one can still ask if this totalization and closure of the space of political life is indeed so seamless.

There do seem to be sites and forces where the seams and ruptures in the space of possible appearances today do promise openings. For instance, at an earlier point in his career, Heidegger often suggested that a capacity to jolt history and set it in motion again remained for the work of art.[34] The imagination and forms of thinking that evade calculation still seem to preserve the capacity to open up the new. One might also point to the failure of technology and the work of human subjectivity to subdue and control nature as yet another way in which the limits of the totalization at work today is found. In short, one needs to ask just how total the colonization of the space of political life and of the earth is today.

But this perhaps begs the question of democracy. Does it still remain a *political* form in which history can be opened anew and responsive to our times? Ours is not the first time in which a sort of extreme seems to have been reached. During the American Civil War, Lincoln remarked that: "The dogmas of the quiet past are inadequate to the stormy present. The occasion is piled high with difficulty, and we must rise with the occasion. As our case is new, so we must think anew, and act anew. We must disenthrall ourselves and then we shall save our country. Fellow citizens, *we* cannot escape history."[35] One needs to ask oneself today whether we are still capable of "disenthralling" ourselves of the forces that hold us in chains today. Democracy has always been about the future, about the turnover of power and, so, the liberation of history. Clearly, democracy has not always (indeed, only rarely) lived up to its name, nonetheless that relation to the future remains central to the very idea of democracy. But for a future to happen, one must first "disenthrall" oneself, one must see beyond the present state of power. For us, this means above all asking about the nature of the globalization and technologization driving our world today. It means asking about the possibilities still inhering in the space of appearance remaining in what Heidegger called the *Gestell*. If we do that, then I believe we will be drawn back into questions about the character of that which might always escape every totalizing force—namely, the singularity that each of us is. This returns us to the root and the aim of democracy: to the recovery of that abyssal truth, that singularity which will remain incalculable, and which it is the task of democracy to preserve. Such singularity is found prior to any pact, prior to any consolidation into a sovereign subject. Out of such singularity, out of the pact that one makes with others, something like a people can, perhaps, be achieved. Globalization reminds us that everyone must count, everyone matters: the Greek concern with asking "who counts" should now be answered. But what remains is the need to recover a sense of that which cannot be counted, but matters just as much. This task, perhaps, will lead democracy today to live up the honor of its name.

Notes

1. "I wish neither to govern, nor be governed." Otanes, cited by Herodotus, *Histories, Book III*, 82–83. I would like to thank Jennifer Mensch and James Risser for their very helpful comments on an earlier version of this paper which was published in *Research in Phenomenology*, 38 (2008), pp. 228–243.

2. *Lincoln on Democracy*, 308.
3. Still, it is important to bear in mind that the role of 'number' should not be underestimated nor undermined: that is why the course of the election of 2000 in the United States when the Supreme Court ordered officials to stop counting the votes represents one of the most fundamental threats to the very idea of democracy.
4. Aeschylus, *The Suppliant Maidens*, line 604.
5. Thucydides, *The Peloponnesian War, Book II*, 2.37.1.
6. On the parallels between Pericles's "Funeral Oration" and Lincoln's "Gettysburg Address," see Wills, *Lincoln at Gettysburg*. It is no accident that two of the most significant public texts on the idea of democracy were delivered on the occasion of the burial of the dead. As Hegel will repeatedly argue, there is a certain *equalization* of everyone in the face of death (this is the reason that the state will always try to control the forces of death, such as suicide and capital punishment). Plato's *Menexenus* needs to be read in this context, as well. See Loraux, *The Invention of Athens: The Funeral Oration in the Classical City*. See also, Schmidt, "Can Law Survive?", 147–158. On the political significance of burial, see Schmidt, "What We Owe the Dead," 111–126.
7. For a detailed discussion of this and of the discovery of this decree in 1970, see Stroud, "Theozotides and the Athenian Orphans," 283–299.
8. For a discussion of the meaning of *kratos*, see Loraux, *The Divided City*, 68–71.
9. On this, see Plato, *Statesman*, 291e–292a.
10. Curiously, this free act does not itself seem to qualify as a democratic act since it is a decision prior to the appearance of any "people."
11. On this difference, see Derrida, *Politics of Friendship*, 104–107.
12. Derrida, *Rogues*, 33.
13. Derrida, *Rogues*, 34.
14. Derrida, *Rogues*, 37.
15. Plato, *Republic*, 557c .
16. *Ibid.*, p. 37.
17. In *Menexenus*, Plato makes the effort to reveal what Pericles's funeral oration suppresses; that is, he insists on the presence of *kratos* in the very notion of democracy and suggests that this will belong to every self-defined *demos*. See *Menexenus*, 238d4ff. See also, Loraux, *Invention of Athens*, 413.
18. This will be the case unless "there is another thought of calculation and of number, another way of apprehending the universality of the singular which, without dooming politics to the incalculable, would still justify the old name of democracy." Derrida, *Politics of Friendship*, 104.
19. Derrida, *Rogues*, 48. Hegel will even refer to the recognition of the singular individual as "the democratic, indeed the *anarchic* principle of individuation" in Hegel, *Werke*, 482.
20. Derrida, *Politics of Friendship*, 22. This is not the place to discuss the obvious parallel between this double bind of democracy and the double bind proper to the very idea of justice. Both are expressions of the need to be universal, equal, and singular *at once*. On this point, see Derrida, "The Force of Law," in *Deconstruction and the Possibility of Justice*.
21. Heidegger's Rectoral Address, in which the philosopher is tacitly set up as a spiritual leader, will only be the most prominent latter day examples of this argument. See Martin Heidegger, *Die Selbstbehauptung der deutschen Universität* (*The Self-Affirmation of the German University*) (Frankfurt A.M.: V. Klostermann, 1983).
22. Plato, *Menexenus*, 238c.

23. It is, I believe, no accident that the philosophical tradition most identified with democracy is American pragmatism with its own anti-foundational tendencies.
24. Plato, *Republic*, 557c.
25. Calasso, *Literature and the Gods*, 53.
26. Heidegger, "Spiegel–Interview (1966)," 668.
27. Heidegger, *Gesamtausgabe* Bd. 65, 100.
28. *Ibid.*, 406.
29. *Ibid.*, 132.
30. *Ibid.*, 69.
31. Here, one would do well to compare Hegel's discussion of a different form of terror in his *Phänomenologie des Geistes*, namely, that of the French Revolution. See the section entitled "Die absolute Freiheit und der Schrecken," where Hegel describes death as the sole work and deed of absolute freedom and as "the flattest and coldest death, without any more significance than slicing a cabbage or a gulp of water." Hegel, *Phänomenologie*, 418–19.
32. Aristotle, *Politics*, 1301b–1317a.
33. Heidegger, "Spiegel–Interview," 652.
34. See, for instance, Heidegger, "Ursprung des Kunstwerkes," 62ff.
35. *Lincoln on Democracy*, 268–69.

CHAPTER 3

PERPETUAL PEACE AND THE INVENTION OF TOTAL WAR

Robert Bernasconi

The Kantian Proposal and the Place of History

The distinguished British historian of war, Michael Howard, began *The Invention of Peace* with an observation from the nineteenth century jurist Sir Henry Maine, who declared: "War appears to be as old as mankind, but peace is a modern invention."[1] After due hesitation, Howard underwrote Maine's claim and, indeed, rendered it more precise: "[I]f anyone could be said to have invented peace as more than a mere pious aspiration, it was Kant."[2] To be sure, Howard neglected to mention the Abbé de Saint-Pierre and Jean-Jacques Rousseau, two thinkers to whom Kant himself referred in his "Idea for a Universal History with a Cosmopolitan Purpose," and who, for that reason alone, merit a place in the genealogy of the idea of a peace that was more than the cessation of war.[3] Nevertheless, even after acknowledging Saint-Pierre and Rousseau's role as Kant's forerunners, together with the fact that Kant was only one of a number of writers discussing peace at that time, one can still say that Kant's idea of peace was new.[4] Its novelty lay not in his proposals for establishing peace through a federation of nations, but in the fact that he located peace at the culminating point of a progressive philosophy of history in the form of "a perfect civic union of mankind."[5]

One consequence of Kant's new historical framework is that one does not find in his writings, as one does in those of Rousseau, a fear that the idea of perpetual peace might promote war. Rousseau expressed admiration for Henri IV's scheme to establish a Christian league in Europe that would preserve peace, but at the same time he acknowledged that it could never be realized, because the means necessary to bring it about would be so violent that there was little prospect of it happening:

> We will not see federative leagues establishing themselves except by revolution, and, on this principle, who would dare to say whether the European league is to be desired or to be feared? It would perhaps cause more harm in one moment than it could prevent for centuries to come.[6]

Kant did not limit the ideal of perpetual peace to Europe as Rousseau did, but the more significant difference between them lies in the hesitation expressed in this passage. Before proceeding to a general discussion of the dangers that follow from the lack of any such concerns, I will show that Kant was freed from having to calculate whether peace was worth the price one might have to pay for it, because his conception of peace was rooted in the idea of a universal history. This is why one must always read "Toward Perpetual Peace" in the context of the 1784 essay, "Idea for a Universal History with Cosmopolitan Purpose," where we find the first philosophy of history that looked to the end of history as a source of meaning. In Kant, the question of the meaning of human existence was separated from theology and referred to history.

In the *Critique of Pure Reason*, Kant identified the lack of a proof for the existence of the external world as the scandal of philosophy and of human reason in general.[7] In "Idea for a Universal History with a Cosmopolitan Purpose," he described another scandal: the fact that everywhere in nature there appears to be an order that can be subsumed under natural laws, except for human affairs, which appear to be a mere succession of events and, to that extent, appears to be directionless. That is to say, Kant's reflections on history were primarily motivated not by a refusal to accept the violence of his times, but by a refusal to accept the idea of an organism without an end within the context of a teleological theory of nature.[8] Kant expressed "indignation" [*unwillen*] that anyone must feel at the vanity and destructiveness of human actions. However, he was encouraged in his attempt to discover "a purpose in nature behind this senseless course of human events" by the emergence of the new science of statistics, whose annual charts enumerating the marriages, births, and deaths in certain large countries provided evidence of a regularity in human affairs lacking to previous generations.[9]

Kant's proposal was that the philosopher should survey the whole of human history and try to find in it evidence of a gradual progress toward the condition of cosmopolitanism. History was now to be rewritten with this idea as its guiding thread. However, one striking consequence of this new perspective opened up by Kant, one that even he recognized as puzzling, was that nature had to be understood as calling on each generation to work for the sake of later generations.[10] In order to make this idea more accessible to his audience, Kant argued that it is a necessary consequence of the assumption that providence decrees "that one animal species was intended to have reason, and that, as a class of rational beings who are mortal as individuals but immortal as a species, it was still meant to develop its capacities completely."[11] It tells us a great deal about the adoption and dissemination of ideas that we tend to take for granted Kant's conclusion that each generation sacrifice itself for later ones, while, nevertheless, rejecting the assumption upon which he based this claim.[12] Indeed, recourse to an idea of providence is so discredited in intellectual circles today that most philosophers writing about Kant do everything they can to minimize its role.

Kant believed that the wars that destroyed communities and even whole societies are instruments of providence that lead the human species to fulfill its capacities. That is to say, antagonism, humankind's asocial sociability, come to be seen for the first time as the means nature chose to bring about law-governed order in society.[13] Kant repeated the argument in the *Critique of Judgment* when he insisted that, although war is inevitable unless a cosmopolitan whole exists, war is also the means by which this cosmopolitan whole is to be realized: war is "an unintentional human endeavor (incited by our unbridled passions), yet it is also a deeply hidden and perhaps intentional endeavor of the supreme wisdom, if not to establish, then at least to prepare the way for lawfulness."[14] However, in the process of trying to find meaning in the apparently senseless course of human affairs, Kant had come dangerously close to offering a new justification for violence. As we shall see later, subsequent authors, particularly politicians, would have no difficulty bridging that gap. What Kant had apparently overlooked was that by giving historical narration the role of making visible an order that had previously been invisible, he had opened the door for individuals or nations to claim to be the agents of the process that would lead to peace. When one adopts the hitherto unsuspected intentions of providence as one's own, one can act with a self-righteousness and sense of conviction that knows no precedent. Whereas previously one might go to war looking forward to some possible changes that might be brought about following the cessation of hostilities, now one could go to war with a view to taking humanity a step further on the path to perpetual peace.

It is not only the role of providence in Kant's philosophy of history that tends to be overlooked today, but also the fact that Kant saw providence as directed toward the complete development of human capacities. Scholars almost always fail to mention that Kant's language in "Idea of a Universal History with a Cosmopolitan Purpose" is the language of natural history: in only ten pages Kant mentioned seeds (*keime*) five times and natural capacities or inclinations (*anlagen*) 15 times. What renders this problematic for current conceptions of Kantian cosmopolitanism is that this is the language of Kant's racial theory, according to which climate and environment determined which seeds and natural capacities were to be realized, thereby giving to each race its distinctive and permanent characteristics, both physical and "moral."[15] Moreover, Kant claimed that the White race alone was equipped with all the impulses and talents.[16] This explains why the perfect civic union involves assimilation to European ideas. As Kant put it, "our continent"—Europe—will give laws to all other continents.[17] Kant was clear that the antagonism rooted in one's unsociability serves the development of one's natural capacities and that, where this propensity for war is absent, the seeds lie dormant.[18] Nevertheless, he did not resolve the problem, so apparent to us, that follows the uneven distribution of those capacities across the different races. Kant seemed to be so far from sharing our sensibilities on these matters that in the *Critique of Judgment*, in the course of presenting "man" as the ultimate purpose of nature, he acknowledged that inequality is necessary if some are to have the opportunity to develop their natural capacities maximally.[19]

Having formulated a new account of racial hierarchy, where the distinctions between the races are permanent, and having also rejected race–mixing as a possible solution to the question of how the allegedly inferior races are to be assimilated into this cosmopolitan civic union, Kant bequeathed to future generations the following puzzle: If the meaning of human existence lies in history, and if certain populations or races seem not to participate in history, then why do those populations exist?[20] Kant asked precisely this question in an anonymous review of Herder's *Ideen zur Geschichte der Menschheit*:

> Does the author really mean that, if the happy inhabitants of Tahiti, never visited
> by more civilized nations, were destined to live in their peaceful indolence for
> thousands of years, it would be possible to give a satisfactory answer to the ques-
> tion of why they should exist at all, and of whether it would not have been just
> as good if this island had been occupied by happy sheep and cattle as by happy
> human beings who merely enjoy themselves?[21]

The fact that Kant made this argument against Herder is particularly significant because Herder was an advocate of the idea that each population has
something vital to contribute to humanity. Kant's opposition to Herder on this
point is underlined by his insistence elsewhere that the world would not lose
anything if Tahiti were to be destroyed.[22] However, although Kant's rhetorical
question seems to imply that the best thing that could happen to the happy
inhabitants of Tahiti was that they be visited by more civilized nations that
would improve them, the perfection of *their* capacities would still not leave
them the equal of Whites. Kant's racial theory entails that, when the four races
were initially developing as a result of climate and other environmental factors, the future possibilities of those races were set permanently. Kant applied
the same perspective to Native Americans, with similar results:

> That their natural disposition has not yet reached a *complete* fitness for any
> climate provides a test that can hardly offer another explanation why this race,
> too weak for hard labor, too phlegmatic for diligence, and unfit for any culture,
> still stands . . . [23]

One consequence of the idea that in the course of history the species should
develop its capacities to perfection was that human history was fundamentally
the history of the White race, as they allegedly were alone in having all the
talents. The other races could at best play only a subordinate role.

I have shown that whereas for Rousseau it seemed possible that the price of
perpetual peace may yet be too high, Kant had no such qualms. I have also
indicated why. Calculations about the price of peace have no role to play for
Kant because the civil union that peace inaugurates is the site where the human
species is meant to attain perfection. In this way, peace becomes integral to the
very possibility of meaning in human affairs. There is no legitimate alternative
insofar as peace alone can bring to human affairs an order similar to that
found in nature, but this peace cannot be attained without violence. Indeed,
the very meaning of human existence is at stake in this process. The consequence, which is not explicit in Kant himself, but which is stated by some of
his heirs, is that to oppose or to resist this process is to side against human
progress. There can be no neutral parties in a war in which the fate of humanity is held to be at issue. Failure to side with the agents of history, who are at
the same time the agents of meaning in human affairs, is to side with the inhuman because it is to refuse to work toward that future that alone makes sense
of the apparent disorder of human affairs. This means that the very logic of
Kant's position committed its proponents to a greater fervor in favor of war

than that possessed by even the most dedicated of fanatics in earlier religious wars. In a religious war there is a great deal at stake, but in a sense one's salvation is secured merely by joining the war, regardless of the outcome. In Kant's schema, there is no such consolation: one must win.

Before Kant, peace had been thought primarily as the simple alternative to war: one was either at war with one's neighbors or at peace with them. One went to war to gain some advantage over them, such as an expansion of one's territory. By contrast, with Kant, war is nature's mechanism, beyond any intention of the participants, to bring about a permanent condition of peace in the distant future. Nevertheless, as the process of universal history becomes conscious through Kant, wars fought for the sake of peace are also fought for the sake of humanity and its ideals, such as freedom or democracy. Kant left unanswered the question of the role that the inferior races would play in the future of humanity, and future generations would take his thought in a direction that would have appalled him. In "Toward Perpetual Peace," Kant rejected wars of punishment: such wars would be possible only if one accepted some states as superior to others, and he ruled this out. However, one suspects that it is only in the context of European states that this relation of inferiority and superiority is ruled out in principle, particularly given the ease with which judgments about the relative superiority and inferiority of peoples are passed elsewhere.[24] Kant also rejected the idea of wars of extermination [*ausrottungskrieg, bellum internecinum*],[25] even though elsewhere he seemed to welcome the possibility that the Native Americans would wipe each other out.[26] Nevertheless, when one reads Charles Dilke's celebration of the Saxons as the only exterminating race, one finds a response to the Kantian question of the place of the allegedly inferior races. It is a response Kant clearly would have rejected, just as he would have rejected the form of imperialism Dilke proposed.[27] But it is the nature of ideas, and particularly the nature of questions, that their authors cannot control where they will lead. My claim in this essay is that Kant, by uniting the relatively new idea of perpetual peace with a teleological philosophy of history, opened the way to a world that he would have been horrified by, but which, nevertheless, he had helped to make possible. By suggesting that no price was too high to pay for peace, he had radically altered the way combatants would approach war, and by raising questions about whether all peoples were capable of sharing equally in the future of humanity, their preservation was put in jeopardy. Today when philosophers and politicians try to promote Kant's answers, they seem to be unaware of the fact that these same ideas are inextricably—one could almost say dialectically, if the term was still understood—linked with the very ideas they are supposed to oppose. These are the dangers that ensue once human beings look to history for validation.

The Ascendance of the Political in Hegel

The Kantian belief in peace as the culmination of human history does not so much search for points of agreement that might allow nations to live together;

it is capable of inventing enemies where none previously existed. Hence, today, the United States of America sometimes considers as its enemies nations that are not seen as democratic or committed to free trade: they are judged to have refused the future in which peace will be secured. The United States can do so because it constitutes itself as at the vanguard of history. It is the representative of the future in the present; it is tomorrow today. By declaring itself the embodiment of the future, this one country claims for itself the right to exercise the jurisdiction of history: It, thus, claims the right to judge other peoples and governments by what they have done to promote or impair cosmopolitanism; the right to impose that judgment by force, if necessary; and the right to be free of the judgment of others because it alone represents this future. This may be a long way from what Kant intended when he declared future generations will judge peoples and governments according to what they have done to promote or to hinder the objectives of cosmopolitanism.[28]

In isolation, Kant's statement could be read as postponing judgment: only the future will provide the retrospective account that reveals the truth of the present. However, since Kant, we have learned to recognize that postponing judgment with the thought that history will judge us only opens the way for those who claim to be the agents of history to take the moral high ground for themselves. The fight for peace is thereby located beyond the sphere of morality, because the temptation immediately arises that one should abandon all constraints in the present in order to secure the future condition in which morality will triumph. Kant insisted on the primacy of morality over politics but the reversal of this ordering in Hegel was all but inevitable.[29] One can see this from the fact that the priority of morality over politics is nowhere reflected in Kant's account of a universal history, which is governed by the asocial sociality that precedes peace.[30] The somewhat simplistic reading of Kant's essay on peace that philosophers have recently developed is possible only because it is read in isolation from the theory of history to which it is inextricably tied.[31] Kant's starting point is that states are in their relation to each other in a state of nature fundamentally no different from that what individuals find themselves in prior to the social contract: "War is only a regrettable expedient for asserting one's rights by force within a state of nature, where no court of justice (*gerichtshof*) is available to judge with legal authority. In such cases, neither party can be declared an unjust enemy, for this would already presuppose a judge's decision (*richterausspruch*); only the *outcome* of the conflict, as in the case of a so-called 'judgment of God' (*Gottesgerichte*), can decide who is in the right."[32] This opened the door to Hegel's adoption of the idea that might is right. Many important nineteenth-century politicians and activists learned from Hegel the idea that there was no contingency in history, and, specifically, that history gave a positive role to violence. For example, Belinsky described how in the course of the summer of 1837, he read Hegel with Bakunin and "a new world opened before us—might is right and right might! No, I cannot describe to you with what emotion I heard these words—it was a liberation."[33]

Ironically, Kant's image as an apostle of peace was largely fostered by the one-sided interpretation imposed on him by his opponents. The distortion is already apparent in the work of Friedrich Gentz in 1800.[34] The dispute was not—and still is not—between peace now or war now. It was between a future perpetual peace brought about by war now and perpetual war broken only by interludes of peaceful coexistence. And yet it seems once again that Kant, by setting up the terms of the debate, had established the framework within which those who rejected his position could operate. So when Hegel rejected what he regarded as the well-meaning but false idea that war is something that ought not to be, on the grounds that war is ethically necessary, because without it, peoples sink into merely private forms of life,[35] he was merely repeating Kant's warning that peace debases the way a people thinks by cultivating selfishness and cowardice.[36] In fact, in spite of his rejection of Kantian cosmopolitanism and perpetual peace, Hegel's *Lectures on the Philosophy of World History* can best be read as his answer to Kant's call for "a philosophical attempt to work out a universal history of the world in accordance with a plan of nature."[37]

The extent to which Hegel adopted proposals that went far beyond anything Kant would have tolerated is not in doubt. Whereas Kant argued in the fifth preliminary article of *Toward Perpetual Peace* that "no state shall forcibly interfere in the constitution and government of another state,"[38] Hegel described how what he called "civilized peoples" have a right to impose a constitution on so-called "unformed peoples," those who have "virtually no constitution," because only a constitution enables other states to live at peace with it.[39] Nor does he stop there. One reads in *The Philosophy of Right* that civilized nations are entitled to treat as barbarians nations that are less advanced than they are.[40] To treat in a barbarous fashion those one regards as barbarians seems to legitimate a descent to what one takes to be their level, while at the same time retaining a sense of superiority. It is also to treat others as one imagines one would be treated by them, while at the same time separating that form of behavior from one's sense of oneself: In a phrase, the war on barbarism justifies barbarism. Hegel is explicit that to identify one's nation with the most advanced stage of world history at any given moment is to appropriate the rights of world spirit, which is the right to deny rights to the other.[41] To be outside history, as Blacks and Native Americans were for Hegel, was to be without justification, without a reason to be.[42] Nevertheless, one should not exaggerate the differences. When Hegel described the extinction of the Native Americans without expressing a clear moral judgment,[43] he was, albeit unwittingly, repeating a gesture Kant had earlier made in his notebooks.[44] According to them both, history would pass its judgment, so there was no need for us to do so. That is why there are no innocent victims of history for Hegel. When lecturing on the philosophy of right in Heidelberg, he said, in the context of Schiller's statement that "World history is a court of world judgment," (*Der Weltgeschichte ist ein Weltgericht*), that "No people ever suffered wrong: what it suffered, it had merited."[45] To describe such an idea as impossible after the Holocaust, as people like to do, is problematic because it seems to imply that it was a legitimate thought before the Holocaust.

Perpetual Peace and Total War

The idea that the end justifies the means in world politics is often associated with forms of Marxism, but it is also operative today, not only in the way that we are told that one is either with the United States of America or against it, but more especially in the way we are told that the treatment afforded to those characterized as the opponents of peace does not have to be in accord with humane values, the values for which one is fighting. This is also what allows civilian deaths to be so easily disregarded in such a war. Civilian deaths are merely collateral damage. In a world in which statistics alone guarantee order, no official statistics are kept on these deaths. They are left uncounted because they do not count. A similar use of the logic of peace to justify war through an appeal to the perspective of a philosophy of history is well illustrated by the following statement made by Madeleine Albright, when President Bill Clinton's Secretary of State. Speaking in February 1998, during what retrospectively seems like a relatively quiet period of American foreign policy, she justified a missile attack on Iraq in the following terms: "If we use force, it is because we are America. We are the indispensable nation. We stand tall, and we see further into the future."[46] The United States of America here occupies the place Kant had given to Europe. The United States, which has long identified itself as the land of the future, represents itself as the future of humanity. Its actions are not, therefore, subject to judgment by other nations, who are in no position to judge it, because judgment comes from the future. It is a way of thinking that Kant helped to originate insofar as he opened up a perspective according to which the unconscious motives driving history have now allegedly become conscious.

The tendency today is to set political idealism in opposition to *Realpolitik*, but the two are not necessarily opposed. Political idealism also has its uses. One can see this conjunction in Henry Kissinger's early thinking on politics. As an undergraduate student at Harvard University, Kissinger wrote a 377-page senior honors thesis under the title "The Meaning of History: Reflections on Spengler, Toynbee and Kant."[47] That was in 1950. In 1957, Kissinger published his doctoral dissertation, *A World Restored. Metternich, Castlereagh and the Problems of Peace 1812–1822*. In the second paragraph, Kissinger announced one of the guiding threads of the book:

> Whenever peace—conceived as the avoidance of war—has been the primary objective of a power or a group of powers, the international system has been at the mercy of the most ruthless member of the international community. Whenever the international order has acknowledged that certain principles could not be compromised even for the sake of peace, stability based on an equilibrium of forces was at least conceivable.[48]

Here, principle is placed above peace as the mere avoidance of war, but not for the sake of principle. It is done in the hope of producing this kind of peace as an effect of not pursuing it. What Kissinger does not add at this point is how another kind of peace, perpetual peace, can serve as one of the principles that cannot be compromised merely to secure the absence of war. Nor did he appear to realize that, when it does so, the result can be massive human devastation.

This is what happened during the course of the First World War.[49] When the United States of America entered the war, President Woodrow Wilson declared his action to be not only "in defense of American honor and American rights," but also "a world struggle . . . a struggle of men who love liberty everywhere." America was "born to serve mankind."[50] This conception led Wilson to insist on the harsh terms imposed on Germany after the First World War: "The settlement must be final. There can be no compromise. No halfway decision would be tolerable. No halfway decision is conceivable."[51] This was a consequence of the sacrifices the United States had made and the conviction, widespread in the United States, that only total victory could lead to total peace. Wilson had come to present the war as a fight for the "national existence" of the United States, fed by "sacrifices such as the world has never known before."[52] His rhetoric employed a certain cosmopolitan language as a way of justifying his country's actions: the United States was an instrument of a higher purpose that coincided with that of humanity at large. However, it was very different before the United States entered the war, as is apparent if one recalls a speech Wilson delivered on January 22, 1917. At that time, he insisted that the liberals and friends of humanity in every nation should want "a peace without victory," "a peace between equals."[53] Wilson explained in a speech in September 1918 that the American people had during the course of the war changed their view of what was supposed to be accomplished by it, precisely because it was "a people's war" fought for "a permanent peace."[54]

This difference between a peace without victory and a settlement that must be final reflects Kant's distinction in the first of the six preliminary articles for perpetual peace, between truce as a suspension of hostilities and peace as an end of all hostilities.[55] The latter notion serves to explain not only a tendency in modern warfare for nations to want to eradicate their enemies, but also their insistence that in doing so, they are acting in the interests of all humanity. It has long been recognized that there is a connection between Kant and Woodrow Wilson, through Kant's proposal of a federation of nations in the *Second Definitive Article for a Perpetual Peace*[56] and the League of Nations established after the First World War: In 1919, Karl Vorländer published a short book under the title *Kant und der Gedanke des Völkerbundes* that included an appendix "Kant and Wilson," which compared Kant's proposals to those of Woodrow Wilson, not without giving the American president credit for surpassing Kant in some respects.[57] But the connection between the two is somewhat deeper than the proposal for a League of Nations. It lies in their ideas of the relation between peace and war, even if Kant himself would surely not have legitimated the idea of a war to end all wars; he had a much clearer sense of how long the process might take.

Since the Second World War, commentators have been much too inclined to read Kant as arguing against war, thereby overlooking the fundamental role he gave to antagonism.[58] To be sure, in the preparation for the First World War, some German commentators, such as Rudolf Eucken, saw Kantian ideas as compromising the development of a war machine. However, later German commentators, who took up Kant's essays on history and on peace between the two world wars, saw more clearly the positive role Kant had given to war. For example, Paul Natorp, who was himself no war-monger, recognized in his 1924 essay *"Kant über Krieg und Frieden"* that, for Kant, life is war.[59] Similarly, Julius Ebbinghaus, who would later leave Germany to escape the Nazis, recognized that Kant saw no way to put an end to wars.[60] Kant was clear: "perpetual peace . . . is indeed an unachievable idea."[61] He did, however, think that alliances which serve for an approximation to that condition were not unachievable.[62]

Clearly, Hegel brings us a great deal closer to the idea of total war, because he is relatively free of the moralizing to which Kant was prone, but my concern here is not to provide the intellectual genealogy of the idea of total war. It is rather to indicate how the idea of total war draws much of its force—dialectically one might say—from the Kantian framework of perpetual peace. What called for total war was the raising of the stakes for which wars were being fought. So long as monarchs fought wars for their relative advantage, there was less investment in victory on the part of the people of a nation than when democratic nations were persuaded that their very survival was at stake. The First World War offers a clear example of how a war that was supposed to be over by Christmas could be sustained for years without decisive results, simply because it was fueled by the relatively new phenomena of national enthusiasm for war. The more casualties sustained, the higher each side raised its expectation of what had to be demanded of the other side in the case of victory, so as to justify those losses. As the demands were elevated, the need for an even more decisive victory developed as the precondition for exacting them. As some commentators have suggested, eighteenth-century princes would have seen the impasse much earlier and would have agreed to a truce.[63] According to Kant, democracies are slow to go to war,[64] but he wrote in democracy's infancy and, so, was unaware of the fact that casualties sometimes make it hard for a democracy to pull back from a war in progress, because it means that the nation has to accept that some of its people had sacrificed themselves in vain. The commitment is intensified when a nation becomes convinced that its very survival as a nation is threatened or is believed threatened. Furthermore, politicians recognize that an additional advantage can be gained by announcing that the fight is one means by which the future of civilization, and perhaps even of humanity itself, can be defended against the forces of barbarism. War could still be presented as a way of resolving disputes or even establishing a new order, but more was at stake if the war was seen as a battle for order against disorder, meaning versus futility, along the lines that the Kantian philosophy of history had inaugurated.

The preeminent theorist of total war was General Erich Ludendorff, but he did not consider himself to be the originator of the practice.[65] The phrase "total war" was first used by a Frenchman, Léon Daudet, while the First World War was still in progress, to refer to the extension of the struggle to every domain: political, economic, commercial, industrial, intellectual, juridic, and financial.[66] Whereas, according to Daudet, it was the Germans who had "mobilized" on every level, according to Ludendorff, it was the failure of the German nation to fight a total war in the First World War that led the German army to defeat under his command by an enemy that believed that it was engaged in a struggle for its existence: the German people believed that they were engaged in a war of aggression and, so, were not fully invested in the fight.[67] Immediately after Germany's loss in 1918, Ludendorff, together with his wife Mathilde, a prolific author in her own right, set about preparing for the next war. This meant attacking Jews, Freemasons, and Roman Catholics as enemies of the state, in large measure because of their alleged lack of total commitment to the state. Indeed, Ludendorff was so convinced that they could not be trusted that he thought that Jews should not be allowed to fight in the armies of Nordic people, nor Blacks in the armies of "white people."[68] In 1930, Ernst Jünger coined the phrase "total mobilization," but what Ludendorff meant by "total war" was not, as with Daudet, just a mobilization of personnel and resources, where every single German is placed at the service of the war leaders,[69] but also a mobilization of the psyche or soul.[70] Although Ludendorff emphasized destruction of the economic life of the enemy country,[71] he also indicated that the bombing of the civil population in open cities is appropriate in war for survival, even though it runs counter to the laws and customs of war.[72] The fact that Jünger's essay was published five years before Ludendorff's on total war does not threaten Ludendorff's claim to originality. Ludendorff had already expounded these ideas in his war memoirs, and indeed Jünger himself appealed to Ludendorff's attempts to fuse the military and the political command as evidence of total mobilization.[73]

Nevertheless, in at least one respect, Jünger's analysis of war over the previous hundred years was more penetrating than Ludendorff's. In his war memoirs, Ludendorff acknowledged the success of the Allied propaganda in undermining the German's resolve by talking of "disarmament after the war" and the League of Nations, but he insisted that the Germans themselves wanted only to restore and to preserve peace.[74] This means that, at least immediately after the war, Ludendorff did not see the connection between the idea of total war and the idea of an absolute, inevitable, peace. By contrast, Jünger argued that Germany's defeat was in part the result of the fact that Germans thought they were fighting for Germany, whereas their opponents had the advantage of thinking that they were taking part in "a struggle of progress, *civilisation*, humanity, and even peace."[75] Writing in 1930, Jünger saw the wars of the early part of the century as presenting clear evidence of the advantage held by "progressive" nations, to the point that it seemed to evoke "a deterministic process such as Darwin's theory of the survival of the 'fittest.' "[76] In other words, from

Jünger's perspective, Ludendorff, for all his insight into modern war, had failed to see that what was ultimately decisive in total war was not primarily the desire to annihilate one's enemy so as not to be annihilated oneself, but the desire to annihilate one's enemy for the sake of progress. Hence Jünger's comment that the genius of war has been penetrated by the spirit of progress.[77]

A *Levinasian Possibility*

Even in a brief essay such as this one, it is not enough to offer a diagnosis that shows that Kant's writings on peace and cosmopolitanism, the place most theorists still go as a resource for addressing our current problems of war and peace, are better understood as part of the problem than part of the cure. So, although I cannot argue that there is a ready-made alternative to which to turn, I shall close by briefly indicating why I believe the writings of Emmanuel Levinas, while far from free of problems of their own, nevertheless indicate another avenue that is well worth exploring.[78]

Levinas began *Totality and Infinity* by questioning the delay to which the introduction of ethics is usually subjected. For Levinas, the politics of being is the politics of war, but he wrote the book to show that there was still a place for ethics. More specifically, he presented an account of war that did not stop at an account of the injuries and deaths it causes, but at the violence it does to the identity of the same, which he explained as follows: "The ontological event that takes form in this black light is a casting into movement of beings hitherto anchored in their identity, a mobilization of absolutes, by an objective order from which there is no escape."[79] The reference to "mobilization" is not accidental. It deliberately evokes Jünger's essay "Total Mobilization" and was introduced because Levinas recognized that the mobilization of resources and the soul of a nation is only made possible by the absolutization of such values as freedom, democracy, or peace itself. Similarly, Levinas recognized that the contemporary tendency to reduce the individual to being a "bearer of forces unbeknown to themselves" is as characteristic of the Kantian discourse of peace as it is of the Hegelian discourse of war. The experience of having seen the dissolution of individuals within larger forces, as happens in total war, forms the basis of Levinas's account of totality.

Although there is no doubt that Levinas's treatment of history is a polemic against Hegel and his idea of the jurisdiction of history,[80] it is less widely acknowledged that Levinas also sought to use his discussion of history to rescue the idea of peace from its Kantian heritage. Nevertheless, that is why on the very next page after his attack on Hegel, he denied that peace takes place "in the objective history disclosed by war, as the end of that war or as the end of history."[81] It is against both Hegel and Kant that Levinas proposed an eschatological notion of judgment that "draws beings out of the jurisdiction of history and the future,"[82] and calls one to responsibility for the victims of war that history tends to forget. It is for the same reason that, instead of locating peace and justice at the end of a history that begins in a Hobbesian war of all against all, as Kant does, Levinas in 1984, in "Peace and Proximity," located peace and justice at the origin.[83] Because peace ultimately arises in Levinas's account as an interruption of history it would be a mistake to suppose that his position is a simple reversal of Kant, although it sometimes might appear that way. Nevertheless, this recognition does not mean that Levinas's account of peace in "Peace and Proximity" is unproblematic, as can be seen by his regrettably all too characteristic rejection of multiculturalism, seemingly without regard for the evil that had been performed in the name of cultural imperialism.[84]

Nevertheless, Levinas restored the suspicion of war that had suffered with Kant. He warned against war being instituted "with a good conscience in the name of historical necessities."[85] This promotion of self-questioning not only marks a decisive difference between Levinas and Kant, but also between Levinas and those politicians who take their nations to war, declaring that they do so for the sake of all humanity, all the while drawing their self-assurance and self-righteousness from a philosophy of history committed to an inevitable progress toward inevitable peace. One should not forget here how Levinas appeals to the agony of conscience in the form of a fear of making the innocent suffer in order to establish the difference between state violence and true revolutionary politics.[86]

Nothing unleashes the horrors of war as readily as a self-confident sense of superiority that has been freed of suspicion about its own motivation. One can persuade oneself that one is superior on the basis of religion, race, culture, or morals, but in each case, the door is opened to the legitimization of brutality. In religious wars, one battles for what one holds most dear—one's soul and the approval of one's God—and one offers one's enemy the choice of conversion or death. In race wars, one worries about the racial purity that is supposed to be at the heart of the capacity of one's own race to survive, so one exterminates those already of mixed race or those who might threaten racial purity through amalgamation. In culture wars, one characterizes certain populations as barbaric or primitive and so places them under an evolutionary death sentence. The next step is to do nature's work for it, speeding up the extinction that is presumed to be their inevitable fate. The war for perpetual peace is a moral war and its proponents believe themselves authorized to distribute certain goods—such as representative democracy or a certain limited kind of liberal freedom—that all human beings are supposed to want by nature, whether they know it or not. That is also why they do not need to be asked what kind of peace, democracy, or freedom they want and under what conditions. It will be given to them in the name of self-determination by people claiming to know better than they do what they want for themselves. In these circumstances, self-questioning of the kind that Levinas encourages is not a betrayal of ethics, but is, rather, the heart of ethics and of peace, and is at least a step in the right direction.[87] Suspicion is nowhere more appropriate than when directed against those who exhibit a Kantian self-righteousness in the pursuit to peace, given its risks. To be sure, the problem is less with Kant than with those who follow him. The Kantian idea of a progressive history that moves toward a perfect civic union subverts, against Kant's own intentions, the opposition of peace and war as an opposition of morality and politics. Once peace no longer alternates with war throughout history, but is postponed to the end of a fundamentally violent history, as its fulfillment, then ethics, too, has been postponed. This is the characteristically modern position on war that is barely 200 years old. Today it would be considered naïve to take an ethical approach to the conduct of war. In the eighteenth century, wars were fought under much stricter rules than they are today, the Geneva conventions notwithstanding. But that was before Kant transformed the terms of the debate.[88]

Notes

1. Howard, *The Invention of Peace*, 1.
2. Howard, *Invention of Peace*, 31. See also Howard, *War and the Liberal Conscience*, 25.
3. Kant, "*Ideen zu einer allgemeinen Geschichte*," 24; and Kant, "Idea for a Universal History with a Cosmopolitan Purpose," 47. (Henceforth, AA followed by the volume number and PW, respectively.)
4. The difference from Kant is particularly obvious in the case of the Abbé de Saint-Pierre, who wanted peace in Europe so that the Europeans could attack the Turks: *Projet pour rendre la paix perpétuelle en Europe*, 689–92. For discussions of peace among Kant's contemporaries, see Dietze, *Ewiger Friede?*
5. AA VIII 29; PW 51.
6. Rousseau, "Jugement sur la Paix perpétuelle," 396; trans. Roosevelt, "Rousseau's 'Critique' of the Abbé de Saint-Pierre, 229.
7. AA III 23.
8. AA VIII 18; PW 42.
9. AA VIII 17–18; PW 41–42. So far as I know, the immediate source for this view has not been established, but it seems likely that he had in mind the work of Johann Peter Süssmilch, *Die göttliche Ordnung*.
10. AA VIII 20; PW 44.
11. AA VIII 20; PW 44.
12. AA VIII 30; PW 53.
13. AA VIII 20; PW 44.
14. AA V 433. Kant, *Critique of Judgment*, 320. (Henceforth, CJ.)
15. See Bernasconi, "Who Invented the Concept of Race?" 11–36.
16. AA XXV/2 1187.
17. AA VIII 29–30; PW 52.
18. AA VIII 20; PW 44–45.
19. AA V 429–30; CJ 317.
20. For Kant's antipathy to race mixing, see further Bernasconi, "Kant as an Unfamiliar Source of Racism," 145–166; and "Will the Real Kant Please Stand Up," 10–19. On Kant's assessment of different races, see the remarks collected by Louden in *Kant's Impure Ethics*, 98–100.
21. AA VIII 65; PW 219–220.
22. AA XV 785.

23. Kant, "Über den Gebrauch teleologischer Principien in der Philosophie," 175–76; Kant, "On the Use of Teleological Principles in Philosophy," 48.
24. AA VIII 346; PW 96.
25. AA VIII 346; PW 96.
26. AA XXV/2 840.
27. Dilke, *Greater* Britain, 308–309. I cite Dilke, as he was one of the foremost early exponents of imperialism. His characterization of the Saxons probably derived from Knox's *The Races of Men*, 466: "But now the aim of the Saxon man is the extermination of the dark races of men—the aborigines—the men of the desert and of the forest." I develop this perspective on Kant further in "Why Do the Happy Inhabitants of Tahiti Bother to Exist at All?" 139–148.
28. AA VIII 31; PW 53.
29. AA VIII 370–386; PW 116–130. Hegel, *Grundlinien der Philosophie des Rechts*, 501–02; Hegel, *Elements of the Philosophy of Right*, 370. (Henceforth, W7 and EPR, respectively.)
30. AA VIII 383–86; PW 137–39.
31. For an interesting exception, although I am not underwriting his interpretation, see Lefort, "The Idea of Humanity and the Project of Universal Peace," 142–158.
32. AA VIII 346; PW 96.
33. Quoted by Kohn, "The Permanent Mission," 285.
34. Gentz, "Über der ewigen Frieden," 461–497. It is perhaps of some interest to note that Kissinger showed a familiarity with Gentz's later writings in his doctoral dissertation.
35. Hegel, *Vorlesungen über Naturrecht und Staatswissenschaft*, 253; Hegel, *Lectures on Natural Right and Political Science*, 303. (Henceforth VI and NR, respectively.)
36. AA V 263; CJ 122.
37. AA VIII 29; PW 51.
38. AA VIII 346; PW 96.
39. VI 251; NR 301.
40. W7, 507–508; EPR, 376.
41. VI 256; NR 206.
42. See Bernasconi, "With What Must the Philosophy of World History Begin?" 171–201.
43. Hegel, *Die Vernunft in der Geschichte*, 200; Hegel, *Lectures on the Philosophy of World History*, 163. See Hoffheimer, "Hegel, Race, Genocide," 37–38.
44. AA XXV/2 878.
45. VI 257; NR 307. Schiller, "Resignation," 168. See also, W7 503; EPR 371.
46. NBC *Today*. Quoted by Todd, *After the Empire*, 204.
47. See the extensive account in Dickson, *Kissinger and the Meaning of History*, and, more briefly, Graubard, *Kissinger, Portrait of a Mind*, 7–8.
48. Kissinger, *A World Restored*, 1.
49. The First World War has often been called the war of the philosophers. According to Kurt Flasch, it gave rise to more than 13,000 philosophical pamphlets in Germany alone. Flasch, *Die geistige Mobilmachung*, 11. See also Hoeres, *Krieg der Philosophen*. The so-called war on terrorism, including the war in Iraq, in spite of its apparent disconnection from the events of September 11, 2001, is often presented as a war of philosophical ideas, insofar as concepts of freedom and democracy are invoked to promote it. However, in comparison with the First World War, philosophers today have been relatively quiet as philosophers. This failure has, for the most part, led the philosophical framework that sustains such arguments to go unexamined.

50. Wilson, "Memorial Address at Arlington National Cemetery," 52–53.
51. Wilson, "The Four-Point Speech," 233.
52. Wilson, "Four-Minute Address by the President," 236–37.
53. Wilson, "Address to the United States Senate," 410. Wilson for some time continued to express similar statements in his speeches. For an overview of this aspect of Wilson's policy, see Martin *Peace Without Victory*.
54. Wilson, "Address Opening the Campaign for the Fourth Liberty Loan," 253–55.
55. AA VIII 343; PW 93.
56. AA VIII 354; PW 102.
57. Vorländer, "Kant und Wilson," 67–85.
58. See, for example, Friedrich, *Inevitable Peace*, 60.
59. Natorp, *Kant über Krieg und Frieden*, 15.
60. Ebbinghaus, *Kants Lehre vom ewigen Frieden und die Kriegsschuldfrage*.
61. AA VI 350. Kant, *Practical Philosophy*, 487.
62. AA VIII 386; PW 130.
63. Howard, *War in European History*, 113.
64. AA VIII 351; PW 100.
65. I do not mean to suggest that Ludendorff's concept of total war is the only viable one. For current discussions of alternatives, see Chickering, "Total War," 13–28. See also Förster, "Introduction" in *Great War, Total War*, 7–9. For some indication of how an understanding of total war might impact contemporary conflicts, including peacekeeping operations, see Smith, *The Utility* Force, 84–91. At one time, von Clausewitz's notion of "absolute war" was seen as a prophecy of total war, but this idea has now been refuted. See Strachan, "Clausewitz and the Dialectics of War," 32–33.
66. Daudet, *La Guerre Totale*, 8.
67. Ludendorff, *Der Totale Krieg*, 87; Ludendorff, *The Nation at War*, 143. (Henceforth, TK and NW, respectively.) For a somewhat dated discussion of Ludendorff that nevertheless gives some indication of the reception of his ideas, see Speier, "Ludendorff," 306–321. On Ludendorff's influence, see Sywotek, *Mobilmachung für den totalen Krieg*, 67. Some commentators do not seem to recognize that Ludendorff thought that the allies had been fighting a total war and that Germany's failure was in not doing so. Hull, *Absolute Destruction*, 205. Other commentators seem to suggest that Ludendorff was in bad faith when he denied that the Germans had practiced total war: *Ibid.*, 330.
68. TK 50n; NW 89n.
69. TK 88; NW 145.
70. TK 26; NW 51.
71. TK 120; NW 189.
72. TK 63n; NW 189n.
73. Jünger, "Die totale Mobilmachung," 15; Jünger, trans. Joel Golb and Richard Wolin, "Total Mobilization," 127. (Henceforth KK and TM, respectively.)
74. Ludendorff, *Meine Kriegserinnerungen*, 3 and 286–87, Ludendorff, *My War Memories*, 4 and 362–63.
75. KK 22; TM 134.
76. KK 17; TM 130. It is extraordinary in the light of recent events today to read Jünger's explanation of "the grotesque idea" of an advertising executive being asked to prepare the propaganda for a modern war, particularly when he introduces the example of the entry of the United States into the First World War, which involved raising its own interests to the rank of a humanitarian principle, in this case "freedom of the seas" (KK 19–20; TM 131–132).

77. KK 11; TM 123.
78. See, for example, Caygill, *Levinas and the Political*; and Bernasconi, "Who Is My Neighbor?" 5–30.
79. Levinas, *Totalité et Infini*, ix; Levinas, *Totality and Infinity*, 21. (Henceforth, TeI and TI, respectively.)
80. TeI xi; TI 23.
81. TeI xii, TI 24.
82. TeI xi; TI 23.
83. Levinas, "Paix et proximité," 346; Levinas, "Peace and Proximity," 169. (Henceforth, PP and BPW, respectively.)
84. PP 340; BPW 163.
85. PP 346; BPW 169.
86. Levinas, *Du sacré au saint*, 38–39; Levinas, *Nine Talmudic Readings*, 110.
87. Bernasconi, "The Ethics of Suspicion," 3–18.
88. Since writing this essay, I have read Bell, *The First Total War*. It provides some of the historical background of the transformation whose philosophical logic I have outlined here. Bell observes that the "Enlightenment theories of history . . . concealed unsuspected changes" by transforming peace from a moral imperative into a historical one. "And so they opened the door to the idea that in the name of future peace, any and all means might be justified—including even exterminating war" (77). As I noted above and as Bell confirms, Kant explicitly drew a line rejecting the use of such means. My point here has been to show both how difficult it is to maintain that line and how closely tied those changes are to the new rhetoric of peace that Kant helped to introduce.

Chapter 4

Violent Thoughts about Slavoj Žižek

Simon Critchley

Slavoj Žižek has been telling lies about me. He attacked a recent book of mine, *Infinitely Demanding* (2007), in the *London Review of Books*.[1] Since then, things have gone from bad to worse, but I will spare the reader the grisly details. What I would like to do here is to use this debate as a lever for trying to think about the difficult question of the nature and plausibility of a politics of nonviolence and try and explore what I see as the complex dialectic of violence and nonviolence. Those with an eye for detail might notice that the following represents both a clarification of and a shift in my position on violence and nonviolence presented in *Infinitely Demanding*.

I begin by discussing Žižek's recently published book *Violence* and then expand and deepen my focus by way of a reading of Walter Benjamin's "Critique of Violence." This leads to a thinking–through of the idea of divine violence and an interpretation of the biblical commandment "Thou shalt not kill," the injunction to nonviolence.[2] In conclusion, I turn to the specifics of the political disagreement between myself and Žižek, which pivot on the question of the relation between authoritarianism and anarchism.

"I Would Prefer Not To"

Žižek enjoys a good joke. Here's one of my favorites: Two men, having had a drink or two, go to the theater, where they become thoroughly bored with the play. One of them feels a pressing need to urinate, so he tells his friend to mind his seat while he goes to find a toilet. "I think I saw one down the corridor outside," says his friend. The man wanders down the corridor, but finds no W.C. Wandering ever further into the recesses of the theater, he walks through a door and sees a plant pot. After copiously urinating into it, he returns to his seat and his friend says to him, "What a pity! You missed the best part. Some fellow just came on the stage and pissed in that plant pot."

This gag perfectly describes the argument of Žižek's book on violence. Drunkenly watching the rather boring spectacle of the world stage, we might feel an overwhelming subjective need to follow the call of nature somewhere discreet. Yet, in our bladder-straining self-interest, we lose sight of the objective reality of the play and our implication in its action. We are oblivious to the fact that we are pissing on stage for the whole world to see.

So it is with violence. Our subjective outrage at the facts of violence—a suicide bombing, a terrorist attack, the assassination of a seemingly innocent political figure—blinds us to the objective violence of the world, a violence where we are perpetrators and not just innocent bystanders. All we see are apparently inexplicable acts of violence that disturb the supposed peace and normal flow of everyday life. We consistently overlook the objective or what Žižek calls "systemic" violence that is endemic to our socio-economic order.

The main ambition of Žižek's book is to refer subjective violence to the objective violence that is its underside and enabling precondition. "Systemic violence is thus something like the notorious 'dark matter' of physics,"[3] Žižek writes, which is invisible to naked eye. In the "Six Sideways Reflections" into which *Violence* is divided, Žižek offers a rather cool and, at times, cruel analysis of the varieties of objective violence. He asks good, tolerant multicultural Western liberals like you, like us, like them (delete, where appropriate) to suspend our outraged and impassioned responses to acts of violence (what he later calls, with Nietzsche, a reactive rather than active force) and turn instead to the real substance of the global situation. In order to understand violence, we need some good old-fashioned dispassionate Marxist materialist critique.

At the heart of Žižek's book is an argument about ideology that has been a powerful constant feature of his work since *The Sublime Object of Ideology*, his first book in English from 1989.[4] Far from existing in some sort of post–ideological world at the end of history where all problems can be diagnosed with neo-liberal economics and self-serving assertions of human rights, ideology completely structures and falsely sutures our lived reality. This ideology might be subjectively invisible, but it is objectively real. Each of us is onstage pissing in that plant pot. Ideology structures or, better, sutures experience, masking what the early Žižek—at the time much, much closer to Laclau than now—saw as the basic antagonism, the *political* antagonism that structures social relations. The great ideological illusion of the present is that there is no time to reflect and we have to act *now*. On the contrary, Žižek asks us to step back from the false reactive urgency of the present with its multiple injunctions to intervene like good humanitarians. In the face of this fake urgency, we should be more like Marx who, with a potential revolution at the gates in 1870, complained to Engels that the activists should wait a couple more years until he had finished *Das Capital*.

Žižek's diagnosis of this ideology is, as ever, quite delightful, producing counter-intuitive inversions that overturn what passes for common sense. Žižek rages against the reduction of love to masturbatory self-interest, the multiple hypocrisies of the Israel/Palestine conflict, and the supposed liberal philanthropy of Bill Gates and George Soros. There is a fascinating analysis of the scenes of torture and humiliation of prisoners at Abu Ghraib, which display, Žižek rightly contends, nothing more than the obscene underside of American culture, the culture of incarceration.

But whither all this dialectical brio? Ay, there's the rub. Žižek concludes the book with an apology for what he calls, following Walter Benjamin, "divine violence." I shall come back to this in some detail below. Divine violence is understood theoretically as, "the heroic assumption of the solitude of the sovereign decision." Practically, Žižek illustrates this with the questionable examples of the radical Jacobin violence of Robespierre in France in the 1790s and the invasion of the dispossessed, a decade or so ago, descending from the impoverished and crime-ridden *favelas* in Rio de Janeiro to disturb the peace of the bourgeois neighborhoods that border them. But, in a final twist, Žižek counsels us to do *nothing* in the face of the objective, systemic violence of the world. We should "just sit and wait" and have the courage to do nothing. The book ends with the words, "Sometimes, doing nothing is the most violent thing to do." True enough, but what can this possibly mean?

Let me briefly turn to the governing concept of Žižek's recent work, the parallax, and what is purportedly his *magnum opus, The Parallax View.*[5] The concept of parallax is a way of giving expression to, at its deepest, the radical non-coincidence of thinking and being. Such is Žižek's metaphysics. If Parmenides and the entire onto-theological tradition that follows him, famously recovered by Heidegger, claims that it is the same thing to think and to be, then Žižek disagrees. Between thinking and being, between, in his parlance, the ticklish subject and the tickling object, there exists a radical non-coincidence, a constitutive lack of identity. Such is, of course, nothing more than the teaching of Lacan, and the parallax view is the expression of the *pas-tout*, the not-all that circles around the traumatic kernel of the Real.

In the conclusion to *The Parallax View,*[6] although it is suggested throughout the book, Žižek claims that the parallax view opens onto a politics, what he calls—echoing Badiou—a subtractive politics, expressed in the figure of Melville's Bartleby, who reappears as the hero in the closing pages of *Violence.*[7] What interests Žižek in Bartleby is his insistent, "I would prefer not to," where Žižek places the emphasis on the "not to" or the "not to do," on Bartleby's impassive, inert, and insistent being, which hovers uncertainly somewhere between passivity and the vague threat of violence. So, at the level of politics, it is ultimately the politics of Bartleby's smile, of his "not" that Žižek wants to oppose to other forms of thinking about politics. Which other forms? Well, mine for example, but we'll come back to that.

At the core of Žižek's relentless, indeed manic, production of books, articles, and lectures is a fantasy, I think, what my psychoanalyst friends would call an obsessional fantasy, a very pure version of the obsessional fantasy. On the one hand, the only authentic stance to take in dark times is to do nothing, to refuse all commitment, to be paralyzed like Bartleby. On the other hand, Žižek dreams of a divine violence, a cataclysmic, purifying violence of the sovereign ethical deed, something like Sophocles' Antigone.

But Shakespearean tragedy is a more illuminating guide here than its ancient Greek predecessor. For Žižek is, I think, a Slovenian Hamlet, utterly paralyzed but dreaming of an avenging violent act for which, finally, he lacks the courage. In short, behind its shimmering dialectical inversions, Žižek's work leaves us in a fearful and fateful deadlock, both a transcendental-philosophical deadlock and a practical-political deadlock: the only thing to do is to do nothing. We should just sit and wait. Don't act, never commit, and continue to dream of an absolute, cataclysmic revolutionary act of violence. Thus speaks the great obsessional. As Hamlet says, 'Readiness is all'. But the truth is that Žižek is never ready. His work lingers in endless postponement and over-production. He ridicules others' attempts at thinking about commitment, resistance and action—people like me and many others—while doing nothing himself. What sustains his work is a dream of divine violence, cruelty, and force. I hope that one day his dreams come true.

Law and Nonviolence in Benjamin

Let me begin to try and deepen and perhaps depolemicize matters by going back to the source of Žižek's notion of divine violence in Benjamin's dense, difficult, and massively over-interpreted essay, *Critique of Violence* (Jacques Derrida, Giorgio Agamben, and Judith Butler have all been over this essay with a fine-tooth comb). The primary thing to keep in mind is that Benjamin's essay is called "*critique* of violence," and to consider what that might mean in relation to the topic of nonviolence. The essay is a critique of the violence of the law, where Benjamin writes, "violence . . . is the origin of the law."[8] This is exemplified in the death penalty as the violence over life and death, and embodied in the activity of the key executive institution of the modern state, the police. In the act of violence, then, the essence of the law is manifested, as well as—to use Hamlet's word—revealing something rotten [*etwas Morsches*] about the law.

Benjamin advances fascinating, but slightly obscure, conceptual distinctions: between law-making and law-preserving violence, between the political and the general strike, and between mythic and divine violence. Let's take them in turn and use them to unravel the argument of Benjamin's essay.

The first distinction between a violence that is *rechtsetzend* and *rechtserhaltend* is, for Benjamin, internal to the theory and practice of law. The claim is that all law is either *law-making* or *law-preserving* and that both these forms are violent. Benjamin makes a fascinating aside about the violent origin of every contract,[9] which recalls Shylock's undermining of Antonio's idealization of law as mercy by returning it to the brute materiality of the contract, of the bond, of the pound of flesh, cut from close to the heart. The same would also go for constitutional law; it requires a violent cut, a moment of decision, and the assertion of power, say, for example, in a revolution or a period of dramatic social transformation.

What Žižek misses, and I suspect he misses deliberately, is the fact that the operation of law-making and law-preserving violence raises a question. Benjamin writes, "the question poses itself whether there are no other than violent means for regulating conflicting human interests." At the beginning of the next paragraph, he writes, "Is any nonviolent resolution of conflict possible?"[10] His answer is that such a nonviolent resolution of conflict is indeed possible in what he calls "relationships among private persons," in courtesy, sympathy, peaceableness, and trust. This leads Benjamin to conclude that "there is a sphere of human agreement that is nonviolent to the extent that it is wholly inaccessible to violence: the proper sphere of 'understanding,' language, [*die Sprache*]."[11] Without wanting to get into the complexities of what Benjamin means by language, particularly his idea of a pure language [*reine Sprache*], we can already see that he is not simply arguing, like Žižek, that all human life is utterly pervaded and determined at every level by systemic or objective violence, but that a sphere of nonviolence is available, at the private, or what Benjamin calls the "subjective," level. Against Žižek, I want to defend this sense of the subjective.

Benjamin continues by turning to Georges Sorel's account of the general strike and makes a distinction between two forms of strike: the political strike and the proletarian general strike. Whereas the political strike is law-making, that is, it simply reinforces state power, the latter attempts to destroy state power and argue for "a wholly transformed work, no longer enforced by the state." As such—and readers of *Infinitely Demanding* will perhaps see where I am heading with this line of thought—where the political strike is law-making, the proletarian general strike is, to use Benjamin's word, "*anarchistic.*"[12] That is, it is revolutionary rather than reformist, committed to nonviolence rather than the violence of law, moral rather than governed by law and the state, and subjective rather than objective. Such anarchism does not require the violence of contracts or indeed constitutions, but aims at the extra-legal resolution of conflict, "Peacefully and without contracts," as he writes, "[o]n the analogy of agreement between private persons."[13]

It is not difficult to imagine why Žižek chooses to avoid and suppress this crucial aspect of Benjamin's essay. What he wants is Bartlebian inertia, on the one hand, and the sexy excitement of the prospect of a dose of ultra-violence, on the other. He wants to live his obsessional deadlock and not give up on his desire for postponement and lack of readiness, a desire that fuels his over-production. However, what I have just tried to explain about Benjamin's essay is the conceptual background against which he introduces his key concept of divine violence. Let's now turn to that idea. Benjamin makes two key assumptions. First, he writes,

> Since, however, every conceivable solution to human problems, not to speak of deliverance from the confines of all the world-historical conditions of existence, obtaining hitherto, remains impossible if violence is totally excluded in principle, the question necessarily arises as to what kinds of violence exist other than those envisaged by legal theory.[14]

So, we cannot expect a radical change in the state of human beings in the world if we exclude violence as a matter of principle. I think this is a crucial point and it has also led to misunderstandings of my defense of nonviolence and neo-anarchism in *Infinitely Demanding*. To be clear, I do not think that in the sphere of politics it makes sense to assert and hold to some principled and *a priori* conception of nonviolence. The standard objection to anarchism always turns on this point: how can you justify your use of violence? Shouldn't you be committed to nonviolence? If you resort to violence, don't you begin to resemble the enemy you are fighting against?

Of course, nonviolence is the aim of anarchist politics, but why should anarchists be the only political agents who have to decide beforehand that they will not be violent, when the specific circumstances of a political situation are still unknown? To this extent, the abstract question of violence versus nonviolence risks reducing anarchism to what Jacob Blumenfeld has called the politics of the spectator position where nonviolence becomes an abstract value, principle, or categorical imperative.[15] In specific political sequences, and it is always and only a case of such specifics—an eventual site, as Badiou might say—the move to violence is often entirely understandable. The turn to violence by protestors, critics, and opponents of a regime is most often simply a response to the provocations of the police and legal violence. Also, it is crucial here to distinguish violence against property from violence against persons. I have no moral problem with the former, but a lot of problems with the latter. As a character in Godard's *Notre Musique* writes, "To kill a human being in order to defend an idea is not to defend an idea, it is to kill a human being." My problem, then, is not so much with violence as with armchair or writing–chair romantic heroicizations of revolutionary violence of the kind that one finds in Žižek's mannerist Leninism. So, to go back to Benjamin's words, if violence cannot be excluded in principle from any social transformation, then what forms of violence exist other than those in legal theory, namely law-making and law-preserving violence? Can we perhaps even speak of what Judith Butler has called, in her highly compelling reading of Benjamin's essay, a "nonviolent violence"?[16] We will come back to that.

The second assumption Benjamin makes brings us to the topic of reason and introduces the key distinction of *Critique of Violence*. He writes: "For it is never reason [*Vernunft*] that decides on the justification of means and the justness of ends: fateful violence [*schicksalhafte Gewalt*] decides on the former, and God on the latter."[17] Although, in the context of the essay, this a peculiar and indeed throwaway remark on a huge topic—and the sudden introduction of the word "God" might appear slightly confusing—Benjamin would appear to be saying that despite the good intentions of someone like Kant, or indeed Rawls and Habermas, reason can never decide on the justification of means or the justness of the ends. The justification of means is the realm of fateful violence, or what Benjamin will call mythic violence, and the justness of ends is the realm of God, or divine violence. Let's try and clarify this distinction.

Mythic violence is illustrated with reference to the Greek myth of Niobe's arrogance in mocking Leto for only having two children, Apollo and Artemis, as opposed to the 14 she had herself. For such a seemingly mild indiscretion, Apollo slaughtered the seven sons and Artemis the seven daughters, and Niobe was turned to a stone statue that wept endless tears. The concept of mythic violence establishes, for Benjamin, the violence that is essentially alloyed to the making of law. Law-making is power-making, and to that extent, necessarily a manifestation of violence. A better example of such mythic violence is perhaps Aeschylus' *Oresteia*, where the condition of possibility for Athena's institution of justice in Athenian democracy is the violent act that decides against the Furies and in favor of Orestes for the simple reason that Athena honors the male principle in all things, having sprung directly from the head of Zeus, without the mediation of the womb. The lesson of the *Oresteia* and Greek tragedy more generally is that the traumatic cycle of revenge and family violence in the house of Atreus and elsewhere can only be suspended by Athena's violent institution of justice. Tragedy is mythic violence that attempts to break the repetitive cycle of family slaughter.

The only thing that can put a halt to the logic of mythic violence, Benjamin thinks, is divine violence, which is not law-making, but law-destroying [*rechtsvernichtend*]. This is lethal and Benjamin gives the biblical example of God's judgment of Korah for rebelling against him. If mythic violence is extremely bloody, then divine violence is bloodless. Korah was not slaughtered by God, rather the earth opened up to swallow him with all his belongings, even the linen was at the launderers and the needles borrowed by people living at some distance from him. Yawveh is nothing if not thorough. This is the function of revolutionary violence for Benjamin, whose origin, he insists, lies in the doctrine of the sanctity of life. If mythic violence is bloody power over human affairs for the sake of state power, then divine violence is the bloodless power over life for the sake of the living, for the sake of life's sacredness, what Butler calls its "sacred transience," a nonviolent violence.

Benjamin's argument in the closing paragraphs of *Critique of Violence* is extremely compact and oracular, but the claim is fascinating. What he is trying to do, in my view, and I am helped here by the closing words of Agamben's *State of Exception*, is "to show law in its non-relation to life and life in its non-relation to law."[18] That is, to open a space between law and life. The name of this space is politics. Namely, if the problem of politics is its eclipse and determination by law, where the political field is determined and regulated by law-making mythic violence for the sake of state power—the experience of the *Oresteia*—then the alternative is an act that, in Agamben's words, "severs the nexus between violence and law."[19] Such is the potentiality—but only the potentiality—of a transformation of the condition of mere or bare life in contemporary bio-politics into a praxis of life's sanctity, its sacredness indeed.

The question, of course, is how to do this. This brings us to a central issue. Towards the end of *Critique of Violence*, Benjamin gives a fascinating analysis of the biblical commandment, "Thou shalt not kill." This divine word is the expression of life's sanctity. But does it necessarily entail that in each and every instance I should not kill, that violence is absolutely prohibited? Matters turn here on how we understand the biblical injunction, and indeed injunctions in general. Is the commandment a criterion of judgment? Is it some sort of categorical imperative that must be followed in all cases? No, Benjamin insists, "Those who base a condemnation of all violent killing of one person by another on the commandment are therefore mistaken."[20] The divine commandment is not a principle, axiom, or categorical imperative, but what Benjamin calls a *Richtschnur des Handelns*, a plumb-line, thumb-line, or guideline for the action of people and communities, "who have to wrestle with it in solitude, and, in exceptional cases, to take on themselves the responsibility for ignoring it."[21]

So, the commandment "Thou shalt not kill," the first and last word of peace and life's sanctity, does not exclude the possibility and the actuality of killing in exceptional circumstances. Nor does it condone such killing. When we wrestle with it in solitude and decide not to follow the commandment, then the responsibility falls on us. The commandment "Thou shalt not kill" is, in Agamben's words, a word that "does not bind, that neither commands nor prohibits anything, but says only itself."[22] That is to say, it might guide an act, a true act, a political act, a praxis outside and beyond the mythic violence of the law. As should be clear, it is this dimension of the act that is missing from Žižek.

A Plumb-Line for Political Action?

What is in question here is the tricky and delicate dialectic of violence and nonviolence, where the achievement of the latter might require the performance of the former. That is, nonviolence paradoxically requires acts of violence. If we are to break the cycle of bloody, mythic violence, if we are to aspire to what Benjamin anarchistically calls in the final paragraph of the essay "the abolition of state power" (in my parlance, creating interstitial distance within the state), if something like politics is to be conceivable outside of law and in relation to life, then this requires the deployment of an economy of violence. That is, the plumb-line to follow in true politics is nonviolence, its aim is anarchism, but this cannot be a new categorical imperative of the Kantian kind. In the solitude of exceptional circumstances—they are not always exceptional, but they often are—the plumb-line of nonviolence might call for violence, for subjective violence against the objective violence of law, the police, and the state. In the final lines of the essays, Benjamin writes, "Divine violence may manifest itself in a true war . . ."[23]

The point is that we are doubly bound, both to follow the plumb-line of the divine commandment and to accept responsibility for choosing not to follow it. We are bound both ways and doubly responsible. The commandment is not a decree that is to be followed once and for all the moment it is made. On the contrary, the commandment is something we struggle with, that we wrestle with. The moral commandment is not an *a priori* moral law from which we derive the *a posteriori* consequences. In many ways, the situation is always the reverse: we always find ourselves in a concrete socio-political-legal situation of violence and we have a plumb-line of nonviolence, of life's sanctity. There are no transcendental guarantees and no clean hands. We act, we invent. What goes for the command also goes for the ethical demand, particularly the infinite ethical demand that I have tried to describe and defend in my recent work.

It is a plumb-line for action that we struggle with in our finitude and the concrete, finite demands that overwhelm us.

On this account, what is divine about divine violence? The name "God" is not the super-juridical source of the moral law. On the contrary, "God" is the first anarchist, calling us into a struggle with the mythic violence of law, the state, and politics by allowing us to glimpse the possibility of something that stands apart, an infinite demand that cannot be fulfilled, that divides the subjectivity that tries to follow it. For example, Christ, in the Sermon on the Mount, says: "Love your enemies, bless them that curse you, do good to them that hate you, and pray for them which despitefully use you, and persecute you" (Matt. 5:44). When he says this, when he is making this infinite and unfulfillable ethical demand, he is not stating something that might be simply followed or carried out. Whether he was the incarnation of God or just a troublesome rabbi in occupied Palestine, Christ was not stupid and must, therefore, have been aware that this is a ridiculous demand. It puts the ethical subject into a situation of sheer ethical overload, as Habermas might say. But, in my view, ethics is all about overload. When Christ in the same sermon says, "Be ye therefore perfect, even as your Father which is in heaven is perfect" (Matt. 5:48), he does not imagine for a moment that such perfection is attainable, at least not in this life, as it would require the equality of the human and the divine. What such a demand does is to expose our imperfection and failure and we wrestle with the demand and the facts of the situation. Otherwise said, ethics is all about the experience of failure, but in failing we learn something. As Beckett writes, "Fail again, fail better."

As I continue to think about Benjamin's essay I do have Emmanuel Levinas in mind, in particular some of his early thoughts in *Totality and Infinity*.[24] Indeed, the two categories in the title of that book seem directly to echo those of Benjamin: mythic violence, for Levinas, would be the experience of totality which is revealed in the experience of violence, war or the generalized state of exception. *Totality and Infinity* begins with the declaration of a state of war, "The visage of being that shows itself in war is fixed in the concept of totality, which dominates Western philosophy."[25] Divine violence, by contrast, would be the surplus to totality, the pacific surplus of being that he seeks to express with the category of infinity, what he also calls "messianic peace." He writes, "Morality will oppose politics in history . . . when the eschatology of messianic peace will have come to superimpose itself upon the ontology of war."[26]

These are handsome words. The problem that Levinas faces is how might categories like eschatology and messianic peace be expressed conceptually or philosophically without simply being explained away as dogma, blind faith, or opinion. Levinas's major claim in *Totality and Infinity* is that, without substituting messianic eschatology for philosophy, it is possible to proceed from the experience of totality, violence, and war back to a situation where totality breaks up, a situation that is the very condition for that totality. Such is Levinas's fragile and provisional transcendental method. He writes, and this is the first time he uses the key concept of the other in *Totality and Infinity*,

"Such a situation is the gleam of exteriority or of transcendence in the face of the other [*autrui*]."[27]

The problem here is that just as the mythic violence of law, the state, and power always seems to nullify or annihilate that which opposes it, so, too, the experience of war and totality refutes and crushes all talk of peace understood as the sanctity of life or the infinity of the relation to the other. In a time of war, in dark times, Carl Schmitt and his stubborn genealogy of political enmity will always appear to be right. This is why Levinas must acknowledge violence in his attempt to give expression to the nonviolent relation to the other. Levinasian ethics is not pacifist. Rather, it walks a Benjaminian tightrope of nonviolent violence.

Levinas affirms that the very experience of welcoming the other is a violence for a mind committed to the ideal of autonomy.[28] With the infinity of the ethical relation to the other, Levinas is suggesting that we are not, and indeed should not be, masters in our own house. To welcome the other is to unseat the *archic* assurance of our place in the world, our sovereignty. Thus, to open oneself to the experience of transcendence, to the pacific itself, is violence. It is what Levinas calls—and it is the word at the centre of my critique of Žižek—an *act*. Such an act is described by Levinas as a shattering of my capacities, as what he calls "a descent into the real" beyond the realm of thought and knowledge. He writes, "The notion of act involves a violence essentially." Levinas continues, "What, in action, breaks forth as *essential violence* [my emphasis] is the surplus of being over the thought that claims to contain it, the marvel of the idea of infinity."[29] Essential violence has the same structure as divine violence. It is a question of a critique of the mythic violence of totality with the difficult aim of nonviolence in view.

For both Benjamin and Levinas, there is something beyond the spheres of mythic violence, totality, the state, law, land, and war. Both of them identify it with an experience of nonviolence, with the placelessness of a commandment, an infinite ethical demand. Both of them describe it as messianic, thinking of the "Theses on the Philosophy of History," where messianic eschatology is not understood as the end time, but as the possibility at each moment that the homogeneous order of objective time might be interrupted by something else. This is why, during the July Revolution of 1830, insurgents turned their rifles on the clock towers: to stop time and inaugurate another temporal order.[30] Both Levinas and Benjamin understand such a possibility as bound up with the experience of language and the realm of the subjective. Both of them see that which would break with mythic violence as anarchistic, where Levinas sees the ethical relation to the neighbor as anarchical in the sense that it places the autarchy and autonomy of the subject in question, unbinding the subject by binding me to the other. Anarchy is a radical disturbance of the state, a disruption of the state's attempt, as Levinas puts it, to set itself up as a Whole.[31]

An anarchistic, subjective messianism of nonviolence as the only way of giving back a sense to politics beyond law and in the name of life. In this way, as I have tried to argue in a debate with Desmond Manderson, we might even speak of an anarchic law, a law against law.[32] Of course, this is a foolish enterprise, but I would like to praise such folly. Yet, what must be emphasized are both the folly and the fragility of what Levinas is describing in his work. Too often, Levinas is seen as the thinker of ethics as first philosophy as if he had some sort of *a priori*, axiomatic-deductive system that explained away all possible objections. Nothing could be further from the truth. Levinas's work is marked by utter fragility, and it is marked by it most profoundly in the experience of the commandment "Thou shalt not kill" or "You shall not commit murder," which stands at the center of *Totality and Infinity*.

For Levinas, the commandment is expressed in the face of the other, indeed *as* the face of the other. It is not expressed in a situation of peace, but in a life and death struggle where I am about to put the other to death, when "the bullet has touched the ventricles or auricles of his heart," as Levinas writes.[33] For Levinas, crucially, "the other is the sole being I can wish to kill,"[34] because he or she refuses my sovereign will in an act of defiance or resistance. At the point of killing the other, they can still resist me, still defy me, even when they die, perhaps especially when they die. Or again, as Levinas succinctly puts it in the 1984 essay, "Peace and Proximity": "The face of the other in its precariousness and defenselessness, is for me at once the temptation to kill and the call to peace, the 'You shall not kill.' "[35] This is why Levinas writes in *Totality and Infinity* that ethical resistance is "the resistance of what has no resistance."[36] This is an extraordinary thought: true resistance is the resistance of that which has no resistance: the powerless, the impoverished, the destitute, the hungry. My point here is that what Levinas is offering, again like Benjamin, is a plumb-line, a guideline, a rule of thumb for action, nothing more. "For the little humanity that adorns the earth," as he puts it in *Otherwise than Being*.[37] The nonviolent relation to the other is what Benjamin famously calls a weak messianic power, nothing more. Messianic power is always weak; it is the power of powerlessness.

It's for this reason that the most pacific ethics has to negotiate with violence and war. Levinas's is an ethics with dirty hands, not some angelic abstraction from the political realm. For Levinas, there is no pure realm of ethics or pure ethical Saying, to use the language of *Otherwise than Being*. It is always a question of its articulation within the Said of politics and law. Just as when Benjamin speaks of divine violence showing itself in a true war, so, too, Levinas, in the closing words of *Otherwise than Being*, writes of "the just war waged against war."[38] War against war, then. Perhaps this is what is meant by a nonviolent violence or violent nonviolence? Slightly earlier in the same text Levinas writes, in an amazing passage,

The true problem for us other Westerners is not so much to refuse violence as to question ourselves about a struggle against violence which—without blanching in non-resistance to Evil—could avoid the institution of violence out of this very struggle.[39]

The question is, can a struggle against violence avoid the institution of violence out of this very struggle? The only honest answer is to acknowledge that we do not know, we cannot be certain. Violence is in the very air we breathe and its unforgiving and bloody political and legal logic is irrefutable. In such a world, Schmittians and political realists will always appear reasonable. All that we have is the folly of a plumb-line of nonviolence, a set of exceptional circumstances and a moral and political struggle, wrestling with the infinite ethical demand. The rest is a matter of tact, of prudence, of understanding the situation and bringing about the conditions under which something like a local victory might be possible. As Wallace Stevens writes, "It is possible, possible, possible. It must/Be possible."

Beyond the Fantasy of False Alternatives

With these thoughts before us, I'd like to turn back to Žižek and to the criticisms he makes of my position in his essay in the *London Review of Books*, entitled "Resistance is Surrender." The title says it all: all forms of political resistance are simply surrender unless they seize hold of the state. Oddly enough, and for quite unrelated reasons, when a friend of mine sent me the link to Žižek's critique of *Infinitely Demanding*, a copy of Lenin's *State and Revolution* was sitting on my desk at home in Brooklyn.[40] One of the striking features of Lenin's text is the fact that his critique of liberals, social democrats, and the bourgeoisie pales in comparison to the venom reserved for the true enemy: the anarchists. Everything turns here on the interpretation of the Paris Commune in 1871. The question is: To whom does the memory and legacy of the Commune belong? Does it belong to the anarchists, and the commune might very easily be understood in Bakunin's terms, or is it a foreshadowing of Lenin's Bolshevism? The key to *State and Revolution* is Marx and Engels's phrase, "the dictatorship of the proletariat" and the issue is whether the legacy of the Commune and the possibility of communism requires a centralist, statist dictatorship of the kind that Lenin envisages, or the decentralized non-state federalism of the anarchists.

As Carl Schmitt reminds us—and we should not forget that the fascist jurist was a great admirer of Lenin, which is only exceeded by his praise for Mao—there are two main traditions on the non-parliamentary, non-liberal left: authoritarianism and anarchism.[41] If Žižek attacks my position with characteristic Leninist violence for belonging to the latter, then it is clear which party he supports. Žižek begins his piece by listing various alternatives on the left for dealing with the seeming indestructibility of capitalism. This listing seems initially plausible—indeed some of it seems to be lifted unacknowledged from the conclusion to *Infinitely Demanding*—until one realizes what it is that Žižek is defending, namely dictatorship and a centralized state defended with military power.

This should come as no surprise, of course. The central issue of Lenin's *The State and Revolution* is the question of the state. Against the anarchist critique of the state, its abolition and replacement with a form of federalism, Lenin defends the state with an admirable sleight of hand. He appears to agree with the anarchists in saying that we should abolish the bourgeois state, but then asserts that a centralist workers' state should be implemented. The goal of such a state, and here's the trick, is purportedly faithful to Marx and Engels's idea of the withering away of the state in communism, but that can only be achieved through a transitional state. This is somewhat laughably called "fuller democracy" by Lenin and in one passage "truly complete democracy."[42] Against what Lenin sees as the bourgeois complicity of the anarchists, an authoritarian interlude is necessary in order to realize the possibility of communism. As history has shown, this was a somewhat long interlude, which gave no indication of coming to an end until state socialism began to collapse from within in the late 1980s.

For authoritarians or what Bakunin calls "crypto-Bismarckians," like Lenin and Žižek, the only choice in politics is between state power or no power. I simply refuse this alternative. For me, politics is fundamentally about the movement between no power and state power and it takes place through the creation of what I call "interstitial distance" within the state. Although Žižek completely misunderstands this point, these interstices are not given or existent; indeed, at the present, the state threatens to saturate totally the space of the social, but they are *created* through political articulation, the activity of what Laclau calls hegemony. Politics is the invention of interstitial distance. In *Infinitely Demanding*, I discuss various examples of such political processes: from indigenous rights movements in Mexico and Australia (but I would now also mention Bolivia's Evo Morales, who is directly answerable to genuine social movements, and Brazil's *movimento sem terra*), to the movement in favor of the *sans papiers* and the *sans abri* (paperless, shelterless persons) in France, to the movement for an alternative globalization and anti-war movement despised by Žižek for its complicity with power and complacency, but which I see as articulating the possibility of a new language of civil disobedience, through to various forms of direct action, civil society groups, and NGOs. To this list I would add the current struggle about the question of immigration in North America and Europe, which I see as the key political issue in these areas in the coming decades, with unstoppable and massive population transfers from the impoverished south to the rich north. Here the political task is precisely the creative articulation of immigrant rights and the exerting of pressure on the state such that extensive immigration reform becomes a reality. I am far from being an expert in the history and ethnography of such movements, but I have tried to listen and learn a little over the years.

But all of this is to no avail to Žižek. He simply does not want to listen and maybe learn something new, something that would challenge his crypto-Bismarckian Leninist authoritarianism. All these forms of resistance are, for him, simply surrender and complicity with established power. Thus, we face an all–or–nothing choice: state power or no power. For me, the activity of politics is working within the state against the state in an articulation, an inventive movement, the forging of a common front that opens a space of resistance and opposition to government and the possibility of significant political change.

Žižek betrays a nostalgia, which is macho and finally manneristic, for dictatorship, political violence and ruthlessness. Once again, he is true to Lenin here, as when the latter calls for the bourgeoisie to be "definitively crushed" by the armed forces of the proletariat and alludes to "seas of blood," as if he were unwittingly attempting a definition of mythic violence and its cycle of bloody retribution.[43] In this connection, listen to Žižek's extraordinary defense of Hugo Chavez's limitation of democracy, which must be "fully endorsed",

> Far from resisting state power, he grabbed it (first by an attempted coup, then democratically), ruthlessly using the Venezualan state apparatuses to promote his goals. Furthermore, he is militarizing the barrios, and organizing the training of armed units there. And, the ultimate scare: now that he is feeling the economic effects of capital's "resistance" to his rule (temporary shortages of some goods in the state-subsidized supermarkets), he has announced plans to consolidate the 24 parties that support him into a single party.[44]

We are here again at the basic obsessional fantasy of Žižek's position: do nothing, sit still, prefer not to, be Bartleby, and silently dream of a ruthless violence, a grabbing of power, a consolidation of state power into one man's hands, a sheer act of brutal physical force of which you are the object or the subject or both at once. Perhaps this is why people play violent video games or go to the cinema and watch movies about psychopaths. As Deleuze and Guattari noted, "philosophy is one long ass-fuck."[45] What Žižek wishes for, which is very odd for a Lacanian, is for someone to occupy the position of master. When Lacan was being heckled by Leninist students at Vincennes in December 1969, he concluded by saying that, "What you aspire to as revolutionaries is a master. You will get one."[46]

However, Žižek does raise a question to which I would like to respond. It's a misunderstanding of my position, but an understandable one. He quotes me as saying, "Anarchic political resistance should not seek to mimic and mirror the archic violent sovereignty it opposes." Žižek goes on from this to object to me in the following terms: "So what should, say, the U.S. Democrats do? Stop campaigning for state power and withdraw to the interstices of the state, leaving state power to the Republicans and start a campaign of anarchic resistance to it?"[47]

Obviously not. On the contrary, I think that the Democrats need to rethink their strategy for obtaining political power. Having been continually out-thought for the past 30 years by a mobile and imaginative conservative right, the Democrats need a wider and more inclusive vision that replaces a right-wing populism with a much more liberal version, perhaps even a left populism. It seems to me that since the defeat of Carter by Reagan in 1980, it is the right that has understood what we might call the motivational or depth dimension to politics, in particular as it is expressed in social issues like religion, identity, sexuality, and moral issues like opposition to gay marriage and abortion.

The Democratic Party has been driven further and further into the abstract institutional procedures and niceties of governance. John Kerry was the worst exponent of this ineptitude and, frankly, deserved to lose in 2004. The Democratic Party needs to learn the lesson from the various forms of interstitial resistance that have arisen (disaffection with the divisiveness of established political parties, and a fatigue and anger against the militaristic neo-liberal exceptionalism of Bush II) and learn to incorporate them into a wider political vision. Are the Democrats capable of this? We will see.

However, Žižek then pulls out the most hackneyed and obvious trump card in all political games in the following terms: "And what would Critchley do if he were facing an adversary like Hitler? Surely in such a case one should 'mimic and mirror the archic violent sovereignty' one opposes?"[48]

Not at all. National Socialism is a powerful example, perhaps the most powerful example, of Benjamin's mythic violence. But should one confront mythic violence with a mythic counter-violence? No. Surely the lesson of Benjamin's essay is the need for a distinction between the mythic violence of archic sovereignty and the anarchism of divine violence, a nonviolent violence. What might this have meant concretely in the situation of Nazi Germany? First, it would have meant not treating fascism as some version of normal politics and seeking to appease it as the British and French did. Second, it would have meant that what fascism reveals is the state of exception which is precisely not the exception but the rule. Third, it would have entailed prosecuting "the just war against war," that is, the adoption of strategies of violence and violent resistance. But—and here the difference with fascism is most clear— this would not lead to the sort of celebration of violence endemic to fascism, but to a responsibility for violence that, in exceptional circumstances, might lead us to break the commandment, "Thou shalt not kill." Would such a strategy have been successful? I don't know. But the point here is that I am not preaching nonviolence in all political cases, and no more am I arguing for a retreat from the state. On the contrary, in fact.

There is a serious debate to be had about the question of violence versus nonviolence, the necessity of the state form, and the nature of radical politics given the seeming permanence of capitalism. This is a debate in which I'd like to engage as my own position on these matters is shifting as I give it more thought. Perhaps when we get beyond the windy rhetorical posturing of Žižek's critique and his description of my position as "post–modern leftism" (I defy anyone to find a word in favor of post–modernism in anything I have written), we can begin to have that debate.

Notes

1. Critchley, *Infinitely Demanding*. Žižek's piece, "Resistance is Surrender" occasioned some interesting responses, notably from T.J. Clark and David Graeber (LRB, Vol 29 No 24, 13 December, 2007; LRB, Vol 30 No 1, 3 January, 2008), to which Žižek replied by accusing Graeber and myself of "the highest form of

corruption" (LRB, Vol. 30 No. 2, 24 January, 2008) Praise indeed! Žižek's critique was then republished in *Harper's Magazine* (February 2008), to which I replied in a later issue (May 2008, pp. 17–20). Žižek published a greatly extended version of his critique of my position in *In Defense of Lost Causes*, 337–350. I hope to respond to Žižek's criticisms of my ethical position and interpretation of Lacan on a separate occasion.

2. Žižek, *Violence*. Walter Benjamin, *Critique of Violence*.
3. Žižek, *Violence*, 2.
4. Žižek, *The Sublime Object of Ideology*.
5. Žižek, *The Parallax View*.
6. *Ibid.*, (375–85).
7. Žižek, *Violence*, 180–83.
8. Benjamin, *Critique of Violence*, 242.
9. *Ibid.*, 243.
10. *Ibid.*
11. *Ibid.*, 245.
12. *Ibid.*, 246.
13. *Ibid.*, 247.
14. *Ibid.*
15. I'd like to thank Jacob Blumenfeld for clarifying my thoughts on this and other issues.
16. Butler, "Critique, Coercion, and Sacred Life," 201–19. I'd also like to thank Judith Butler for sending me some of her unpublished writing on the question of violence and nonviolence.
17. Benjamin, *Critique of Violence*, 247.
18. Agamben, *State of Exception*, 88.
19. *Ibid.*
20. Benjamin, *Critique of Violence*, 250.
21. *Ibid.*
22. Agamben, *State of Exception*, 88.
23. Benjamin, *Critique of Violence*, 252.
24. Levinas, *Totality and Infinity*.
25. *Ibid.*, 21.
26. *Ibid.*, 22.
27. *Ibid.*, 24.
28. *Ibid.*, 25.
29. *Ibid.*, 27.
30. Walter, "Theses on the Philosophy of History," 263–64.
31. Levinas, *Otherwise than Being*, 194.
32. Critchely, "Anarchic Law," 248–255.
33. Levinas, *Totality and Infinity*, 199.
34. *Ibid.*, 198.
35. Levinas, *Basic Philosophical Writings*, 167.
36. Levinas, *Totality and Infinity*, 199.
37. Levinas, *Otherwise Than Being*, 185.
38. *Ibid.*
39. *Ibid.*, 184.
40. Lenin, *The State and Revolution*.
41. See Schmitt, *Theory of the Partisan*, 54–61.
42. Lenin, *The State and Revolution*, 80.

43. *Ibid.*
44. Žižek, "Resistance is Surrender."
45. Deleuze and Guattari. *A Thousand Plateaus*, x.
46. Lacan, *The Other Side of Psychoanalysis*, 207.
47. Žižek, "Resistance is Surrender."
48. *Ibid.*

PART II

At the Borders of Enmity, Otherness, and Identity

Chapter 5

Fragile Identity: Respect for the Other and Cultural Identity[1]

Paul Ricœur

I am delighted that our meeting of the International Federation of Actions by Christians to Abolish Torture chose for its theme the question of identity linked to recognizing the other. This question really puts us face to face with a great conundrum, which can be expressed best as the question: "Who are we?" Even more seriously, we are straight away confronted by the presumed, alleged, and supposed character of the demands of identity. This presumption is found in the responses that aim to mask the anxiety of the question. To the question "who?"—Who am I?—we shift to a response in terms of "what?" In the form: this is what we are, all of us. This is who we are, like this and not otherwise. The fragility of identity, which will be our focus in a moment, shows up in the fragility of these responses in the form of "what" that pretends to give us the secret formula for this identity that is proclaimed again and again.

The Question of Memory

I would like to focus the first of my remarks on the splitting of the question into personal and collective identity. The question "who?" may be asked of the first person singular (me, I) or of the first person plural (we, all of us). The truth of this split is put to the test when one confronts the problem of memory, which will play an important role in our discussion of narrative and history.

Already on the level of memory, the question of the meaning of identity is not an easy one in the sense that, in the first place at least, memory would be not only a personal but also an intimate form of identity: remembering is in the first place remembering oneself [*se souvenir, c'est d'emblée se souvenir de soi*]. This is already the teaching of St. Augustine in the *Confessions*, and once again in the modern era it is found in the English philosopher of language, John Locke. In his *Essay Concerning Human Understanding*, Locke proposes to equate all of the terms of the series: identity, consciousness, memory, and self.[2] By identity, he understands the primacy of the same over what he calls diversity (what we call alterity). It is that according to which a thing is the same as itself and not something else. This identity with itself, which one can follow in the atom of the oak that remains the same from the seed to the tree, culminates with the self that recognizes itself as the same in the moments of reflection stretching across different places and times. It is memory that affirms the continuity of existence and the permanence of the self. Taken in a radical fashion, this series of equivalences does not allow for a collective memory, nor, by the same token, does it allow for a notion of identity applied to groups, collectivities, communities, or nations. At best, it would represent an analogy that would be quite possibly deceptive. Our common experience, however, belies this semantic Puritanism. Memory is not only personal or private remembering but also commemorating, that is, shared memory. We see it in our stories, legends and histories—in which the heroes are just as much the people itself as they are particular individuals. We also see it in our festivals with their celebrations, their rituals. Not only does the idea of collective memory seem appropriate to a direct and immediate experience of shared memory, but one can also legitimately wonder if personal or private memory isn't in large part a social product. Think of the role of language in memory's declarative phase: a memory is expressed in one's maternal tongue, the common language. Our earliest memories—those of childhood—show us bound up in the lives of others—in our family, school, or city. It is often the case that together we evoke a shared past. Finally, looking at a particular case such as psychoanalysis reveals that even the most private acts of remembering are not easy and require the assistance, possibly even the authorization, of another. Succinctly put, our memory is always already mixed up with that of others. In order to bring this initial discussion to an end, I would like to say that attributing memory to someone is a very complex operation that may be carried out quite properly across all the grammatical persons: I remember, she or he remembers, we remember, they remember. In what follows, this multiple attribution of memory will be our guide in our analyses and will allow for an unceasing movement back and forth between the level of the individual and that of the community. We shall see that this entanglement is such that in certain cases collective identity will present us with the problem of its justification (even its purification, pacification, or healing) in a more lively and disquieting fashion than personal memory in so far as it is true that our collective—even more so than our individual—memories are wounded or sick.

Having sorted out in a provisional manner the appropriateness of this equal attribution of memory (and, thus, to identity by way of memory) to persons as well as communities, we can tackle the major difficulty, namely, the fragility of identity. It is in this second part of our investigation that we will be confronted by the alterity of the other both on the individual as well as on the collective plane.

What is the Source of the Fragility of Identity?

We must name as the first cause of the fragility of identity its difficult relationship with time. It is this basic difficulty that justifies turning to memory in its role—by way of the evaluation of the present and the projection of the future—as temporal constituent of identity. Now the relation to time causes difficulty because of the equivocal nature of the concept of the same implicit in the notion of identity. What does it mean to remain the same through time?

I undertook to investigate this enigma before, and I proposed a distinction between two types of identity: the same [*le même*] as *idem*, same [in English], *gleich*, and the same [*le même*] as *ipse*, self [in English], *selbst*. It seems to me that the holding together of the self in time rests on an ambiguous game between staying the same [*mêmeté* and *ipseity*] (if one is allowed such barbarisms). In this complex game, the practical and affective [*pathique*] aspects are more formidable than the conceptual or epistemic ones. I will say that the temptation of identifying—the "obsession with identifying," as Jacques Legoff says—consists in the collapsing together of *ipse* and *idem* identity; or, if you prefer, in the sliding or diverting that leads the flexibility native to the upholding of oneself in the promise to slip into the inflexible rigidity of character in the quasi-typographical meaning of the term.

Let's pause a moment at this initial cause of fragility. In virtue of what we will be saying in regards to the overlapping of individual and collective memory, this difficult negotiation of time concerns both types of memory. We have learned from psychoanalysis how difficult it is, on the level of the individual, to remember and to confront one's true past. The subject, exposed to traumas and emotional wounds, has the tendency, as Freud noted in his famous essay, *Remembering, Repeating, and Working Through* [*Errinern, Wiederholen, Durcharbeiten*], to give in to the compulsion of repetition that Freud attributes to the resistance of repression. What follows from this is that the individual repeats the fantasies rather than working through them and, further, allows them to become active in the gestures that threaten both themselves and others. The analogy to the level of collective memory is clear: the memories of a people are wounded memories that haunt the recollection of glories and humiliations long past. We can even be astounded and unnerved by what the collective memory presents; namely, a caricatured version of this mode of repetition and the passage to action in the form of a haunting by a past that is indefinitely brooded over. One must even acknowledge the fact that the work of memory is more difficult to carry out on the collective level than on the individual level and that the resources that the analytic cure offers have no equivalent here. Where will one find something similar to transference? Or the session? Who is the analyst? Who can direct the process of working through [*perlaboration*]? The question becomes even more worrisome when we link the idea of the work of memory to that of the work of mourning, which, as Freud spells out in another essay, consists in the emotional treatment of the lost object of desire and, thus, also of the loss of what we detest. The subject is invited to break, one by one, the ties caused by her or his libidinous attachments under the direction of the harsh constraint of the reality principle that opposes the pleasure principle. This is the price one must pay for a liberating detachment, if one does not wish to follow the path from mourning to melancholy to depression, where the very sense of self (what Freud calls *Ichgefühle*) is tied to what has been lost. On this point, a note from this essay should be a warning to us; speaking of melancholic subjects, Freud says that their "complaints are accusations" (*ihre Klagen sind Anklagen*). It seems as if the hatred of oneself mutates into a hatred of the other in the morbid chemistry of melancholy. It follows from this analysis that the work of memory on the self does not occur without a work of mourning, which is not at all the simple expression of feelings but rather consists in a working on the loss until a reconciliation with the lost object reaches the point of its being interiorized completely.

There are plenty of parallels at the level of collective memory. The idea of the lost object finds a direct connection in the "losses" that also affect power, land, and the people who make up the substance of the state. The difficulties of mourning are even more serious here than on the level of the individual. Hence the equivocal character of the great funeral processions around which a battered people gather, where the phrase "complaints are accusations" (*ihre Klagen sind Anklagen*) echoes in a sinister way. What is troubling here is that the wounded memory is much longer and more tenacious on the collective level than it is on the individual one: thus, on the collective level, enmities span millennia and are inconsolable, giving the impression of excess—too much memory here, too much forgetting there. The same repetitive memory, the same melancholic memory, leads some to visible acts of violence that do not remain merely symbolic, while leading others to a murderous brooding over old wounds. It is on the level of collective memory, perhaps more seriously than on the individual level, that the intersecting between the work of mourning and the work of memory takes on its full meaning. One can quite justifiably speak of the loss of the beloved object when one speaks of the wounds to national pride [*amour propre*]. It is always such losses that wounded memory is forced to confront. What memory lacks is the knowledge of how to do the work demanded by the reality test—namely, to give over the attachments that continually bind the libido to the lost object in so far as the loss has not been completely interiorized. But we must also note here that this submission to the reality principle, which is at the heart of the work of mourning, is also an integral part of the work of memory. As regards the melancholy collection of troubles that affect collective memory, one may well worry about the lack of any parallel to therapy. At the very least, can one not call for patience towards others and oneself? The work of mourning does not demand any less time than the work of memory.

Experiencing Others as a Menace

I will now set out a second source of the fragility of identity: the sense of menace in our encounter with the other. It is a fact that the other, because she or he is other, comes to be seen as a danger for true identity—our collective identity as much as my own identity. We can be shocked by this and ask if it's really the case that our identity is so fragile that it cannot put up with or stand the fact that others lead their lives, understand themselves, and inscribe their own identity in the web of life in different ways than we do. But that's how it is. It truly is the humiliations, the slights—real or imagined—to our self esteem, brought on by the impact of poorly tolerated differences, that cause the relation of the same with the other to twist from welcome to rejection and exclusion—the relation that the same maintains towards the other.

Could we push the analysis further back before this hostile reaction to the other? One might find a biological root of this hostility in the immune system's defense of the organism, seen in the rejection of the intruder in the case of a transplant. The organism fiercely defends its identity, with at least two exceptions that are, in fact, more than exceptions: cancer and the gestation of the embryo. Along these same lines, AIDS presents a troubling example of the burglar's tricks that enable the virus to slip past our immune system's defenses. Something happens here along the border of the cell or organism: the operations of recognition and identification function here according to very precise codes. This defense of identity takes on its properly human form when the phenomenon of language enters the scene. Despite the relative successes of translation and linguistic exchanges, languages are not hospitable to each other. Something like the biological defenses of our immune system occurs here, and yet language is the essential mediation between memory and narrative. Hannah Arendt notes somewhere that a narrative says the "who" of action. Now narrative easily contributes to the binding together of the identity of a memory to itself—my memories are not yours and, if need be, they exclude yours. Making things more complicated is the fact that the relation of envy, which is just as much an obstacle to receiving the other, is added to the sense of menace that arises from an alterity that is poorly tolerated. Envy, according to one dictionary, is a sense of sadness, irritation, or enmity against another who possesses a good that I lack. Envy makes another's happiness intolerable. One must add the refusal to share happiness to the refusal to share unhappiness. We must show in this context that the active moment of rivalry over possessions connects to the passive moment of envy seen as a type of sadness. René Girard builds his theory of mimesis and his interpretation of the phenomenon of the scapegoat (the mimetic rivalry that creates the coalescing of all against the one) on this desire to enjoy an equal share of the benefits or pleasures possessed by others.

These phenomena of defense, rejection, and envy tempt us to close the distance between individual and collective identity. The common phenomenon is this menace—the simple existence of another different than me—that threatens self-identity. This menace rises up on a massive scale at the collective level. Collectivities also have a problem of defending their immunity that is quasi-biological. It is precisely on this grand scale that one is able to see phenomena that scarcely have an equivalent on the personal level apart from some feedback from the collective level of identity to the personal. I'm speaking of acts of manipulation that can be recognized as a disturbing and multiform factor that operates between the demand of identity and public expressions of memory. The phenomenon of manipulation is in part tied up with ideology, the workings of which remain purposively hidden away. In contrast to utopia, with which it ought to be linked, ideology remains unspoken. It hides itself in its turning against, and denouncing of, the other on the battlefield of ideologies, and it operates on multiple levels. It's always the other person who's up to her or his neck in ideology. Closer to the sphere of action, manipulation is an invincible strategy, in as much as it is a symbolic mediation that falls under what Clifford Geertz calls a "semiotic of culture."[3] It is in this role as a mode of integration that ideology can play the role of the guardian of identity, but this protective function would be useless without the means of justification that occur in actual systems of order and power—no matter if these take the form of property, family, authority, the state, or religion. All ideologies in the end revolve around power, and from here one passes easily to the more obvious incidents of the distorting of reality, of which both sides delight in accusing each other.

One sees right away just at what point the ideologues can break into the process of self-identification of a historic community; namely, at the level of narrative function. The ideology of memory is made possible by the resources found in the variation that is offered to the work of configuring a narrative. All narrating is selecting. One does not tell everything but only the salient moments of action that allow for the setting of the plot; including not only the events that one is talking about but also the protagonists of the action, the characters. It is because of this that one can always tell the story differently. It is this narrative function of selecting that provides the opening and the means for manipulation to devise its cunning strategy, which is at first a strategy of forgetting just as much as it is a strategy of recollecting. From these strategies there arises the attempts by certain pressure groups (whether they be in power, in opposition, or found in activist minorities) to enact an "authorized" or official history to be taught and celebrated publically. A practiced memory is, on the institutional level, a taught memory. Obligatory memorization is hereby enlisted in the service of remembering the events of common history understood as the founding moments of collective identity. The finalizing of the narrative is, thus, put into the service of the finalizing of a common identity. History taught, history learned, but also history celebrated. Traditional commemorations are added to the obligatory memorization. A powerful pact is formed in this fashion between remembering, memorizing, and commemorating. This hand laid on history is not a unique feature of totalitarian regimes, but is equally the prerogative of all those hungry for glory.

We've said enough about this second cause of the unreliability of memory and how it is exploited by ideology. One of the responses to these manipulations is to look precisely at the point where it is being exploited; namely, in narrative. We noted above that we can always tell the story in a different way, but it is exactly this resource that is offered to the critic of manipulation just as much as it used as a means of distorting what is the case. By telling in a different way, by confronting divergent stories—as historians have learned to do with conflicting testimonies—the stories become documented and archived. Confronting the stories means, first of all, allowing them to be told by others, and, in particular, allowing others to tell our founding stories, thereby allowing for the events that lie at the heart of our communal or national celebrations to be construed differently. We are broaching here the manner in which history may act as a corrective to memory. Beyond its breadth in space and time, history brings with it the spur of comparisons, thanks to which we are invited to reinterpret our identity in terms of difference in relation to opposing identities. It is perhaps along this path that we will find that the initial tendency to resent being confronted by another as a sort of threat to our own identity (just as much our collective identity as my own) might turn back on itself. "Strengthening One's Identity Without Refusing or Mistreating the Other" reads the title of our session. This is something that our critical narrative might be able to bring about when it confronts the narratives of an "irrational identity."

The Inheritance of Founding Violence

In conclusion, I would like to put forward a final cause of the fragility of identity: the inheritance of founding violence. These final thoughts bring us into contact with the principal concerns of our International Federation of ACAT, namely, torture. We are placing this concern in a larger context that refers to the inheritance of a founding violence. It is a fact that there is no historical community that is not born out of what we may say is an original relationship to war. What we celebrate under the name of founding events are in reality essentially acts of violence that have been given legitimacy after the fact by a state of precarious authority—based, at the limit, simply on its ancient or time-worn status. If the founders of political philosophy (Hobbes, first of all) have put the fear of death at the heart of the instinctive desire for security in which the various and divergent forms of the principle of sovereignty are anchored, it is not by accident. In the strongest sense of the term, it is security that individuals seek in the state—no matter the particular manner in which each state goes about its repetition of the fear of violent death at the institutional level.

By evoking this fear, one is reminded of the place of murder in the genesis of the political. One can legitimately ask if this scar is every truly effaced even in a lawful state. Marks of violence are evident everywhere. At the level of the individual, it is the persistence of the spirit of revenge at the heart of the spirit of justice. Of course, the state has disarmed its citizens by denying them the possibility of taking justice into their own hands, but it has concentrated in its own hands the right to exercise this so-called legitimate use of violence. Every punishment, no matter how well it fits the offence or crime, adds yet more suffering to what has already been inflicted by the aggressor. Among the sanctions, the death penalty, which was permitted in all of Europe up to the beginning of the century, continues to be practiced in many states otherwise understood to be democratic. In other words, the practice of violent death has not been wiped out from our lawful states.

This presents us with a very particular sort of discordance that distinguishes in a radical manner the political from the private sphere in terms of their respective relations to what is exterior. What I mean by this is that the hostile behavior between peoples or states is of a different sort than the enmity between individuals, which remains open to compromise or negotiation. At the level of the state, the prevailing relation is friend/foe, which becomes explosive whenever the survival or integrity of the community is in question (we know how a political thinker like Carl Schmitt has focused on this line of thinking). Whatever we might think of this, we still need to spell out the serious problem of war and its cruel demands [*droit cruel*]. In particular, what are we to say about the license to murder granted in the state of war? Killing is not simply permitted but is, in fact, commanded. Now we are fully aware that it is precisely under the cover of the so-called rules of war [*droits de la guerre*] that torture has been, and continues to be, practiced. Of course, the limits to these so-called rules are imposed by the international community under the name of war crimes (to say nothing of the crime of genocide and crimes against humanity). Torture and inhumane treatment are war crimes, but the right not to be tortured or treated inhumanely is without any real sanction. It is defended solely by the protest that arises from morality. We must at least know why we protest and march. It is in the name of human dignity—even for those who are guilty—and for the right of all to our consideration. For behind every act of inflicting suffering on another hides the humiliation that wants the one persecuted to lose all self-respect, to come to hate herself or himself.

—*Translated by* Mark Gedney

Notes

1. Paper given October 2000 in Prague at the Congress of the International Federation of Actions by Christians to Abolition Torture (ACAT). It was published in the "Les droits de la personne en question—Europe Europa 2000" by FIACAT. Translation into English by Mark Gedney, 2008. For more information on FIACAT see http://www.fiacat.org/en/.
2. See, Locke, *An Essay Concerning Human Understanding*, 330–331.
3. See, Clifford Geertz, "Description: Toward and Interpretive Theory of Culture," *in The Interpretation of Culture*, (NY: Basic Books, 1973).

Strangeness, Hospitality, and Enmity

Bernhard Waldenfels

To the German ear, it sometimes it sounds as if *Fremdheit* (strangeness) should rhyme with *Feindschaft* (enmity), but is this really the case? These reflections will focus on the relation between the stranger and the enemy, with the guest in the background as a transitional figure.[1] At the same time, I shall reflect on the relationship between individuals and groups, as well as on the interchange between cultures. The philosophically shaped Western tradition suggests to distinguish, similar to the case of the savage, between the good and the evil stranger. In the first case, one finds fundamentally the possibility of comprehending another person and of reaching a mutual understanding, while in the second this possibility is excluded. The good stranger is on the whole one of us, but the evil stranger is not. The evil stranger is simply the other. The Manichean-like demonizing of the evil stranger goes very well with a general disparaging of the stranger. Good strangers are the responsibility of the translator, while evil strangers are dealt with by the police (who include the acting guardians—often operating in secret—of ideology). Obviously, it is at this point that theoretical investigations would intersect with our everyday dealings with strangers. Still, it is worth asking if it isn't the case rather that hostility arises from an initial ambivalence towards what is strange, and thus on the hither side of good and evil. We will develop this question in three stages, in the course of which the problematic will become increasingly sharper.

The Stranger in Twilight

The phenomenology of what is strange is a task that struggles to find its way, since the view of the stranger or what is strange has been blocked from time immemorial until today. One sees what one guesses to know. The first stage of our reflection will be limited to formulating concisely a few specific points of contention. They can be determined in the following way: Do we involve ourselves with what is strange or do we persistently avoid it?[2]

Relative and Radical Strangeness

Strangeness that presents itself as only provisional or temporary and that, in the long run and under favorable circumstances, can be overcome, I call "relative." The relative character of this strangeness proceeds first of all in

Western thought from a global order; namely, from the presumption of a cosmos that includes myself and the other, as well as what is mine and what is strange. The strange is in this fashion *integrated*. In Modernity, the Ego stands at the center of a sphere of ownness to which all that is accounted strange, even the alter Ego, appears as a secondary reflection or modification. The strange would thus be *subordinated* each time to what is our own. Modernity answers the dreadful fragmentation of the world into individual perspectives and interests with a return to a foundational and legal order, in which I, as well as everyone else, am bound up. In this manner strangeness would be *neutralized*. The law-like categorical imperative only comprehends rational beings and does not recognize anybody that is strange. Radical strangeness, on the other hand, means something other. It signifies a strangeness that touches the "root of all things." It belongs, phenomenologically speaking, to the thing in itself and not at all to our limited access to the world. This form of strangeness assumes that each way of ordering (as a limited ordering) selects some possibilities while excluding others and that no one is master in his or her house. In this way the two foundation stones of an all-encompassing reason and autonomous subjects become unstable, and thus different dimensions of strangeness emerge. Order sets an *extraordinary* strangeness free. I am other to myself in the form of an *ecstatic* strangeness. The other, who in its distant closeness assumes the shadowy shape of the doppelganger, presents us ultimately with a particular form of *duplicative* strangeness.[3] A radical form of strangeness is, thus, not thinkable without reconceiving reason, the subject, and intersubjectivity. The aversion to such a different mode of thinking makes it clear that strangeness has been consistently understated or even resisted.

The Ambiguity of the Strange

If one follows traditional ways of thinking, the strange always appears as a *lack*; as something that is not (or not yet) available to, or understandable by, us. If one begins with what is strange, as it is encountered pre-conceptually in experience, it appears as a form of *withdrawal*. The strange shows itself as something that evades proper or common modes of accessibility just as much as it evades the framework of the prevailing order. What is strange appears through its effect on us, by its appearing from, and disappearing into, the distance and through its "bodily absence" (like the past and the future). With the concept of what is strange, the concept of the *outside* equally begins to totter. This concerns the being-outside of myself as much as the ex-clusion of certain possibilities.[4] Traditionally speaking, the negative aspect of mere exteriority has been linked to what is outside, which at best belongs to a necessary transitional stage of externalizing. It is another matter entirely if we begin with the radical form of strangeness. The extraordinary, implied—like a shadow—by every ordering system, does not signify something outside the order but rather signifies that the order itself, as the endowment and preservation of order, is without ground. The being outside-of-ourselves does not mean that we are losing ourselves but rather that we begin from elsewhere. However, possibilities that are excluded are not erased. The temptation of an absolutely inclusive community, to which nothing or nobody is exterior, belongs to ideas that fade as soon as one attempts to realize them.[5]

The Ambiguity of the Between [Zwischen]

The subject of the between leads us to the contemporary consideration of this theme in all of its many facets: as pure between (*Zwischen*), as the interworld (*intermonde*) or intermediary realm (*Zwischenreich*); or, in its Latin form, as intersubjectivity, intercorporeality, or intercultural life.[6] This between amounts to very little if it is conceived only as the empty space between things or as a tying together of independent realities—and not rather as the field in which something or someone becomes what it is. This includes the fact that something happened between us that cannot be traced back to merely individual activity. Taken literally, the intercultural means something more than a bare, multicultural situation made up of a plurality of cultures. Rather than a receptacle, it more resembles a magnetic field. When we ascribe to the between a role that is constitutive we move into an ambiguity that is linked to the ambiguity of strangeness. The between can be understood as *mediating*, as Logos—the law or right that regulates the exchange between substantial beings without itself arising from this exchange. The idea of a symmetrically arranged dialogue, in which each partner can take up the reverse role in truth, can only be understood as a monologue with assigned roles. Taken as a monologue, the happening of the between would not be truly creative. Equally, this intersubjectivity could no longer be seen as a plurality of subjects that become related in a transubjective instant. What we have in mind, with an appreciative nod to von Kleist, could be called a "production of thoughts in dialogue."[7] Thus, we are referring not only to something that happens *between us* but also to a threshold that is crossed with each utterance; but this production of thinking would never be seen as the overcoming of an obstacle standing in our way. A word gives what is other without one following from the other. We thus arrive at an *entretien infini* (infinite conversation), in the sense of Maurice Blanchot, or an inter-communication that is going on by interruptions. Between what belongs and what is strange there is as little a synthesis as between waking and sleeping, life and death, young and old. There is a synthesis only insofar as our speaking and doing have a meaning and follow a rule, but not simply because something happens in word and deed. The synthesis belongs to the said and the deed, not the saying and the doing. The synthesis is subjected to the standpoint of a *third*. This mediating third intervenes as an observer or judge in that event that occurred between us, but without standing over it. The standpoint of the universal is not to be confused with a universal standpoint in which what belongs and what is strange—one's own and foreign speech, one's own and foreign countries, one's own and foreign culture—would be reduced to mere particulars. The strange stands for the un-mediated in the middle of all mediation. What is strange permits itself neither to be localized nor globalized for it is always elsewhere.[8]

Intertwining of What is One's Own and What is Strange

Once what is strange appears in one's own house and as the "foreign territory within," what is properly one's own and the strange become bound together as in a net whose lines and straps wind themselves together. There is both a more and a less in what is strange, just as in the domain of language. Spanish is more closely related to Italian than it is to German, and Italian and German are closer to each other than either are to Chinese. Moreover, our point of view as to which to take as nearer or farther changes according to practical interest, historical tradition, and geographic vicinity. We can only think about perfect similarity and perfect difference as limits. A *foreign* language that is supposed to be absolutely unintelligible would cease to be a foreign *language*. Speech sounds would dissolve into mere sounds. One must not, therefore, confuse the radically foreign with the absolutely foreign. The foreign does not mean that something is *absolutely other* but rather that it is in some originary manner elsewhere [*anderswo*]. Precisely for this reason, we need a topology or topography of the foreign, something that thwarts the long study of the play of the self and other. There has always been this intertwining of what belongs to us and what is foreign that unmasks any so-called purity of language, culture, religion, or the obsession that is the product of this delusional desire for purity. What we call "Europe" was never a structure with an inner homogeneity and clear borders. It never had a simple center—despite its having a favorable location like Athens, Rome, Jerusalem, or Byzantium—and was never really the center point of the world. Such a controlling idea is part of the forgetting of what is foreign that overshadows every experience of it. What we are experiencing in Europe today is an unusual increasing and decreasing of the foreign: increasing insofar as what is foreign to us impinges ever more on our lived experience, and decreasing insofar as what is foreign runs the risk of sinking into something ordinary and becoming pulled along in the wake of globalization until it becomes worn away by indifference. In doing away with what is foreign we would also, however, be doing away with what belongs to us.

Iterative Strangeness

Strange experience does not end with the experience of what is *strange* but equally confronts us in the iterative form of the *strangeness of the strange*, of the strangeness both for others and in others. Whatever escapes the other also escapes me in an indirect manner, and this holds for all strange wonders and terrors. We are reminded of Plato's phrase: "Philosophy begins with wonder," but the question is: Which one? If we had only a single wonder—perhaps the wonder at the orderly procession of the stars—then we would have only one philosophy. And what about anxiety? Here we find the anxiety over death by some strange hand (which is at the very heart of Hobbes's thought) or the anxiety over eternal damnation that stifles life (which the sellers of indulgences in Martin Luther's time hammered into a profit). We can picture Paul at the Areopagus or Luther in Rome transformed into a scene of interreligious strangeness in which the strangeness would not simply be doubled but rather intertwined. We'll remain in the present. Germans, who meet millions of Turks in their own land, also encounter a foreignness within Turkish people between Atatürk's modernist descendents, traditional rural people, and religious fanatics. These iterative experiences of strangeness would be illegitimately thought through if one straight away proceeded to the level of judgment, of being for or against, as happens when one refuses what is not compatible with one's convictions.

Strangeness as Pathos

The key moment comes last. In other words, one must already have begun to question in order to ask the question where one has begun or should begin. Every question that touches on the strangeness of what is proper or belongs [*des Eigenen*] is a questioning back [*eine Rückfrage*] in the sense of Husserl. A beginning has already been made whenever I am asking about it. Insofar as the proper experience begins with what is strange, it begins as strange experience. Yet how does one experience what is strange? Does one experience it insofar as one searches, intends, questions, or judges it? I would say the following: if one begins with this point of view, one has already passed by the strange. What is strange emerges by befalling us, amazing us, frightening us, or tempting us. It is in this sense that I am speaking of a pathos of what is strange. The strange is that out of which we come, before it is that to which we go. Or, to vary a saying of Nietzsche, what is strange comes when *it* wishes, not when *I* wish. What is strange, therefore, has something archaic or unexpected about it. Normalizing, or making what is unfamiliar into something familiar, does not put a stop to strangeness. Just as the process of normalization, should it prevail, would only drive out what is strange, so, too, would a methodologically produced amazement not master wonder but rather abolish it. Just as there is an learning that comes through suffering, but which is not an learning of suffering, so, too, is there an learning that comes through the encounter with what is strange that is not an learning of what is strange. Strange experience is an experience *à rebours*, an experience that goes against the grain.

The Guest—The Stranger on the Threshold

The question at this point concerns how it has come about that what is strange or foreign has swung over into hostility [*Feindschaft*] both in individual, but more importantly in collective consciousness. With this question, I am approaching the detour related to the figure of the guest and the institution of hospitality. The guest unfolds as a transitional figure that invokes the *rites de passage*. As we shall see, the vocabulary used in the West to approach this figure is truly variable. For the Greeks, ξένος/ξένη means the stranger, but it also means the guest and the host.[9] It seems here that the guest, the one who comes from outside, embodies strangeness in a preeminent sense. In Latin, we go a step further. Not only do we find here a linguistic affinity between *hostis* and *hospes*, but both can stand equally for the stranger as well as the guest and host (just as *hôte* in French and *ospite* in Italian). Moreover, the meaning of *hostis* expands to the point where it means enemy or opponent. From this point on, it appears as if the stranger might be a potential enemy. Who comes first, however, the stranger, the guest, or the enemy? Obviously, this is not a simple matter of giving a definition but of taking a stand on the issue.

We return here to the matter at hand. Georg Simmel, in his celebrated study of the stranger,[10] describes the outsider as one who "arrives today and stays to-morrow." The author, himself an assimilated Jew (as one traditionally puts it), leaves no doubt about the fact that the stranger violates the rules of normal hospitality when she or he stays. But what this brief text puts into question is precisely this assumption that such a state of normalcy exists. The stranger, as the "potential wanderer," is certainly a "part of the group," but a "part" of a totally different sort. She or he belongs to the group in a manner that includes "exteriority and opposition." Even this *incomplete belonging*, this belong in not-belonging, denotes the status of a guest; one who stays in a strange house, in a strange state, and in a strange land, without truly belonging. The guest is at home in the other's house.[11] The guest dwells as the stranger on the threshold, neither truly inside nor truly outside. This fractured mode of belonging has corresponding spatial and temporal aspects. The guest is here and elsewhere, already there, where tomorrow or soon they will be. We recognize the unease that the guest, who is "on the edge," brings, and we try to put an end to this suspended present that makes us so uncomfortable by saying things like: "Take your place," or "Make yourself comfortable."

Hospitality has to be considered as a *para-institution*. It never stands on its own foundation but is grafted, rather, onto normal places: a family's house, an ethnic community, the public places of a city, or the open territory of a country. At the same time, hospitality breaks free from normality so that in similar fashion it approaches as something of a parasite (παράσιτος) that has taken the food from the host's table (σῖτος).[12] The guest would lose her or his special status should she or he become integrated into the host group. The guest receives steadily more as one becomes indebted to her or him. Hospitality is not only positioned near what is normal; it equally departs from it. The guest is troublesome in the sense that Levinas generally speaks of the stranger and the other. If Derrida, following Levinas, insists that hospitality is unconditional, he is not speaking as a moralist but rather as a phenomenologist. For a hospitality that was subjected to specific preconditions would presuppose, incorrectly, that the guest who comes from outside could properly partake of the life of the group that she or he is visiting. This in no way should be taken to mean that there are no conditions of hospitality. Whoever receives another must own a place into which the guest can be invited and received. Still, it is quite right to say that hospitality is un-conditioned and exceeds normal limits. Just as the stranger generally, the guest is either more than a normal group member or rather less—but never simply one among others.

In the end, it is quite astonishing, this gliding passage from the one who grants to the one who receives hospitality; something that often is directly deposited, as we have seen, in language (for example, in the Latin word, *hospes* and its derivatives). Émile Benveniste spells out this indeterminacy of meaning by noting that one gives to the foreign guest the same rights that were enjoyed by the Roman citizen with the expectation that Romans would be treated in a like manner when they sojourned in foreign lands.[13] I certainly don't believe that a legal or quasi-legal perspective will suffice to comprehend what is at play here. One must most of all take into account the fact that the host is no longer fully "master of her or his home," insofar as the guest crosses the threshold that separates what belongs to the host from what is foreign. In a way, the host gives what she or he doesn't have, insofar as what is proper and what belongs to her or him will be put into question by the demand of the stranger. This is why the figure of the guest signifies more than an ordinary institutional role. The figure of the guest appears as a preliminary shape of a radical strangeness that exceeds the limits of the fixed order. Hospitality constitutes a transitional phenomenon that no one can get past but which allows for many different responses. This permits us to suspect that the transformation of the stranger into the enemy has something to do with the rejection of the guest.

The Enemy—the Stranger from the Other Shore

In order to disperse the ideological fog that envelops the question of enmity, we must shift from a questionable ontology of enmity to a genealogy of enmity. Rash questions such as, "Who is my enemy?" or "What is an enemy?" presuppose, "How does one become the enemy?" This is truly an enormous question, and I will be able to deal with only one of its facets. I will take as a starting point a famous aphorism of Pascal: "Why are you killing me? Well! Don't you live across the water? My friend, if you lived on this side, I would be an assassin and to kill you like this would be an injustice. Since you live on the other side, however, I am brave and this is just."[14] What is worth noting in this short exchange is the fact that I know myself as addressed through the other before I myself address him. "*Pourquoi* me *tuez-vous?*" "Why are you killing *me?*"

The insight that is expressed in the general statement, "Every ego [*moi*] is the enemy and wishes to be the tyrant over every other,"[15] is already the product of what we could call the laboratory of hostility. "Mon ami, *si vous demeuriez de ce côté . . .*", "*My friend,* if you lived on this side . . ." In the answer that I would send over the water, the other would be addressed as a friend, but a friend under certain restrictions. The restrictions or conditions, which here block us from moving past simply calling each other friend to actually being friends, is a barrier—a river or mountain just like the Pyrenees. It is the bank (*rive*) of the river that creates the rivalry.[16] In contrast to the threshold—which is something that one can cross over—the line that marks out the enemy is an either/or: either on this side or on the other. Whoever is not for us is against us. What remains is thus the tepid neutrality of an observer who avoids the conflict instead of overcoming it. Nevertheless, this is not to deny that fact that linguistically, and not only linguistically, *hostis* and *inimicus* remain connected to the *hospes* and the *amicus*. There lingers here a certain memory, no matter how dim it may be.

So, where does enmity come from? We will need to deal with a variety of sources. We discover a first source when we take up the function of order. Conflicts of all sorts lie at the bottom of any given order: jealousy among family members or lovers, business competitors, political rivals, lawsuits, academic disputes, quarrels over words, the battle for cultural hegemony, and, not least, theological controversies and wars of religion. The great cultural passions—which Kant described as ambition, the desire for mastery, and avarice—ensure continual conflict between people. Still, so long as one does not leave the grounds of a common order, one only runs up against an *opponent*, not an *enemy*. The opponent is determined by the fact that what we say, do, desire, and think varies from individual to individual and from group to group. These divergences are not simply various perspectives or coping mechanisms that affect the meaning of what each particular person pursues. At the most basic level, what comes into conflict are alternatives that are involved with the actualization of meaning and the implementation of a new order. Thinking otherwise also means thinking against: against myself, against the other, against my ancestors, against the tradition, or, as was the charge against Socrates, against the belief in the gods of the city. The contingency at the heart of every order contradicts any pre-established harmony. All those who content themselves with the question of how to understand the other—or of how to reach an understanding with the other—may be men and women of good will, but their concerns are quite naïve as concerns both a sufficient experience of strangeness and equally the experience of hostile power. In his *Critique of Pure Reason*, Kant speaks of a transcendental illusion that never ceases to tempt us with a knowledge that would reach beyond the limits of experience. The moment we move from a critique of pure reason to a critique of cultural and intercultural reason, we will find ourselves also fighting against a hermeneutical illusion that dupes us into believing in a harmony beyond all practical conflicts.

All of this remains, however, in the foreground, for the opponent is not yet the enemy. How does the opponent become transformed into the enemy? First of all, we must maintain that the opponent, for all of her or his antagonistic aspects, does not present a hostile form of strangeness because she or he is not totally reduced to what she or he says or does. One would say, using Levinas's terminology, that the encounter with the opponent operates at the level of the *said* rather than that of *saying*. As a result, we are not prohibited from saying "no" to what the opponent says or does but only from saying "no" to the other herself or himself. Saying "no" to the other as other would in the end mean the destruction of the other. The relative "no" of everyday speech resounds in the absolute "no" of violence.[17] The fatal move from opponent to enemy is facilitated by the medium of words, in risings in the midst of sense. This occurs in such a way that heretofore opponents become reduced to what they say and do. The opponent is not necessarily reduced to a slave or an "embodied tool." She or he can also be reduced to a vehicle of meaning or cultural value.[18] In this sense the opponent has only a price and not dignity in the Kantian sense. What has a price can be used and, when it is used up, discarded. One can also destroy it the moment it becomes dangerous.[19]

The enemy is the opponent who does not have a place to hide away. Instead of being situated like the stranger, equally inside and outside of the order, the other splits itself into two halves. As a friend or *alter ego*, the other is found within, but as enemy it stands without. Taking up Pascal's imagery, the other as friend is on this side, while the other as enemy is on the other side. This means that enmity is defined in an absolutely negative fashion. The *extraordinary*, which surpasses the given order, degenerates into the *disorderly*, which represents a mere privation. In this way, we arrive at a great divide that produces a series of binary categories: reason versus violence, reasonable folk versus barbarians, Christians and Muslims versus pagans, civilized people versus savages, the law-abiding versus the lawless, or simply the functional versus the dysfunctional. This social Manichaeism survives today in the war of freedom versus terrorism, in the struggle between proper states and rogue states, and so on. In the end, however, it manifests itself as something like the revenge of violence and hostility. The exclusion of the other and of foreign culture returns to the instant of exclusion. The antagonism towards what is outside is bound up with the antagonism towards what is inside from which the strangeness in ourselves arises. The psychoanalysis of hate contributes to this discussion with its clarification of this originary binding together.

In addition, hostility differs from one culture to the other. One could then say: this many types of order, so this many types of strangeness, and this many types of enmity. Each type of order has special mechanisms by which it produces a picture and a concept of the enemy. This is the work of a social imaginary (in the sense of Cornelius Castoriadis), but it is a dark and destructive imaginary. There is much to be said concerning these mechanisms. I will limit myself to a few suggestions that come once again from my conception of order.[20]

The hostility that arises from *ethnocentrism* sets the tone for traditional societies. The enemy is somebody who, based on the simple fact that she or he is different, puts into question our own form of life. Even the attempt to understand the stranger is liable to be taboo. In societies like classical Greece that have come to question themselves, enmity achieves the rank of a *cosmocentric* enmity. Our enemy is not only our enemy but even more the enemy of all true *Logos* and *Ethos*. The overall order that is anchored in nature implies the admission of what Plato calls the "enemies of nature,"[21] which is similar to the "slaves of nature" found in Aristotle's politics. The idea of a natural enmity is part of the shadow that follows on the light of majestic reason. These days, we have become more modest. In modern times, order, which has been limited for necessary but not sufficient conditions of possibility, opens up the field for a plurality of beliefs, ideas, and practices. What remains is a circumscribed form of *legal* hostility that is directed at the enemies of democracy, law, freedom, and, ultimately, against the enemies of humanity.[22] Things are not so simple, however, when it comes to humanity. For humanity cannot be equivalent to some limitless "We" that would be capable of representing and speaking for itself. We don't escape from what is foreign by appealing to humanity. It is always at a particular point in time that a claim is made, without seeking anyone's approval, to speak and to fight "for one and all." Embodied humanity takes on many forms. A humanity that would only be expressed in a single form is nothing more than an *idée fixe*, though a powerful one all the same. In this way, irrespective of the interests that hide behind it, the globalism of the "free world" remains a source of enmity. This globalism would come into question if there were something strange that resisted its integration efforts.

Finally, we must take into account that the various orders, broadly sketched above, do not only follow each other diachronically but are equally arrayed on a synchronic, or better, heterochronic plane. Civilizations do not bounce off one another like billiard balls, but rather they are interconnected in myriad ways. Still, the lack of a central cultural measure affects the conflicts between cultures. One often does not fight at the same level or with the same weapons. We must distinguish between a *heated* form of enmity that is characterized by direct, immediate, and physical force—especially when the actual means used is oneself (as in the case of the suicide bomber), and a *cool* form of enmity that operates indirectly using technically sophisticated tools. If one takes so-called collateral damage into account, including both the innocent victims and the subsequent suffering that the perpetrators feel,[23] then the cold enmity is truly a violent enmity that promotes the arousal of a heated reaction from those who have been assaulted. The channeling of enmity through various technical means and media belies the affective surplus that lurks in the background of violence. It allows us to forget that there is a paroxysm of violence that does not simply seek out the value of the other for its own profit, but rather the obliteration of the other. Passionate hatred is just as uncalculated as passionate love. So, the annihilation of the enemy and self-annihilation pass over into each other in a certain manner; something that directly contradicts the modern principle of self-preservation. What's more, this topography of violence and terror belongs to the topography of what is strange. It is a long stretch of road that has taken us from the stranger by way of the guest to the enemy. The connection that arises here is very clear. Enmity means more than a lack of understanding and poor recognition. It stands for repressed strangeness and refused hospitality.

—Translated by Mark Gedney

Notes

1. Translator's Note. Of the three key terms of this essay, *Fremdheit*, *Gastfreund-schaft*, and *Feindschaft*, the last two cause little difficulty and are translated consistently as *hospitality* and *enmity*, respectively (though on one or two occasions I translate *Feindschaft* with its other natural English cognate, "hostility"). *Fremdheit* is a bit more difficult, for two reasons. First of all, the word very naturally can be translated as "strange" or as "foreign." Generally speaking, I have translated it as "strange" except in those passages of a political nature where the word "foreign" fits best. The second issue concerns the distinction between the neutral notion of "what is strange or foreign" (*das Fremde*) in contrast to people who are strangers or foreigners (*ein Fremder or eine Fremde*). Again, I have used "the foreigner" in those cases where the political context is clear and "the stranger" in most other contexts.
2. As a supplement to this sketch, see the following: Waldenfels, *Topographie des Fremden* and Waldenfels, *Verfremdung der Moderne* and *Grundmotive einer Phänomenologie des Fremden.*
3. On the distinction between the two different dimensions of strangeness, see an earlier version in Waldenfels, *Bruchlinien der Erfahrung*, chapters V–VI.
4. Two witnesses to this different way of thinking [*umdenken*]: Levinas, in his first great work, *Totalité et Infini* (1961), which had the subtitle *Essai sur l'extériorité*, and Foucault, who wrote a piece in 1966 for *Critique*, a magazine edited by Blanchot, *entitled*, *"Penser au dehors."* The common aim of these works does not preclude important differences.
5. Compare on this point, Habermas, *Die Einbeziehung des Anderen.* The author refers to a moral community that is purely inclusive. The strangeness of the other and every other form of strangeness melts under the sun of communicative reason.
6. On the various forms of the between, see *Topographie des Fremden*, 85f.
7. I am thinking here of Heinrich von Kleist's essay *Über die allmähliche Verfertigung der Gedanken beim Reden* (1805–1806). The essay is written from the perspective of the speaker, but from a speaker that knows how to listen to this or that other, and thus conceives of the other's thinking in this production. I call this a creative responsiveness.
8. I am referring here to my essay on Europe, Waldenfels, "Anderswo statt Überall," 13–19.
9. Further support for this linguistic distinction in Greek can be found in my essay, Waldenfels, "Das Phänomen des Fremden und seine Spuren in der klassischen griechischen Philosophie."
10. See Simmel, "Gesamtausgabe," 764–771.
11. In French, one says, *L'hôte est chez soi chez l'autre.* The preposition, *chez*, is linked to the Latin word, *casa* (= hut).

12. The normalizing and simultaneous degenerating of hospitality allows that the parasite can be more happily understood as a flatterer. It is called, therefore, in Greek also κόλαξ, that is, "flatterer".
13. See Benveniste, "Don et échange dans le vocabulaire indo-européen."
14. Blaise Pascal, *Pensées* in *Oeuvres Complètes*, edited by Gilberte Pascal Périer and Louis Lafuma, 51.
15. *Ibid.*, 597.
16. In Latin, *rivalis* most probably is derived from *rivus*.
17. I would point out the investigation into the "Aporien der Gewalt," in Dabag et al. *Gewalt*. On the language of power, see also, Platt, *Reden von Gewalt*; Hirsch, *Recht auf Gewalt?*; and Kapust, *Der Krieg und der Ausfall der Sprache*.
18. One should remember that the Romans happily employed Greek slaves as tutors.
19. Compare as well, Locke, *The Second Treatise of Government*, III, 16: Anyone in a state of emergency can appeal to a natural law, so that for Locke it holds that "one may destroy a man who makes war upon him, or has discovered an enmity to his being, for the same reason that he may kill a wolf or a lion . . ."
20. For the wider context, see Brehl and Platt, *Feindschaft*.
21. Plato, *Politics*, 470c.
22. These days, some people in certain quarters are discussing the monstrous idea of a "penal system for enemies" [*Feindstrafrechts*]. This lies along the path of the Guantanamo prisons, where one creates an exterior space for non-persons, and where obligations that apply to prisoners are put aside for those suspected of being terrorists.
23. One thinks of the continuing psychotherapeutic care for soldiers who only reenter normal life with difficulty. On this alienation that soldiers had to expect on their return to everyday life, see the essay that was published in English already in 1945, "Der Heimkehrer" by Schütz. In German, it can be found in *Gesammelte Aufsätze*, vol. 2. Also from the same author, see *Der Fremde und der Heimkehrer* (Den Haag, Martinus Nijhof, 1971). See also B. Waldenfels, "Der Fremde und der Heimkehrer. Fremdheitsfiguren bei Alfred Schütz," in I. Srubar, St. Vaitkus (editor), *Phänomenologie und soziale Wirklichkeit* (Opladen, 2003).

CHAPTER 7

BEYOND CONFLICT: RADICAL HOSPITALITY AND RELIGIOUS IDENTITY

Richard Kearney

Among the many alarming, incisive, and even subtle ways in which the problem of violence is manifest today, there is the cumbersome though vital question of how to navigate the intersection of religious belief and secular norms. Common experience and philosophical discourse alike will testify that this threshold marks an uneasy site of translation, perhaps even a collision course, charged with the familiar tensions between public and private spheres, confessional and constitutional commitments, and what philosophers have described as the longstanding reductive dualism between what is same and what is other. Arguably one of the most interesting philosophical contributions to the contemporary discussion concerning the role of religion and secularity is that made by Jürgen Habermas in his debates with figures like Jacques Derrida and Joseph Ratzinger. Interestingly, both Habermas and Derrida agree on the central importance of "hospitality" in our modern world. For Derrida, it is the best alternative to the friend–foe distinction, made intellectually familiar by figures like Leo Strauss, Francis Fukayama and Samuel Huntington, and perilously enacted by political figures on both sides of the "axis of evil."[1] Faced with the Huntington thesis that "we only know who we are . . . when we know whom we are against," the ethic of hospitality replies that the stranger is precisely the one who reminds us—not as enemy but as host—that the self is never an autonomous identity but a guest graciously hostaged to its host.[2] Thus, at a practical level, the ethics of hospitality opposes the apocalyptic dualism of pure/impure invoked by President George W. Bush and Osama Bin Laden after 9/11 and among other religious and political leaders since. Hospitality opposes such gnostic divides between friend and enemy, where God is always my ally and the stranger forever my adversary.

My aim in this chapter is to redirect the path of approach to these matters of religious conflict and identity. Though I am unable to treat the face of religious violence with the rigor it deserves, my discussion is oriented precisely by an attunement to those confessional roots and practical experiences of religious difference that so often yield aggressive and antagonistic expressions. With Habermas's goal of institutionalized secular discourse as a point of departure, I will suggest that the priority of securing peaceful creedal coexistence is insufficiently served by effecting a program of rational assimilation. Alternatively, I argue that a hermeneutic practice of radical hospitality and religious auto-critique is not only more appropriate to the gyre of religious difference, but also more intrinsic to the resources of faith traditions themselves. I propose a model of translation that plumbs the depths of religious identity, a pilgrimage to the "deep ground" of faith that is pluralistic without being syncretistic, singular without being dualistic, and ultimately a kenotic practice that retrieves interreligious translation on the basis of humility.

Translation and the Risk of 'Rational' Assimilation

Treating the question of religious identity and practice within the larger paradigm of secular or public discourse involves opening oneself to the promise and peril of what is at root a matter of hospitality and translation. Aspiring to normative social–political safeguards, by the same token, may well involve an intended retreat from the pathologies of dogmatism, but also entails a potentially violent or reductive positioning of one norm over another, one *logos* adjudicating the terms of another. Habermas, for his part, appeals to an ethic of hospitality to overcome the state of nature and its multiple frictions on the basis of mutual respect.[3] While Derrida acknowledges the deeply "messianic" structure of hospitality as an affirmation of the "impossible," Habermas prefers to sublate and liquefy the religious roots of hospitality into a discourse ethics of rational norms and universalisable laws. He holds that religion, defined as a "comprehensive worldview which claims to structure a life in its entirety," must be translatable into the language of secular society, where it can be adjudicated and negotiated. But Habermas does concede that political liberalism goes too far if it maintains that *only* secular reason counts in the public sphere. Religious identity, he admits, is something *other* than socio–political–normative existence.[4] "The liberal state," he clarifies, "must not transform the requisite *institutional* separation of religion and politics into an undue *mental* and *psychological* burden for those of its citizens who follow a faith."[5] In this way, he is attuned to the subtle though consequential risk of enabling dualistic suppression in the name of singular liberal affirmation. And here Habermas introduces what he calls the "institutional translation proviso," which allows religious believers, who accept that only "secular reasons count beyond the institutional threshold," to express their beliefs in a specifically confessional language if they find "secular translations for them."[6] Nontranslatable religious convictions (what Habermas terms "private reasons") may, thus, be admitted to the public sphere for functional and discursive purposes. This admission aims to avoid an unbridgeable chasm between private (religious faith) and public (political reason) and is accompanied with the proviso that religious beliefs remain open to possibilities of further translation and assimilation. Once admitted, under the guise of confessional language, it remains the task of a democratic liberal society to encourage the "religious consciousness to become reflective and the secular consciousness to transcend its limitation in a mutual learning process."[7]

While this seems like a fair apportioning of responsibilities, it nevertheless remains more a one-way street. A close reading will show that for Habermas, the goal of such "mutual" learning is for religion to become more and more translatable into the rational normative pedagogical process, not for secular reason to "transcend its limitations." The pedagogical process is surely admirable, but it should, I submit, work in *both* directions at once. Secularity should be humble enough, in other words, to acknowledge the possibility of a certain untranslatable remainder, a *surplus* of meaning that surpasses the limits of normative rationality. For Habermas, it becomes clear, the ultimate goal of a democratic society is to integrate a plurality of faiths and cultures into an institutionalized discourse of deliberative decision-making and generally accessible language.[8] And here he explicitly cites Judeo–Christianity as a suitable candidate for such progressive pedagogy, since many of its religious legacies have already been translated into core principles of democratic enlightenment. "For the normative self-understanding of modernity," writes Habermas, "Christianity has functioned as more than just a precursor or a catalyst. Universalistic egalitarianism, from which sprang ideals of freedom and a collective life in solidarity, the autonomous conduct of life and emancipation, the individual morality of conscience, human rights and democracy, is the direct legacy of the Judaic ethic of justice and the Christian ethic of love. This legacy . . . has been the object of a continual critical reappropriation and reinterpretation. Up to this very day, there is no alternative to it. And in light of current challenges of a post–national constellation, we must draw sustenance now, as in the past, from this substance. Everything else is idle postmodern talk."[9]

However, the underlying difficulty haunting such a view (quite apart from the neglect of the Islamic legacy) is this: how do we react to the radically new and surprising? How do we respect the stranger without trying to translate him or her into our terms? How do we respond to what Derrida and Walter Benjamin call the "messianic"? In short, it would seem that for Habermas, the final aim of philosophical and political reason is to "completely assimilate, translate, rework and sublate all desirable religious content."[10] If this assimilation is indeed the endgame of his project, one is left wondering about the hermeneutic and phenomenological elisions it assumes and/or enables. How then, for example, can the divine remain a transcendent Other who comes to us? A visitor from outside our home [*unheimlich*], opening doors to novel events and inviting us to epiphanies "never dreamt of in the philosophies" of Horatio or Habermas? How, in a word, is secular reason to account for that aspect of alterity, which—precisely as foreign and sacred—always remains partially unassimilable and inaccessible to our normative or normalizing grasp? Such a remainder may not be *the* operable keystone joining the arches of creedal confession and religious identity, but it is in the very least a vital cornerstone to the architecture of belief. Can others only become our guests as *Gästarbeiter* tolerated in so far as they surrender their irreducible uniqueness and difference? It is not clear that Habermas's pubic sphere can really welcome strange gods or practices fated to strangeness on the basis of otherwise-communicable standards. He does not seem, that is, to have a host language to respond to what Benjamin calls the "untranslatable kernel" at the heart of every guest language, namely, that inimitable transcendence that puts us into question, shatters our self-security, and opens us to the incoming other.[11]

If there is a decision to evade the unsettling horizon of alterity fundamental to religion, there is also an adjacent, and perhaps resulting, decision to overlook the insecurity Habermas's telos of "universal rational translatability" would face when responding to religions other than the European tradition of Judeo–Christian humanism. What of the religions of the East or, closer to home, the religion of Islam both inside and outside the borders of the Western "postnational constellation"? Are only those believers to be accepted whose translation from faith into reason has "already occurred . . . in the political public sphere itself"?[12] On this score, Lovisa Bergdahl is right to say that Habermas has a limited and somewhat Euro–centric notion of religious pluralism, one that prefers familiar religious neighbors to unfamiliar strangers. The real task of translation, as Benjamin and Bergdahl note, is to acknowledge the *double* call of the stranger: translate me/do not translate me! For the real challenge is to respect "the unfathomable, the mysterious and the poetic" superfluity of meanings while making as much sense as we can.[13] In short, the biggest temptation for the translator—in politics no less than in poetics—is to conserve the meaning presiding in one's host language without allowing it be transformed by the foreignness of the guest tongue.[14] To yield to such temptation is to close the door on the stranger. It is to decline, even violently, interlinguistic and interconfessional hospitality. One *telos*, conceived according to one *logos*, that is, entertains and employs the terms of a constructive project while at the same time harboring a potentially destructive course of arbitration.

The Wager of Alterity

Its instigating integrity notwithstanding, the pitfalls of Habermas's design for institutionalized discourse necessarily return us to the more hermeneutic question of religious meaning, a question that remains vital, difficult, and, to an important extent, incongruous with the game of classifying and managing religious "identity." If religion is to mean anything in the third millennium it should, I believe, mean more than a set of common norms. Such norms are necessary but not sufficient. In searching for a shared "essence" or "universal structure" of religion, it would be folly to neglect what is most strange and different in each faith. Interconfessional hospitality means respecting the otherness of each other as much as acknowledging the sameness in all. For without the former there would be no guest to be invited and no host to receive. In other words, it is not enough to distill the overlapping moral elements of the great religions into one syncretist brew. It is also crucial to acknowledge the very distinct paths that each wisdom tradition takes to reach that shared ethical vision. Without this appreciation of deep confessional and cultural *difference*, there can be no real sense of hospitality at work between religions. For, I repeat, without the recognition of alterity, there can be no experience of the stranger and, so, no opening to what is not ourselves.

But, I hasten to add, alterity is not always on the side of the angels. If religious difference bears the potential for welcoming aliens, it also bears the opposite potential to enclose, exclude, and expel. The double plot of hospitality and hostility does not dissolve as one reaches the roots of diversity; it thickens. The retreat from the pathologies of assimilation and reduction under rational norms is by no means assured by a naïve expansion of the many into one. Reinstating a productive posture of hospitality within the practical horizon of interreligious identity and difference, rather, turns on an ongoing decision to live, move, and speak in proximity to the tensions of pluralism.

Let me try to put this in another way: if all religions are reduced to the same—be it via discursive assimilation or via radical equivalence—there is no way of recognizing the equiprimordial potential for both love and hate inherent in each religion. There are seeds of dogmatic exclusivity and violent self-assertion within any confessional tradition. That is why every religion needs to carry on a radical autocritique of its own violent tendencies if it is to rescue what is genuinely tolerant and emancipatory at its core. In short, any faith must be prepared to purge itself of the inherent temptation to violently impose its own version of the "absolute" on others. For only then is it capable of acknowledging the multiple receptions of the Word in faiths not its own. As Anthony Steinbock puts it, obedience to a Word that surpasses human language is the source of both "vertical" *and* "idolatrous" interpretations.[15] Hence the deep ambivalence of such religious terms as "surrender," "submission," and "sacrifice." There is always a hermeneutic wager. And if one opts to follow the path of hospitality, of listening to others, one must be open to the possibility of discovering in the other faith something which is not—or not yet adequately—discovered in one's own. Believers in the Bible, for example, may well discover in Buddhism a sense of unconditional compassion for "all sentient beings" still dormant or undeveloped in the Abrahamic religions, just as Buddhists may discover in biblical religion a greater attention to the realization of a Kingdom of justice in history or to the emancipatory power of divine desire.[16] It is possible such autocritique might disclose some of the norms Habermas means to privilege and translate in secular discourse, but it is important to bear in mind that religious autocritique is an exercise of reflection that has affirmation, not simply distillation, in view.

One might also mention here how Hindu sages like Vivekananda, Tagore, and Ramakrishna confessed that their understanding of Vedantic religion was amplified by their exposure to Abrahamic faiths and practices (see the example of Gandhi). And this gesture of interconfessional exchange between East and West was reciprocated, in turn, by pioneering figures like Abhishiktanada, Bede Griffiths, and Sarah Grant, who believed their Christian convictions were greatly deepened (and at times critically revised) by exposure to the Hindu tradition of Advaita.[17] These are anecdotal illustrations, but they serve to indicate how the disrupting the dualism of same and other is already a constitutive concern for believers—how the very strength of what may be termed religious identity is in part anchored on a mode of interconfessional hospitality.

The Word of Hospitality

Though I have highlighted the perils of seeking an institutionalized public discourse, and have suggested a more hermeneutic and practical alternative centered on hospitality, it is important to recognize that the distillation of all religions into a set of common denominators does have its purpose. But the distillation I have in mind is only effective if it is instigated by communities of believers and not by theoreticians or policymakers seeking to contain and translate religious identity at the expense of intrinsic alterity. An impressive example of this is the project of the Parliament of World Religions, convened in 1992, to develop a global ethic of peace based on the Golden Rule that we should treat all others as ourselves. The project echoed similar attempts to establish principles of interfaith dialogue such as the Snowmass Conference of 1986, the Scorboro Interfaith movement of the 1990s, and more recently the "A Common Word" document of 2007 signed by 138 prominent Muslims reaching out to non-Muslims to come together on the basis of certain basic shared religious principles. These mark crucial steps in the reconciliation of competing and often warring religions in our world and should be applauded as measures against the seeds of exclusivity that so often bloom into factional-ism, even violence. But there is a further step to be taken that supplements the move towards universal principles. And this second step, much like the need for autocritique outlined above, involves a radical descent into the specificities of each spiritual tradition—a descent into difference, in addition to the ascent towards oneness: a plunge which seeks, at the root of each religion, a silent, speechless openness to a Word, which surpasses us. The hermeneutic wager of radical hospitality is, therefore, that in the deep belonging to a faith conviction unique to one's confession, there may arise the humility to counter the violence of exclusivity with a generosity of attention. For if it is true that all religions involve a special acoustic of obedience to a Word beyond our finite language, this may lead to a modest ability to listen to otherness as much as to a claim that our religion alone has an absolute take on the absolute. Hosting the radi-cal stranger means that verticality leads to latitude.

I do not for a moment wish to deny that most religions have, at one time or another, invoked creedal partisanship to prove their superiority over others, and sometimes assure it in violent words and ways. *In hic signo. We have God on our side. There is no God in all the earth apart from ours.* These are not catchcries of the past. One need only mention the ongoing struggles between Hindus and Muslims in Kashmire, between Buddhist Singhalese and Hindu Tamils in Sri Lanka, between Muslims and Jews in Jerusalem, between Christians and Muslims in Kosovo—not to mention countless examples of intra-religious wars in places like Northern Ireland, Iraq, and the Balkans.

These are sorry truths, and there is no point pretending that our secular post–Enlightenment world has exorcised such atavistic passions. There is, it would seem, a tendency in the "inaugural energy" of almost every religion (with possible exceptions like Buddhism and Jainism) towards some form of exclusivism, exceptionalism, or absolutism.[18] It is one side of the Janus–face of religion. But there is, I am arguing, another side: the ability of each confession to delve into its own hidden foundation and discover there, in a moment of bold auto-critique, a countervailing drive towards hospitality and healing.

That such healing hospitality emerges from each religion's unique depths rather than from a surpassing of these depths may seem paradoxical. It marks a retrieval of what is best against the very worst that belief can offer: difference cuts both ways. And this is what I might call an ana-theist recovery of a religion *before* religion—a recovery stemming from a foundation without secure foundation, namely, a foundation founded on something *other* than itself. It is this mystical *fond sans fond*, I suggest, which ultimately invites our wager that the other—the foreigner—has more to offer us than we can ever find in ourselves alone. In this sense, ana-theism may be said to come before as well as after religion.

Retrieving the Original Remainder

My approach to the problem of religious identity by way of radical hospitality and interreligious dialogue has at root a simple premise: the hermeneutic maxim that the shortest route from self to self is through the other. Just as in linguistic translation we discover something in the "guest" language that has never been said in our "host" tongue, so, too, in interconfessional translation we may discover in another faith something not dreamt of in our own. Though, as we have just seen, we have to dwell deeply in our own faith to be able to recognize such disclosure as *new*, as basically *other* than our own. The discovery of the wisdom of the stranger presupposes that the self knows itself as different from the stranger. Thus, certain messages in one's own faith—say, in the case of a Christian, the wise detachment preached in the Sermon on the Mount—may find confirmation of this otherwise "impossible" message in the teaching of a very different tradition, for example, the Buddhist notions of compassion, detachment, and *sunyata* [the emptying of self]. In fact, to pursue this example further, I would say that the biblical messages of *kenosis* and *Zimzum* might actually *need* exposure to foreign teachings like the Heart Sutra ("Emptiness is form and form is emptiness") in order to better understand themselves. Confessional adherents do not need to pledge their allegiance to secular norms in order to preserve and enact this depth of dialogue, or to appreciate the constitutive way in which it prevents aggressive demarcations.

The ethics of radical hospitality suggests that religions can best recover their own unique secrets through reciprocal exposure to others. (Just think of the illuminating readings of the Gospels by Thich Nhat Hanh or of Eastern texts by Thomas Merton). Reciprocity is the key here. In faith as in love, you discover your true self in the self revealed to you by the beloved. Self-discovery presupposes the discovery of one's other (and vice versa). This other may be a million miles away or in our very midst, or both: a paradox Camus poignantly captures when he writes of those moments when "under the familiar face of a woman, we see as a stranger her we had loved months or years ago, and perhaps come even to desire what suddenly leaves us so alone."[19]

This is where ana-theist hospitality returns to the appreciation of not just others' theism but of atheism *tout court*. For in the otherness of the atheist who does not know (unlike the anti-theist who knows everything), we encounter an estranging and dispossessive challenge that: (a) compels autocritique, and (b) reveals our innermost convictions in a movement of response and recovery. So, rather than too rapidly renouncing our respective convictions—in the name of one global religion or morality—might it not be wise to equally acknowledge what differentiates us? For in thus recognizing the existence of otherness in each other, we may mutually attest to a *surplus of meaning* that exceeds all our different beliefs. A surplus that is other than every other. Stranger than every stranger. This something "more" is what enables humans to do the impossible, to break with conditioned patterns of thinking and behavior (any AA member will attest to this). This discovery of something "different," "ulterior," "more," is stronger, I suggest, when it is made from *inside* each confession than when imposed from *outside* by some abstract God's-eye view. In short, an ethics of radical hospitality proposes the challenging route of embracing complexity, diversity, and ambiguity rather than prematurely endorsing a spiritual Esperanto of global norms. It holds that the universal can only be reached through singular others—that is, others that are other to each other.

If this is so, it means that the answer to religious conflict requires more than a sociology of comparative religions based on some common "essence." One also needs to take the internal journey to the silent, unspoken root of each religion. For we might then be in a better position to practice a hospitality of translation between different root convictions deeper than a set of universal principles, though in no way counter to it. The road to an ultimate reality preceding and exceeding our belief systems passes through each of these beliefs.

To return, then, to the hospitality wager we might say that when we translate—interconfessionally—we export ourselves into strangers and import strangers into ourselves. And in daring to translate across borders, we encounter the limits of translatability. This invariably implies risk, as aptly expressed in Antoine Berman's phrase "*l'épreuve de l'étranger.*" The process of interreligious hospitality summons us on a pilgrimage to the depths of the inaugural moments of different religions rather than to some super-theological summit adjudicating rival claims from On High. For it is in the depths, as Paul Ricoeur insists, that we "touch on something unsaid . . . a mystical ground (*un fond mystique*) of what is most fundamental in each religion and which is not easily translatable into language but rather borders on a common profound silence."[20]

In other words, the best way to tackle the violent tendency within religious conviction is to go all the way down to the source which that religion does not master and which refuses to be rendered into dogmatic formulae or ideological manifestos. Each religion will have its own unique access to this ineffable genesis-point: the work of illumination for the Buddhist, the prayer of Thanksgiving for the Christian, the learned meditation on scriptural texts for the Muslim or Jew, the practice of yoga for the Hindu. In each case, the specific way acknowledges a source which it does not initiate or control, but which it heeds with modest vigilance. And it is in this hearkening to a source beyond and beneath oneself, a superfluity that one does not possess or manipulate that we may find new resources for nonviolent resistance and peace.

The most effective antidote to fundamentalist perversions, therefore, may well be to attend to the "deep ground," which no religion can ever appropriate or contain. Every religion is capable of taking this action against itself, brushing against its own dogmatic grain, purging itself of its pathologies so as to reach the silent source that not only surpasses but disarms it.[21] This implies a conversion of the heart whereby each religion finds at the ineffable root of its belief the means to reverse the violent impulses that inform religious claims to master absolute truth. It involves a moment of critical and therapeutic self-retrieval (what Ricoeur calls *"un mouvement de retournement contre la composante de violence d'une conviction"*).[22] Precisely here we discover a complementary partnership between an inner descent to ineffable mystery and an outer ascent to enlightened awareness. And it is at this ana-theist chiasmus, I would argue, that theism and atheism can become, once again, salutary allies.[23]

The autocritique of religious power is, I conclude, doubly assisted in this way—from both within and without. And this bilateral gesture is crucial for the critical self-surpassing of religion. In encountering strange gods, we are invited to discover hidden aspects of our own God (often congealed in convention and defended with dogmatism); while the recovery of such hidden depths opens us further to stranger gods. But this two-way encounter does not imply sublation into some all-embracing infinite. We are reminded here again of the necessary limits of translation. For at the root of every translation between self and stranger, within or without, there remains that "untranslatable kernel," that irreducible alterity that resists complete assimilation into a home whose doors could finally be closed. This fundamental alterity is what makes translation between religions at once necessary and always inadequate. There is always something *more* to be said and understood, some inexhaustible remainder never to be known. And it is this "more"—which many religions call "God"—that allows the stranger to remain (in part, at least) always strange to us. This is why every authentic religious experience is a *re-legere*, a returning again and again from surplus to signification to surplus, an ongoing odyssey of reading that makes translation endless.[24]

All great ethical teachings share a set of precepts—do not kill, tell the truth, be just, look after the weak. What religions, anatheistically retrieved, can add to such common principles, as inscribed in world charters of human justice, is a deep mystical appreciation of something Other than our finite, human being: some Other we can welcome as a stranger if we can overcome our natural response of fear and trauma. For beyond the indispensable provisions of juridical, ethical, and political peace, there are deep spiritual resources that can bring an extra dimension to the peace table—the surprise of the stranger, the gracious surplus of faith, hope, and caritas.

If peace is ever achieved on our planet, it will not, I suspect, be brokered solely by global politicians and constitutional lawyers. It will also be a peace brought about by what Karl Jaspers called a "loving combat" (*liebender Kampf*) between different faiths and non-faiths. Radical hospitality is not about a facile consensus that ignores the reality of conflicting convictions. It is an effort to retrieve a unique hospitality towards the stranger at the very root of each belief, a counterweight to the violent specters of antagonism that we assume (rightly or not) will accompany the partisan fate of religious identities. In thus exposing ourselves to the gods of other traditions, we take the risk of dying unto our own. And in such instants of kenotic hospitality, where we exchange our God with others—sometimes not knowing for a moment which is true—we open ourselves to the gracious possibility of receiving our own God back again; but as a gift from the other this time, as a God of life beyond death. In losing our faith we may gain it back again. First faith ceding to second faith, in the name of the stranger. That is the wager of ana-theism. And the risk. For in surrendering our own God to a stranger god, no god may come back again. Or the god who comes back may come back in ways that surprise us.

Notes

1. Habermas and Derrida, *Philosophy in a Time of Terror*, 55f. See also de Vries and Sullivan, *Political Theologies;* this volume which soberly demonstrates how excessive the political take on religion has become. I am grateful to Lovisa Bergdahl for several of these references.
2. Huntington, *The Clash of Civilisations and the Remaking of World Order*, 21. I am grateful to Donatien Cicura for this reference. Cicura explains in his *Identity and Historicity: Hermeneutics of Contemporary African Marginality*: "According to Huntington, the process of creating enemies is an inherent component of the process of being a self, of acquiring or appropriating an identity. Identity is made of allies (those who belong to my group) and enemies (those with whom I compete either individually or as a member of a group). In this line of thought, Huntington's idea of identity is analogous to the interpretation Francis Fukuyama gave of Plato's *thumos* in *The End of History and the Last Man* (New York: Penguin, 2002). Human beings identify themselves in thyumotic terms, that is, they need self-esteem, recognition, and approbation. To this extent, conflict wth an enemy reinforces the above qualities in a group, and procures comfort and a sense of gratification" (Cicura, 75). As Huntington himself puts it: "The need of individuals for self-esteem leads them to believe that their group is better than other groups.Their sense of self rises and

falls . . . with the extent to which other people are excluded from their group" (Huntington, *Who Are We?* 25). For recent critiques of this adversarial model of politics and of religion, see Sen, *Identity and Violence*; Bhaba, *The Location of Culture*; Nussbaum, *For Love of Country*; and Kearney, chapters 1, 3 and 5 in *Strangers, Gods and Monsters*, 23–140.

3. Habermas and Derrida, 55.
4. Habermas, "Religion in the Public Sphere," 6.
5. *Ibid.*, 55.
6. *Ibid.*, 9–10.
7. *Ibid.*, 18.
8. *Ibid.*, 10.
9. Habermas, "A Conversation about God and the World," 148–149. On the need for a complementary rational dialogue between secular and religious citizens, see also Habermas and Ratzinger, *The Dialectics of Secularisation*, 43–47.
10. Habermas, cited Bergdahl, "Lost in Translation," 3–4. I am very grateful to Lovisa Bergdahl for bringing these arguments and texts to my attention.
11. See Benjamin, "The Task of the Translator."
12. Habermas, "Religion in the Public Sphere," 10–12; also Habermas, *Between Naturalism and Religion*; cited and commented on by Bergdahl, "Lost in Translation," 3.
13. Benjamin, "Task of Translator," 70. On the limits of interrelgious translatability as both a possibility and impossibility of symmetrical dialogue, see Cornille, *The Im-Possibility of Religious Dialogue*. See also Edith Stein in *On the Problem of Empathy* where she describes our phenomenological encounter with the other as a "primordial experience of the non-primordial," that is, as a direct sense of the indirectness and elusiveness of the "stranger" within every person we encounter, be they familiar or foreign. On this theme, see also Scheler, *The Nature of Sympathy* and Derrida's discussion of Husserl's Fifth *Cartesian Meditation* in "Hospitality, Justice and Responsibility," in *Questioning Ethics*, ed. R. Kearney and Mark Dooley (London: Routledge, 1999), 66–83.
14. Benjamin, "The Task of the Translator," 75, 81.
15. Steinbock, *Phenomenology and Mysticism*, 211f.
16. Ricoeur, "Entretien Hans Küng–Paul Ricoeur," 211–230.
17. See Kearney, Introduction to *Traversing the Heart: Journeys of the Inter-Religious Imagination*, entitled "Journey to the Heart," 3–33.
18. Ricoeur, "Entretien Hans Küng–Paul Ricoeur."
19. Camus, *The Myth of Sisyphus*, 441f.
20. Ricoeur, "Entretien. "
21. *Ibid.*, (*"non seulement ce message me dépasse mais auusi il me désarme"*).
22. *Ibid.*
23. *Ibid.*: "Je crois que nous avons besoin de la parole de *l'Aufklärung*. Et la grande chance du christianisme c'est d'avoir été confronté dès le début, grâce à la Grèce et a tout l'héritage du rationalisme, à ce conflit de ce que j'ai appelé le conflit de la conviction et de la critique. C'est dans la mesure où nous menons ce combat de l'intérieur de la conviction, et avec l'appui de ceux du dehors, et du dehors de toute religion, que nous avons besoin de l'athée, pour nous comprendre, nous croyants, et pour comprendre les autres croyants qui sont dans d'autres croyances que notre croyance."
24. Benjamin, "The Task of the Translator." Contrast this with Habermas's view of translation between religions as a process of mutual public exchange and exposure in "Religion in the Public Sphere." The ana-theist approach seeks a middle route between the positions of Habermas and Benjamin.

Chapter 8

Towards an Anthropology of Violence: Existential Analyses of Levinas, Girard, and Freud

Jeffrey Bloechl

When political order and the promulgation of law are treated as essentially a matter of power, politics appears incapable of solving the problem of violence for the simple reason that it is itself already implicated in violence. On that line of reasoning, peace such as we may fairly be expected to achieve it in this world would become a matter of economizing the violence that is our inevitable lot. One does not overcome violence so much as turn it against itself, and one does not expect peace without a price. Any other vision, we would have to admit, reveals a dangerous innocence. Order and law would be exigencies of the human condition, and politics the study of their application.

If, however, it is proposed that these exigencies do not only resist the constant possibility of violence but also point toward an absolute peace after all, and if it is argued that what is sometimes denounced as innocence in fact finds warrant in the truest labor of concepts, then political philosophy is required to contemplate a horizon that it may well consider as literally out of this world. Contemporary philosophy recognizes this extraordinary counterproposal in attempts to reinstate a theory of eschatology. Such an eschatology does not contest the view that violence is a constant condition of our existence in this world, but it does contend that we are more than that existence. What ground is there for accepting this contention? Nothing prevents philosophy from attending to an example: when in the presence of a vulnerable stranger, I respond with a compassion that transcends both violence and the need to impose order on it. Love is inordinate, we are told. Our care for one another is not to be contained within the limits of the world.

It is well known that such a claim rests on a provocative and highly debatable account of the human face that elicits our compassion. Before turning to that account as it appears in the philosophy of Levinas, it is worth pausing over two important complications that it brings to the problem of violence. First, it must not be forgotten that the same human face that is said to open the way to peace is also a precondition for the extreme violence that strikes even, *and especially* at, the vulnerable and forsaken. Second, this in turn suggests that political responses to violence must be submitted to careful critique, not only because they are limited by their own implication in violence, but also because the political response always arrives late on the scene—that is, after the instant in which my response to a vulnerable human being turns toward respect and support, and thus away from the annihilation that ensues when that vulnerability is refused or even attacked. I do not intend on this occasion to ask whether we have no properly political solution to the problem of such an excessive violence, or instead are simply in need of a partially different politics than is generally invoked in these discussions (I have already suggested that what I have called the "eschatological response" to the problem of evil concedes a great deal to a certain politics). For the moment, it will be enough to try to clarify the nature of that excessive violence, and then seek an account of our humanity that will be attentive to it.

The Face of the Other

I will begin by opposing myself to a common premise: The possibility of overcoming violence does not rest securely on our capacity to recognize the other person as truly another person—that is, on our capacity to recognize and respect her as someone who has her own needs and desires, her own concerns, and in the final account her own vulnerability to everything from the world itself, as well as to any number of impulses or tendencies in herself. It is true, of course, that violence *can* give way to nonviolence—true that peace does become *possible*—in and through this kind of recognition, but that outcome is somewhat less assured than we might like to think. My neighbor's humanity, I readily agree, can become an occasion for me to reverse, or at least stem, the tide of violence we have all met in this world. But it does not always do so. And sometimes its emergence seems to actually incite violence where previously there seemed to be none. What might this say about us, about our humanity, and the effort to live well with one another?

This is not yet a thesis but only a claim in need of substantiation or, if one prefers, an insistence on phenomena still in need of interpretation. The first examples that come to mind are dramatic. Psychiatrists, for example, are familiar with the sudden, murderous rage of certain patients, arising the moment they catch sight of the singular humanity of their therapist. What, specifically, the patient cannot accept is the vulnerability of the one who faces him. In such cases, vulnerability, as an essential figure of our humanity, elicits neither care nor solicitude, but an active, unreserved violence that is their strict opposite. In quite another context, Jean Améry, in his autobiographical essay "On Torture," recounts how the spectacle of his own helplessness provoked in his Nazi torturers what he calls an "existential sadism," aimed at eradicating his very subjectivity.[1] The moral significance of what happened at Breendonk and other places is not grasped until one recognizes the insidious role of technique and the dark urges that exploited it. Arrested on suspicion of working for the resistance, Améry was immediately submitted to a process that skillfully undermined his very self-assurance as a free and rational being, whereupon his captors found the worst sort of excesses not merely possible but virtually irresistible. Only their profession as "cops" answerable to higher officers set limits on their abuse. Now existential sadism is not murderous rage; it is undoubtedly more measured, and it does not aim at the death of the victim but at the annihilation of his humanity. The two experiences I have invoked are, thus, not quite the same, yet they do bring to mind the same unsettling thought: *something in us can respond to the recognition of another human being, precisely as vulnerable, with a strong urge to negate it.*

Are we entitled to associate these astonishing and rare experiences with what we observe in less dramatic and, after all, less restricted circumstances? It should be admitted up front that the phenomenon is difficult both to verify in others and admit in ourselves, and not merely because one would rather not own up to their existence: how can we be sure that it is specifically vulnerability that provokes an intensely violent response? Numerous other motives quickly come to mind: Perhaps the victim said something incendiary, even if unintentionally and only by gesture or deed; perhaps the aggression is not excessive but confused, mistaking the victim as an instance of something not strictly present; etc. There is no way around this (phenomenological) difficulty, except by way of further clarification of the notion itself. I think we stay on the right track if we ask whether the form of violence I have invoked can truly be distinguished from two other forms whose existence could hardly be more assured. There is, to begin with, the violence that is wrought with a heavy heart and a stiff upper lip, in the conviction—to be sure, often enough confused or mistaken—that it is the price to be paid for a higher good. I do not wish to underestimate the savagery of this allegedly well-intended violence, and still less the contentious nature of the reasoning sometimes guiding it, but I do not think it is especially difficult to understand how it becomes possible. Secondly, there is the violence that is wrought by human beings who are simply, terribly blind to the humanity of those who are injured by their actions. I do not underestimate this sort of violence either, but once again find it relatively easy to grasp it in its genesis: a range of coldly inhuman structures—social, political, economic—and deeply self-interested impulses combine to make decisions and adopt courses of action, without ever taking into consideration their consequences for any number of people near and far. But neither of these is quite the violence that is wrought by human beings responding specifically to a humanity that truly presents itself to them, precisely because it presents itself to them, and certainly without regret. Strikingly enough, the genesis of this third sort of violence must be thought together with the genesis of the true nonviolence that becomes possible at the same moment, when with the dawn of recognition, respect, and compassion become at least thinkable. Here then, with this third sort of violence, it is a matter of an impulse to destroy life and reject humanity just as it comes into view and, thus, also just when it becomes equally possible to promote life and affirm humanity. And to repeat, this is no longer the violence that we find among individuals and groups caught up in ordinary conflict. I have in mind the possibility of another, darker violence that seems to accompany the very possibility of overcoming that more familiar violence— one that arises alongside the initial promise of peace and immediately, essentially, contests it. So I now reformulate the question I asked a moment ago: Would such an impulse be present wherever and whenever we have the chance for peace? And I have to follow it with another: What would this say about us, about our humanity?

These questions are not wholly absent from every philosophy that is attentive to the problem of violence. In a startling passage of *Totality and Infinity*, Levinas observes that the face of my neighbor, who comes to me impoverished and destitute, both calls me to care for her and tempts me to murder. Murder, after all, has as its proper object another human being, and according to Levinas, that unique presence is revealed when she faces me. This is more than a banality, for it cannot be understood without some reflection on the distribution and exercise of power in human relations. Power is a matter for the very movement of our being before and apart from any question of wielding it against others. When I encounter another person, I am already sustained by a world and possessions, and already exercise a certain power over the situation in which they are mine. The face of that person does, of course, enter my world and, thus, does in some sense hand itself over to the power with which I maintain my place at the center of that world. Yet it does so in the form of a withdrawal from my world and, thus, a refusal of my power. The face of an interlocutor is in my world but not wholly of my world. According to Levinas, this can only appear to me in the form, as I have already said, of poverty and destitution: she has none of what I have, and is not at home here where I am. At the same time, this poverty and destitution render her ultimately mysterious to me, or in the phenomenological sense, beyond my comprehension. Nothing of what I know extends to another person insofar as she is other. There is, thus, something fundamentally ambivalent about the other person such as I encounter her: on one hand, her poverty and destitution are, of course, figures of powerlessness; on the other hand, they are figures of an unfathomable mystery, and in that sense indicate the power to resist or withdraw from me. Paradoxical as it may sound, the powerlessness of another person that presents itself to me in her face marks the limit of *my own* power. It is this that murder would refuse. Murder is insistence on one's own power where power has neither the right nor the means to satisfy itself. "Murder," says Levinas, "exercises power over what escapes power."[2]

This is already enough for us to understand how it could be that the face of another person not only opens the possibility of murder as a necessary condition, but even tempts me to the act. In its very appearance as flesh and surface, the face by which the poor and homeless other enters my world and indeed my consciousness challenges me in the exercise of a power that is dedicated to my own security—or, more specifically, enters the movement of that power in a manner that puts it immediately in question. This experience, like the face itself, is ambivalent. To the degree that the face does touch me, the other person has, at least at the noetic level, already fallen under my power. But to the degree that that touch occurs specifically in the mode of withdrawal, I am made newly unstable, and perhaps even left resentful at this change in my situation. It would be at such a moment, in which my very identity hangs in the balance, that the temptation to violence might well present itself.

Having followed Levinas this far, one is entitled to ask how it is that the utmost violence does not in fact occur far more often than it does. What prevents the self-interested subject, acting under its own power and attached to its own place at the center of its world, from a murder that would have to be both expedient and reassuring? It comes as a surprise to us moderns to find that Levinas continues to appeal solely to the face of the other person—to what is expressed first and solely in her face—and not for instance to either some notion of natural right or civil law. The face itself, he says, not only tempts me to murder but also prohibits me from murder. Without immediately understanding this, we can nonetheless begin to recognize the enormous scope of the position it announces: if peace is born in a decision that is made without appeal to rights and laws, then it yields a response that is in turn unlimited by either rights or laws. This proposal of a relation anterior to any set of norms suggests an ethics that would be strictly universalist. Yet that same ethics would also define a bold pluralism: true peace, if it is to be had, must be born in recognizing and responding to the other person in her immediate uniqueness, which is to say before and apart from her identity as, for instance, one among many citizens. How, then, does the same face that tempts me to annihilate him in his uniqueness also prohibit me from doing so? According to Levinas, the very weakness by which he hands himself over to my understanding has the capacity to shock me as I continue to exercise my power over him. In my neighbor's defenseless eyes are mirrored my potential for murder. In meeting his gaze, I catch sight of myself and that vision can give me pause, so that it is now possible for me to continue with a violence that serves my own interests *or* relinquish that course of action in favor of the respect for his uniqueness that for Levinas constitutes true nonviolence.

This brings us to a point of some difficulty in Levinas's position (and, as is well known, some contention in Levinas scholarship): it is not immediately clear what would motivate a subject in that destabilized predicament to turn away from violence toward peace—or, at the level of Levinas's application, from interest in myself to respect for the other. If the first and necessary condition of peace is a decision and a response rooted before and outside of one's attachment to everything that comes between oneself and one's interlocutor, *in his uniqueness*, then what motivates the decision and the response must seek something that is not contained any of those other attachments. In short, one must be called and respond from before and outside of anything already present in the world to which one does well and good belong. Levinas fittingly speaks here of a call and an ordering to the good that is beyond being, and of a goodness that is otherwise than being. Without entering into the difficulties of such a notion—metaphysical, logical, phenomenological, none of which are overlooked in Levinas's texts—we are able to recognize in it the final gesture of an attempt to contain the possibility of violence, associated with the very movement of our being, within the vision of a more fundamental and inextinguishable possibility to overcome it. This is not a theodicy, since violence is never justified within some higher economy, and since in any case Levinas rejects any basis for *certainty* that the good will indeed prevail.[3] Instead, salvation from evil, from violence and the suffering that is its consequence, depends on me—or let us say: on each of us, but always in the first person singular.

I must commit the very power of my being to respect for my poor and impoverished neighbor. I must no longer concern myself with what is good for me or good for my group, but must attend to what is good specifically for her. And this means: I must seek a goodness that neither belongs to me nor lies in my world. Levinas calls the desire that aims at such a goodness, at a peace that would not be possible in the world alone, "metaphysical." If this is to be the desire that motivates one to decide for the other and respond to the other at the very moment when utmost violence is also possible, it can succeed only to the degree that it manages to suspend the other, self-centered desire that attaches us to the world and everything in it—that is to say, in the most general sense, to objects. Peace, then, is to be won at the cost of suspending relations with objects. The good beyond being, after all, is precisely not an object. Everything in Levinas's approach to violence and nonviolence depends on establishing this desire and the good that it seeks. We may accept the coherence of his ideas, and indeed the expected characterization of their price—expiation, self-abnegation, kenosis (terms that appear on virtually every page of *Otherwise than Being or Beyond Essence*)—and still hesitate on a single point: what becomes of the unreserved violence said to be surfacing in the murderous subject before he turns to respect and care for the other person? Neither Levinas's own account of the life of the subject nor, I submit, common experience permits us to suppose that it simply disappears. Having nowhere else to go, it seems bound to turn inward and visit itself on the subject. Or perhaps it finds its way to expression after all, but in covert form: as we all know, an outwardly nonviolent act such as turning the other cheek can be animated by an angry defiance that is anything but peaceful. But failing even that, one can expect the violent impulse in question here to become self-destructive. This is not the occasion to pursue the many features of Levinas's philosophy that plainly invite an investigation of just this possibility, from a call to make oneself the hostage of the other to a characterization of responsibility by trauma. In any case, it is not certain to me that he has overlooked the danger signaled here, but there is no mistaking how close he is to it: it is not impossible that there, in the nonviolence that asks for unremitting self-sacrifice, peace for the other coincides with violence for the subject.

Should we not hope for a peace that extends to me, too?

A Notion of the Sacred

Should we wish to lift the pressure imposed on the problem of violence and nonviolence by the foregoing defense of an absolute good, but nonetheless continue to ask whether there may be an utmost violence that arises at the same moment as does the possibility of respect and care, we can take an interest in some elements of the position adopted by René Girard. In effect, what Girard proposes is a theory of human violence that locates the possibility of nonviolence through neither *suspension* nor *conversion*, but *expenditure*.

Real, viable peace, he suggests, is achieved by way of focused and well-managed release, such as occurs in ritual scapegoating and sacrifice. There interest of this thesis is evident enough: if there is to be peace for the other person *and for me*, the violence within me must be directed away from the other without the chance of folding it back in on me. Hence, as far as Girard is concerned, the continued importance of symbolic victims, and of the rituals which make them available to us—modern anti-religious prejudices notwithstanding.

This much already makes it plain that for Girard violence is a genuinely original feature of our condition, and not only, as Levinas would have it, the natural but corrigible tendency of a being that has forgotten its prior debt to others. And this is easily confirmed by following the logical progression of what he calls "mimetic rivalry," whereby our humanity is said to emerge and subsist through imitation of others. According to Girard, who would not be the first to have said this much, this imitation is animated by a powerful sense of rivalry; I want what the other wants, even and especially if he already possesses it. From here, human relations seem bound either for a competition that will intensify until friction gives over to the fire of open violence, or else for a nonviolence resulting from some diversion of the impulse to violence. What sort of subject is so thoroughly imbued with violence? Though much of Girard's anthropology is surprisingly close to Levinas, there are important differences where it matters most for us here. He does not fail to note, for instance, that neither mimesis nor violence would be possible without a primal moment of recognition in which I have identified the other person who is now my rival as alter ego, another me. It must be said immediately that this implies a symmetry for our encounter with the other which Levinas, for his part, is generally at great pains to resist. Yet Girard does agree with Levinas that it is the presence of a desiring other that calls me toward what can become murderous violence, and indeed that her presence has that effect on me before and outside of the cultural determinations that contribute so greatly to our specific identities. But an essential difference does show up in their respective phenomenologies of that experience: whereas for Levinas the desiring other is an other in need, an other who is vulnerable, impoverished and destitute, Girard places the accent on that desire as potential and as menace: the other person wants what I want—or I want what she seems to want—and I respond first to the impression that she may soon take possession of it if indeed she has not already done so; she is always and already my rival. This means that against Levinas's suggestion that it is the weakness of the other that tempts me to violence, Girard contends that it is what I take to be her strength, her power, which has that effect on me.

Girard's ensuing attempt to link generative violence to some version of catharsis—whether purgation or purification—is too familiar to detain us for long: passing a certain threshold, violence is directed collectively toward a single object or, as I have noted, a victim submitted to a highly ritualized set of procedures which channel, but also prolong and, thus, release over time, the violence that otherwise threatens to erupt in all directions without restraint.

In this way, the potentially murderous violence stimulated by the presence of my neighbor who is my rival is shifted on to one who, bearing it, becomes both the polluted exile and the revered victim—that is, according to what is, after all, a somewhat familiar conception of the sacred. The sacred, Girard proposes, is the effect of generative violence and the solution to it; the sacred is, perhaps literally, the apotheosis of violence and yet, since it gathers all violence to itself, it is also the only means to peace.

At this juncture, it is useful to consider the fact that Levinas is strongly opposed to any notion of the sacred, which he associates with frenzied violence and an affective fusion in which properly human relations decline into a swirl of "anonymous realities."[4] Girard, for his part, evidently considers the sacred to be the sole and proper *insurance* against such a decline. In his view, we are always in danger of losing our humanity so long as we are *without* sacrifice and a common orientation to the sacred. What shall we make of this difference? Is the violence that becomes possible when we catch sight of another person, as a desiring being, prohibited already in the same face that incites us to that violence, or is it manageable only by diversion, according to logic of the sacred, onto some third party? The question highlights the fact that, for Girard, violence is a constant and inextinguishable possibility, and responsibility—or nonviolence—could never call for its suspension. One does not overcome violence, but reduces it to a level permitting comfortable respect for rules, including prohibitions, and indeed the possibility of creative solicitude—of a willingness to recognize and commit oneself to the needs of others. As a matter of the attachments that Levinas would have us put aside for the neighbor in need, Girard seems far less willing to direct human aspiration to willful dispossession. Levinas, I have said, would have us strive to empty ourselves of all objects in favor a goodness that is precisely not an object. Girard, in contrast, suggests that we ought never pretend to abandon the primacy of desire for objects, but does offer reason to seek a moderation of that desire by way of the release gained in an approach to the sacred. This distinction could hardly be more important: the state of objectlessness that for Levinas is at least an ideal and perhaps more than that, is for Girard a dangerous lure into psychosis (a word that Levinas, incidentally, does not refuse).[5] Psychotic desire, says Girard, is desire withdrawn from any attachment to an object of my own, leaving only an attachment to the model whom I imitate, so that my desire is now strictly and without qualification the desire of the other.[6] One thus surmises that healthy desire is desire that remains attached to the object, with its tonality and even its intensity shaped at least to some degree by imitation of the other. And nonviolence, then, would in no small part be a matter of that degree. Any moderation of the mimetic desire that propels us into rivalry would also be a loosening of our attachment to objects whereby room is made for the possibility of a livable peace. Before examining this more closely, let me not fail to note the following: it is true that Girard seems far from the self-destruction one may fear in Levinas's vision of an impulse to nonviolence that is first and above all for the other, but he is also far from any notion of an impulse to nonviolence that could be more than a complication of a deeper, more fundamental impulse to violence.

An Interrogation of Narcissism

Now, it would be surprising to find that in this attention to the phenomenon of our attachment to objects Girard directs us to something Levinas would have simply failed to consider. Such attachments, Levinas has said, define a condition that stands in need of ethical critique. Possession must give way to dispossession, time and again, for real peace to come into view. But in studying these two views, we do not have to immediately decide between dispossession and moderation, the loosening that is not a complete letting-go. And in the very appearance of this difference, there is at last some phenomenological terra firma on which to address the violence and nonviolence that become possible, together and at once, in the moment of recognition of another person. The knot between desire and attachment to objects is, already before it is a question of peace for me and peace for the other, an index of narcissism, as the inner constitution of our subjectivity. Narcissism, we know, involves desire for a primary object—an object unlike any other object—that sets the condition for desire of all other objects. It is possible, in the most preliminary manner, to situate Levinas and Girard on either side of this proposal for our condition. Would the question of violence and nonviolence then come down to an interrogation of narcissism? As it happens, the concept itself is present in both Levinas and Girard. Unfortunately, in both cases it is *assumed* rather than, as I have just put it, interrogated and then perhaps grounded.

For Levinas, the word "narcissism" designates one's tendency to affirm and reinforce what he calls "the sameness of the same," that is to say a tendency to install oneself at the center of a world in which everything gives itself to me and gets its meaning from me.[7] "Narcissism" is, thus, a name for what we have already understood as the movement of our being to assert and establish its own interests before those of the other person. In the philosophy of Levinas, it is a name for the exercise of power by which we try to erase an ulterior sense of disorder insecurity. But then it is also a name for what must be given up, whether suspended or reversed, in favor of a greater goodness that cannot be reached by any feat of power but nonetheless draws near in the call of a helpless neighbor. Evidently enough, what matters in all of this, as a matter of objects and desire, is only that there is some possession followed by a call to dispossession. What matters far less, if at all, is the particularity of objects and the particularity of our attachments to them. Should we not wonder about this? This is not a question merely of insisting on detail where Levinas is content to be schematic; if the subjectivity of the subject is constituted by its relation to objects—by the character of a desire that takes possession of the things it encounters—then one wants to know about the unicity of the subject who desires these particular objects with this or that particular intensity. For Levinas, this is of, at best, secondary importance. His analyses begin with a subject already structured by a narcissism that is, as far as the argument needs to be concerned, only quite general. It is this thesis of a general form of narcissism that makes possible his move straightaway to interpret the entire structure, including its inner dynamism, in the context of a primordial exposure to the other person who is, again as far as the essential structure is concerned, at least as general and undefined as is that narcissism. The absolute, unqualified otherness of the other person precedes and later emerges to challenge the general narcissism of the self-interested subject. None of this helps us understand how there is *particular* attachment to *particular* objects in the first place—how there is the *particular* identity said to be called into question, called to empty itself of itself, by the face of the other person. It is a considerable surprise to find that the same philosopher who insists that violence is always my violence, offers us only very little about either the origin or the minimal conditions by which I, already in the spontaneity of my own being—that is, before I am awakened to responsibility for my neighbor—am already precisely myself, with urges and objects that are quite evidently my own.

But Girard, too, arrives at the theme of a fundamental narcissism having already deprived himself of the means to investigate its anterior conditions. This occurs at the very heart of the theory: if the conditions for subjectivity—Girard even suggests *humanity*—are set by mimetic rivalry, then one's identity is always strictly a function of a relation to what others seem to want: I am this one who desires what they desire, though it is true that I desire it differently than they desire it. If the theme of narcissism arises inevitably for this theory that is so concerned with the intersubjective dimension of desire and objects, still it never presents that theory with much difficulty because it is enough to say that all desire aims at *some* object, and that all objects become present through the desire of *some* other. If narcissism in its usual sense entails a sense of the specificity of desire and objects—even a hierarchy among them—for Girard that is nonetheless a circumscribed problem. And indeed, this must also be true when it comes to the specificity of violence. As far as the theory is concerned, the *particular* violence that I commit counts only as an instance of a mechanism that is essentially *general* (and I mean the "process" itself, and not merely the theory that proposes it). On this last point, there is unexpectedly almost perfect agreement with Levinas: we can be sure that violence is always my violence, but this can be said without having to probe my personal identity, as one who can become aggressive or not.

What I have been suggesting is that in their consideration of desire, possession and relations to objects, Levinas and Girard, along lines of reflection that are often directly opposed, each resist any primacy for what Freud calls personal psychic "investment" or "cathexis" in objects. There is no need here to go into the fact that Levinas had almost no serious encounter with psychoanalysis and the fact Girard's famously massive encounter touches on the metapsychology almost not at all[8], since we have already understood that when they define the being of the subject purely and simply by a natural tendency to violence, they necessarily exclude any interest in the possibility that that being owes its unicity to some prior, or deeper investment by which all the other investments (for Freud: *Besetzungen*) are oriented. I am tempted to suggest that there may be another, more important reason for this, but will instead propose it as a consequence. Bear with me for a moment: If we recognize that a primary investment in some first object that orients all other investments— this being essential for the very formation of narcissism—necessarily implies an event or occurrence rooted outside consciousness, we come unavoidably to some sense of the unconscious. More specifically, since this is also a matter of an investment that sets the tone and pattern for conscious desire, we also come to some sense of what is properly called "drive" or "pulsion" [*trieb*]. More than inner complications of the self-determining life of the subject, the unconscious and the drives must be considered before and outside of that life—thus, before and outside of the subjectivity that Levinas wishes to associate with the sameness of the same and then put in question by the face of the other, and also before the very advent of mimetic desire such as Girard wishes to trace from rivalry to violence, and so forth. But this is more than an anthropological problem, for especially a theory of the drives would complicate—or frankly, limit— our conception of human freedom. And it is to an extraordinarily capacious freedom that both Levinas and Girard finally appeal to in order to account for the possibility of nonviolence arising in a subject that they have first defined by an extraordinary capacity for violence. The question is obvious: if our subjectivity exhibits a fundamentally narcissistic structure, if narcissism is constituted around a primary investment in some first object—paradigmatically, for Freud, the mother, as the one thing that ought to matter most for everyone because it matters most to me—and if that primary investment must involve a theory of drives anterior to the freedom with which we try to take up a relation to them, *then we have to wonder just how much we can actively do about the difference between nonviolence and violence, when they arise as distinct possibilities for our response to the presence of another person.* I hasten to clarify: it is not that nothing at all can be done, but that our prospects probably do have real limits. In different ways, Levinas and Girard can appear to protect themselves from the consequences of such a thought.

The psychoanalyst's proposal is deceptively simple. Freedom, like maturity itself, depends on self-knowledge. One makes considerable progress already in learning how one tends to react to certain situations, let alone what that finally says about how one is put together. Is not everything that the word "narcissism" seems to represent an excellent clarification of what we undergo when frustrated or wounded? The world will not answer wholly to my own wishes, will not become what I want or at least center itself on what I want. Or the world, perhaps someone in it, gives sudden evidence of refusing that subterranean wish in me. In the former case, I struggle with a rising aggression. In the latter case, it often rushes past me before I can stop it. Is this not tantamount to saying that the other person can incite me to rage simply by showing up as other, as someone with her own desires, desires not answerable to my own—that is, tantamount to saying that the possibility of violence opens up at the same time and in response to the same event as opens up the possibility of nonviolence? Other people are not always who or what we want them to be, for better and for worse, and this is especially the case with others who are close to us or especially esteemed by us. This is so not because of some fault in them, and in a certain sense also not necessarily because of some fault in me—but simply because people are put together under conditions for which they cannot be held entirely accountable. Or rather, they cannot be held accountable for the arrival of those conditions that are formative of their character with which they meet life and its exigencies. We can, of course, reasonably expect that each of us seeks a good understanding of herself, learns to live in an awareness of the vulnerability and the tensions that cannot be banished but only accepted and thereby diminished. Presented with this, Freud would surely have observed that we thus reminded that, in fact, all of us are struggling with our narcissism, but in different ways. There are those who resist its very presence, whether by flight or by denial. There are others who somehow manage to accept it, and sometimes even care for it. It would be a mistake to reduce such acceptance to simple insistence and recalcitrance. In the struggle to manage oneself and one's situation in all its complexity, one may recognize a moving confession of our exposure to what we neither have chosen nor can fully escape, and of the proper root of our need of help from others—those same others who find themselves equally in struggle and exposure and thus also in need of help. Should it not count among he fundamental tasks of our politics to nurture the friendships that this calls for, and indeed the wherewithal it takes to seek them?

Notes

1. J. Améry, "On Torture," 35–36. The expression comes from Bataille, with whom Améry sides against the adequacy of a psycho–sexual interpretation.
2. Levinas, *Totality and Infinity*, 198.
3. Levinas has written of a "temptation to theodicy" by which we would explain to ourselves, and in that way justify, the suffering of the other. Levinas, "Useless Suffering," 168.
4. Levinas, "Levy-Bruhl and Contemporary Thought," 46.
5. See, Levinas, *Otherwise than Being*, 142.
6. Girard, *Things Hidden Since the Foundation of the World*, 310–311.
7. See especially the programmatic usage at Levinas, "Philosophy and the Idea of Infinity," 49–53.
8. In both *Things Hidden Since the Foundation of the World* and *Violence and the Sacred*, Girard manages to discuss Freud at some length and with great sophistication without, however, entering into a serious discussion the theme of narcissism. To be sure, *Things Hidden* does touch on Freud's essay "On Narcissism: An Introduction," but then only to submit it to the reduction I have outlined (367–383).

Chapter 9

Agamben on Violence, Language, and Human Rights

Peg Birmingham

The concept of the refugee (and the figure of life that this concept represents) must be resolutely separated from the concepts of the rights of man . . . The refugee must be considered for what he is: nothing less than a limit concept that radically calls into question the fundamental categories of the nation-state, from the birth–nation to the man–citizen link, and that thereby makes it possible to clear the way for a long-overdue renewal of categories in the service of a politics in which bare life is no longer separated and excepted, either in the state order or in the figure of human rights.[1]

Giorgio Agamben

As we see in the above epigrah, Agamben's thought is marked by two consistent claims: first, the figure of the refugee is the political subject of contemporary politics, and secondly, that this political subject cannot be understood as a subject of rights. Agamben's call for severing the figure of the refugee from human rights discourse is rooted in his argument that the modern declaration of human rights collapses the universal claim of the rights of the human being as such into the particular claim of the rights of citizens. Following Arendt and agreeing entirely with her on this point, Agamben points out that human rights have always been inseparability linked with nativity, which, in turn, has been inseparable from the notion of the nation–state. In other words, the *native* is inscribed into the juridical order of the nation–state: "The fiction is that birth comes into being immediately as nation, so that there may not be any difference between the two moments. Rights . . . are attributed to the human being only to the degree to which he or she is the immediately vanishing presupposition (and, in fact, the presupposition that must never come to light as such) of the citizen."[2] Only nationals have rights and no one knew this better than the refugees, such as Arendt herself, who had to flee for their lives. In the very situation where the claim to universal human rights ought to have offered remedy and protection, refugees were left only with their bare life, or as Agamben states, "the pure fact of being human." He goes on to claim, ". . . there is no autonomous space in the political order of the nation–state for something like the pure human in itself . . ."[3]

I want to suggest, however, that the subject of rights in Agamben's thought is more complicated, arguing in this essay that Agamben's critique is not with the concept of human rights *per se*, but with the *declaration* of modern rights. In other words, and this accounts for Agamben's continuous preoccupation with language, the *declaration* seems incapable of doing anything other than declaring rights of particular peoples in particular political spaces and this last precisely due to Western philosophy's understanding of *logos* itself. When Aristotle makes the claim in the *Politics* that the human being is a political being because the human being is *zoon logon echon*, it is not often noted that Aristotle goes on immediately to make the claim that *logos* is inherently violent: *Logos* distinguishes the just from the unjust, good from evil, the beneficial from the useless.[4] Distinguishing *logos* (speech) from voice, Aristotle suggests that the sovereign decision is inherent to *logos* itself. As Zizek points out, "[L]anguage is the great divider" and as such is violent.[5] Rank and dominance seem to be built into language itself. Following Heidegger's insight that language is the house of being and brings things into their essence, Zizek claims that through language the world is "given a partial twist, it loses its balanced innocence, [and] a partial color gives the tone of the whole."[6] In this framework, stretching from Aristotle to Heidegger, the declaration of the rights of man cannot then be anything other than partial and violent, dividing those who belong to the city from those who stand outside, distinguishing those who possess true political speech from the senseless voices beyond the gates, separating those who possess human rights from those endowed only with bare life.

As mentioned above, it is my contention in this essay that Agamben's reflections on language offer his readers not only a radically new framework out of which to think *logos*, but also a new framework out of which to think human rights. In other words, shifting from *logos* understood as speech to *logos* understood first as voice, Agamben allows for a non-sovereign, nonviolent *logos* that, in turn, allows for a conception of human rights tied to the figure of the refugee rather than to the citizen. Agamben's most extensive analysis of this non-sovereign, nonviolent *logos* is given in his analysis of the *Muselmann*, "the human being who is the inhuman; the one whose humanity is completely destroyed is the one who is truly human."[7] His analysis of the Muselmann renders problematic the *declaration* of human rights, a declaration that is itself tied to sovereignty, the nation–state and the citizen that from its inception has been constituted out of a "state of exception." This analysis suggests that when thinking the notion of right, we must move from the declaration of right rooted in *logos* to the *material* dimension of language that makes such a declaration possible. Here, I suggest, we find a new basis for thinking human rights. In other words, there is for Agamben a dimension of language that infuses both speech and the law, a dimension that can never be declared but which makes declaration and the law possible. This dimension, I argue, is the exposure of rightful appearance itself, an exposure that emerges in communicability itself. To allow rightful appearance to appear is the task of the coming politics.

The second part of the essay will, therefore, examine Agamben's analysis of language, especially the play of *langue* and *parole*. How do we understand the passage from communicability [*langue*] to discourse [*parole*]? In other words, how do we understand this "I" who speaks? For Agamben, in the appropriating of discourse, the I slips away: "I speak a language, but I do not speak. The impossibility of speaking comes to light in speaking."[8] In discourse, then, the "I" requires the event of speech and yet the "I" is not present. Calling into question Aristotle's claim that the human being is political because the human being is *zoon logon echon*, Agamben's analysis shows that there is no place where the "I" can transform itself into speech. There is always a "non-place" of articulation that is not something outside the polis, but at the very heart of the polis itself. This non-place marks the exposure of the human, as such. Following Agamben, I will argue that human rights are not declared, but are exposed in our very appearance, our very being-manifest. Here I will examine Agamben's notion of language as the seizing of our own appearance, our exposition, in which language is the "communicability of exposure," arguing that a new notion of human rights is rooted in the ontological condition of appearance which carries with it the right of exposure, without identity, to appear. This is the inalienable, human right of the refugee.

The Muselmann: De-subjectification and Human Rights

In his analysis of the Muselmann, who, like the refugee, is for Agamben the limit figure of the political today, he carries out this task of returning appearance itself to appearance. The question he raises through the figure of the Muselmann is whether there is a "humanity of the human" over and above the claim of belonging either to the nation or to a biological species. The question reveals the dilemma presented by the Muselmann. To say simply that the Muselmann is inhuman is to repeat and validate the Nazi experiment that places the Muselmann outside the limits of the human and the ethical–political status that accompanies this category. Instead, Agamben argues, the Muselmann indicates a fundamental indistinction between the human and the inhuman and in this indistinction our ethical–political categories are brought to crisis: "[The Muselmann] is the non-human who obstinately appears as human; he is the human that cannot be told apart from the inhuman."[9] The Muselmann is the site where "morality and humanity in themselves are called into question."[10] We cannot deny the humanity of the Muselmann, and yet this figure is a zone of the human where dignity and self-respect do not make sense. Insofar as no ethics can exclude a part of humanity, an ethics based on the dignity of the individual fails in the figure of the Muselmann.

Extending Arendt's claim that that the unprecedented nature of the death camps lies in the "fabrication of corpses," Agamben argues that in the camps there is no distinction between death and deceasing, "the ways of dying render superfluous the thought of death as such—death becomes a bureaucratic, everyday affair."[11] In the camps, there is no longer any sacredness of death, no burial of the individual who has died. Death is now in a living area and the humanity of human beings is called into radical question. Again, the Muselmann is the human who cannot be told apart from the inhuman: "[B]iopower's supreme ambition is to produce, in a human body, the absolute separation of the living being and the speaking being, *zoe* and *bios*, the inhuman and the human— survival."[12] Biopower's supreme ambition in the camps is to produce a living corpse that falls outside Aristotle's definition of the human being as *zoon logon echon*, the being who has speech. Lacking speech, the Muselmann lacks both humanity and any rightful claim to the political. No longer able to appeal to dignity, self-respect, or even speech for the rightful claim to humanity, Agamben argues that for the Muselmann, there is only shame. And it is out of this shame that Agamben finds a new subject of rights.

Referring to Robert Anthelme's account of the young Italian student from Bologna who blushes when he is called out of line just before being shot, Agamben argues that the blush of shame is the embarrassment of having to die. We who live on after him bear witness to this blush: "It is as if the flush on his cheeks momentarily betrayed a limit that was reached, as if something like a *new ethical material* were touched upon in the living being . . ."[13] Shame provides the new ethical material for thinking the subject of right; it reveals what is most intimate about us in our subjectivity and yet we can never assume it or adopt it as our own. The feeling of shame originates in being caught in one's own radical passivity or sensibility; it is to be caught in one's own "desubjectification," in the nakedness of one's own subjectivity. I quote the text at length:

> To be ashamed means to be consigned to something that cannot be assumed. But what cannot be assumed is not something external. Rather, it originates in its own intimacy; it is what is most intimate in us (for example, our own physiological life). Here the "I" is thus overcome by its own passivity, its ownmost sensibility, yet this expropriation and desubjectification is also an extreme and irreducible presence of the "I" to its self. It is as if our consciousness collapsed and, seeking to flee in all directions, was simultaneously summoned by an irrefutable order to be present at its own defacement, at the expropriation of what is most its own. In shame, the subject thus has no other content than its own desubjectification; it becomes witness to its own disorder, its own oblivion as a subject.[14]

The student from Bologna, called out of line by a call that will end his life, is utterly exposed in his subjectivity as it is being stripped away. Caught in this movement of exposure and being stripped away [this is to radicalize Arendt's claim that the refugee is reduced to the naked human being], the student blushes. The blush reveals the double sense of the subject: "The fundamental sentient of being a subject, is in the two apparently opposed senses of this phrase: to be subjected and to be sovereign. Shame is what is produced in the absolute concomitance of subjectification and desubjectification, self-loss and self-possession, servitude and sovereignty."[15]

The blush indicates that to be a subject carries two different senses of subjection. First, I am subject to whatever happens. I am subject to the rain in the sense that I can do nothing about it. I am passive in relation to it. Secondly, I am sovereign in the sense that I am the subject of my own life—I make something happen. I am active in the relation to building and creating of my life. This is the fundamental difference between Agamben and Kant. Kant recognized the duality of the *political subject* as both a sovereign and a subjected member in the community of ends. In other words, at the level of the political, Kant's subject is doubled, but at the ontological level, this subject remains autonomous and sovereign. By contrast, Agamben's analysis shows that the duality of the subject as both sovereign and subject is at the very ontological level of subjectivity itself. The double movement of subjectification and desubjectification, passivity and activity, being seen and seeing, self-loss and self-possession are at the heart of the subject itself. This is what it means to be a subject. Further, Agamben argues, "every act of speech implies something like a desubjectification."[16] There is a "desubjectifying experience implicit in the simplest act of speech."[17] At the very heart of *logos* resides the inhuman, the barbarian.

Indebted to Benveniste, Agamben elaborates on this point by analyzing the double structure of language as both *langue* and *parole*. At the level of *langue*, language is a series of signs or indicators of enunciation: "table," "chair," "lake," "light."[18] Signs, however, in themselves mean nothing. The sign is not a positive term, it refers only to other signs in a formal system, and it is constituted in its identify by its difference: A is not B, a table is not chair, a chair is not table. The sign indicates nothing. There is no significance. In order for significance to occur, there has to be the *taking* place of language. In other words, there must be an "I" who speaks. But in becoming the subject of enunciation, paradoxically, the "I" is never appropriated in the discourse: "But, once stripped of all extra-linguistic meaning and constituted as a subject of enunciation, the subject discovers that he has gained access not so much to a possibility of speaking as to an impossibility of speaking—or, rather, that he has gained access to being always already anticipated by a glossolalic potentiality over which he has neither control or mastery."[19] Once the "I" is introduced into language—becomes the subject of enunciation—nothing will allow the "I" to pass over into discourse. Still further, the event of enunciation is an event that is always taking place, without "its ever being possible to assign it any lexical reality."[20] The event of enunciation is the "pure event of language," which Agamben claims is the outside of language, its brute facticity. The outside of language, he claims, is the plane of language as potentiality of speech.[21] In the appropriating of discourse, the "I" slips away. I speak a language, but I do not speak. The subject of enunciation is composed in discourse, but once the subject is in discourse, "he can say nothing; he cannot speak."[22]

Extending Hegel's analysis of sense–certainty, Agamben argues that in addition to the "this," "here," "now," there is an "I" that is asserting this in discourse [*parole*]. And in the act of enunciation of the "this, here, now," the "I," too, slips away. Just as the "this, here, now" is marked by an irreducible negativity and distance from itself, so too is the "I" that seemed to be so firm and upon which so many modern hopes were pinned is also seen to be fragile and fleeting.[23] Engaged in idle chatter or not, the "I" and its lived experiences is never present. Subjectification, therefore, is "a trauma of which human beings are no easily cured; this is why the fragile text of consciousness incessantly crumbles and erases itself, bringing to light the disjunction on which it is erected: the constitutive desubjectification in every subjectification."[24]

This experience of subjectification and desubjectification is also experienced at the level of biological existence, the sensation of my own lived body. How can the subject be introduced into the biological flow? I have a sensation of myself physically, and yet the speaking subject can never appropriate completely this biological flow. In other words, there is never a complete coincidence between the biological and the speaking subject. Here, too, the speaking subject experiences an intimacy with its living being, but never an identity: "Indeed, 'I' signifies precisely the irreducible disjunction between vital functions and inner history, between the living being's becoming a speaking being and the speaking being's sensation of itself as living."[25] The intimacy between the speaking being and the sensual being marks neither an identity nor a difference between the two dimensions of the subject; rather, the intimacy marks that dimension in which life is always already sensed (and thereby communicated) without necessarily being the life of the speaking being. It is impossible to separate the *bios politicos* from *zoe*. In *The Human Race*, Robert Anthelme provides an account of this impossibility when he points to the "almost biological" that marks his existence in the death camps. Contested in his very appearance as a human being, Anthelme writes: "The calling into question of our quality as men provokes an almost biological claim of belonging to the human race. After that it serves to make us think about the limitations of that race, about its distance from 'nature' and its relation to 'nature.'"[26] Our bodily existence is never simply biological, but always already a form-of-life. Contrary to Aristotle's position, for Agamben there is an "irreducible disjunction" but nevertheless no strict separation between the vegetative, biological part of the soul and the "properly human" part of the soul.

Agamben then turns to Aristotle's definition of the human being as *zoon logon echon*, the definition that makes human beings fit for the *bios politicos* rather than mere life, *zoe*. Agamben points out that what is left unthought in Aristotle's definition is precisely the *echon*, the *having* of speech. The having of speech is simply the promise that language joins the living being (*zoon*) and the speaking being (*logon*) through the voice, but there is no moment when the voice can be appropriated: ". . . nowhere, in the living being and in language, can we reach a point in which something like an articulation truly takes place. Outside theology and the incarnation of the Verb, there is no moment in which language is inscribed in the living voice, no place in which the living being is able to render itself linguistic, transforming itself into speech."[27] There is no place where the "I" can transform itself into speech. There is always a non-place of articulation. This is not a place outside the walls of the *polis*, but at the very heart of the *polis* itself. Again, at the very heart of the speech that founds the *polis* is the purely human as such, without any linguistic qualifications. We can now begin to understand Agamben's claim that the Muselmann occupies the zone of indistinction between the human and the inhuman. Lacking speech, the Muselmann is not outside language altogether. The figure of the Muselmann occupies the taking–place of language, a taking–place in which rightful appearance itself appears.

The Taking-Place of Language and the Revelation of Rightful Appearance

Agamben's two seminal essays on language, "The Thing Itself," and "The Idea of Language," not only illuminate the "desubjectification of the subject in language itself," but go further, developing the outside of language, that is, the openness and potentiality of language. This, in turn, illuminates the zone of indistinction between the human and the inhuman. In the essay, "The Thing Itself," Agamben, reading Plato's *Seventh Letter*, gives five conditions of knowing the thing itself: (1) the name or the signifier, (2) the definition [*logos*] signified, (3) the image–denotation or actual reference, (4) knowledge, and (5) the thing itself. The first four must be conceived as a single thing, and together, he argues, the fifth aspect, the thing itself, is revealed. Agamben gives the example of the circle. The name, the definition, the image, and the knowledge of the circle conceived together give the circle itself. The circle itself, however, is not presupposed by the name, the definition, the image, or knowledge, but instead, is revealed or illuminated through them. The thing itself—the *auto*—is "the very medium of its knowability—in the pure light of its self-manifestation and announcement to consciousness."[28] The weakness of language [*logos*] consists in the fact that it is not capable of bringing this very knowability, the thing itself, to expression. *Logos* transforms the thing itself into a presupposition, as that which is placed beneath *logos* and which is spoken *about*. Agamben disagrees. The thing itself is not what is presupposed in language; instead, it is the very sayability of language: "The thing itself is not a thing; it is the very sayability, the very openness at issue in language, which, in language, we always presuppose and forget, perhaps because it is at bottom its own oblivion and abandonment."[29]

The problem then is how is it possible "to speak without pre-supposing, without hypothesizing and subjectifying that about which one speaks?" In other words, how can we say the thing itself? Agamben gives his answer in the "The Idea of Language," an essay that begins with a consideration of the meaning of revelation. For Agamben, the thing itself is revealed not through linguistic propositions, but instead through the revelation of a truth "that cannot be expressed in the form of linguistic propositions about a being (even about a supreme being), but is, instead, a truth that concerns language itself, the very fact that language (and therefore knowledge exists). The meaning of revelation is that humans can reveal beings through language but cannot reveal language itself. In other words: humans see the world through language but do not see language."[30] Revealed is the unveiling itself, the very fact of that there is openness to a world and to knowledge: "The proper sense of revelation is therefore that all human speech and knowledge has at its root and foundation an openness that infinitely transcends it. But at the same time, this openness concerns only language itself, its possibility and its existence."[31]

Certainly, contemporary philosophy is acutely aware of the limits of language. Agamben's critique of hermeneutics and of deconstruction however is that both reach this limit and leave in place an unsayable foundation. Language is experienced as a *negative* arche, something that cannot be gotten at or made intelligible. Critically referring to Derrida's position in *Speech and Phenomena*, for whom, "there is no voice for language—the voice is always already tied up with the signifier/signified," Agamben asks whether the recognition of limit of language exhausts philosophy's task. Is it enough to recognize that "all comprehension is grounded in the incomprehensible?"[32] Is this the last word on the subject? Agamben says, "No." The limit of language marks both incomprehension and intelligibility. The Copernican Revolution that marks contemporary thought is to find ourselves alone and abandoned with our words. For the first time, language itself is revealed as the thing itself and "the essential matter of human beings."[33] The revelation of language, without presupposition, is the *arche anypothetus* that constitutes the authentic human community:

Agamben's analysis of language, and by extension, his analysis of right and law, allows him to argue the claim of human rights exists prior to their *declaration*. In other words, for Agamben, the coming community will not be declared on the basis of a presupposition or a representation:

> There can be no true human community on the basis of a presupposition—be it a nation, a language, or even the *a priori* of communication of which hermeneutics speaks. What unites human beings among themselves is not a nature, a voice, a common imprisonment in signifying language; it is the vision of language itself and, therefore, the experience of language's limits, its *end*. A true community can only be a community that is not presupposed.[34]

Agamben maintains that the arche of the coming community is the taking–place of language itself, without presupposition, without being tied to the signifying declarative and representative language of a people or a nation–state. The pure event of language precedes meaning (itself always significant and, thereby, representative), but it is not, therefore, senseless. In other words, the taking–place of language precedes the signifying space, and yet there is intelligibility.

The child Hurbenik who utters the word *mastiklo*, understood by no one in the camps, is the first citizen of the coming community. He reveals without being understood. "*Mastiklo*" is the pure event of language, without signification, but nevertheless, with intelligibility. Still further, *mastiklo* is "*no longer the experience of mere sound and *not yet* the experience of meaning.*"[35] The child Hurbenik and his word reveal the desubjectification in the event of language, a desubjectification that is intelligible without making sense: "No longer the experience of pure sound nor is it the experience of signification, but it is the experience of the voice, of the event of language."[36] The event of language is the *factum loguendi*, the appearance of language itself. Hurbenik is the barbarian, the inhuman, who has *echon* [language] without *logos*. Hurbenik is the first citizen of a coming community that is not founded on either the presupposition of a national language nor of any declaration of the identity of the people. Agamben argues that this community is one where all languages will return to the *argot*, the pure event or appearance of language itself.

Agamben links the appearance or taking–place of language to gesture. And, it is perhaps most of all in his analysis of gesture that we can begin to think the connection of the figure of the refugee or the Muselmann to the revelation of rights. Still further, by understanding gesture and its relation to language, we can begin the political task of returning appearance to itself, a return that will no longer permit separating bare life from a notion of right. Indeed, this age of bio-power in which appearance has been lost and where existence is reduced to bare life is for Agamben an age that has lost its gestures. An age which has lost its gesture is the age in which we all have become marionettes—no life seems attached to our limbs. Without gesture, life is bare life "ready for the massacre"—no strings attached.

In his essay on gesture, Agamben claims that "[g]esture is not absolutely a linguistic element but, rather, something closely tied to language. It is first of all a forceful presence in language itself, one that is older and more originary than conceptual expression . . . Linguistic gesture is the stratum of language that is not exhausted in communication and that captures language, so to speak . . . in its solitary moments."[37] With the discussion of gesture, Agamben returns again to the desubjectification at work in subjectivity. In gestures, there is the experience of the "I" as a kind of deformation of the inside with respect to all presentations of the "I." In other words, looking into the mirror and observing one's gestures, the "I" experiences a "disjunction between appearance and essence . . . the small sign of the corporeal points to the indescribable."[38] The indescribable is the zone between gesture and interiority. One's gestures mark the threshold between the inside and the outside. Gesture, he argues (citing Max Kommerell), "is not a nameable substance, but rather, a figure of annihilated human existence, its 'negative outline' and, at the same time, its self-transcendence not toward a beyond but in 'the intimacy of living here and now,' in a profane mystery whose sole object is existence itself."[39] This negative, unnameable outline of the "I" is what is most intimate about the "I," while at the same time it is most on view. The walk, the turn of a head, the movement of the hand is what is most singular, unique, and recognizable about the person. The "I" is never a *res* (thing), but a *res gesta* (thing done). And yet, gesture itself is speechless and there is no speech that can adequately describe it. Agamben argues that gesture is the "profane mystery whose sole object is existence itself."

Moreover, gesture subtends both *praxis* (practice, doing) and *poiesis* (making, creating). Here Agamben provides a supplement to Arendt's account of action. In gesture, nothing is being produced or acted upon; rather, gesture supports and subtends both spheres. Gesture is not *praxis* insofar as it is not an end without means. At the same time, it is not *poiesis* insofar as gesture is not a means that produces in view of an end. Instead, it is the domain of pure mediality that evades the means–ends relation altogether: *"The gesture is the exhibition of mediality; it is the process of making a means visible as such. It allows the emergence of the being-in-a-medium of human beings and thus it opens the ethical dimension for them."*[40] Opening the ethical dimension, "gesture . . . opens the sphere of that which is human."[41] Gesture is the opening of the space of the purely human itself. And, significantly, Agamben argues that gesture is the *linguistic* dimension of an "I," which subtends discourse. In other words, gesture is the medium of language, its taking–place. Hurbinek's stammer, the speechless shuffle of the Muselmann, and the bone–weary flight of the refugee are examples of the taking–place of language itself. Subtending discourse, gesture is the arche upon which the declaration constitutes itself. Still further, gesture brings right and law to the light of day and reveals that birth and right are already present prior to the signifying act that declares the "good people." The act of signification is subtended by a rightful gesture that gives birth to the law. Gesture breaks the link between nativity, citizenship, and the state of right. Subtending all performative acts, gesture exposes the birth of rightful appearance as such.

The face is for Agamben another word for gesture. Like gesture, the face is the domain of the taking–place of language. In fact, for Agamben, the face is exposed through its gestures. There is a face whenever something reaches the level of exposition, and this level, he argues, is the true location of the coming community: "The face is at once the irreparable being–exposed of humans and the very opening in which they hide and stay hidden. The face is the only location of community, the only possible city."[42] The face, he argues, is the "revelation of language."[43] Agamben's analysis of the face mirrors his analysis of language as *parole*. The face is the threshold of depropriation and de-identification; it is the zone of indistinction between the subject and desubjectification. The face is, therefore, another way to think the exposition of the "I" in its desubjectification; it marks the location of an "irreducible impropriety" that exposes the human being as such without essence, nature, or destiny. There is only exposure, only appearance. Thus, when Agamben argues that the task of politics today is "to return appearance itself to appearance, to cause appearance itself to appear," he is arguing that the task of politics today is to return gesture and the face to itself, to cause gesture and the face to appear. This occurs at the level of the taking–place of language. Language is the seizing of our own appearance, our exposition, our being–manifest. Language, he argues, is the "communicability of exposure."[44]

Contra Aristotle, Agamben argues that the space of the political is not the realm of *logos* with its violent division of the good from the evil, the just from the unjust, the beneficial from the useless. Instead, it is the realm of communicability, which is never about something, but rather is the exposure or the taking–place of a "commonality of singularities."[45] This taking place is the taking place of language in which the thing itself, appearing singularities as such, is revealed. The figure of rights is this exposed appearance who in its desubjectification stands at the threshold of the law. Prior to the declaration, the figure of rights is this exposure and communicability of right. Without *logos* or proper identity papers, nevertheless, the Muselmann, the refugee, and the child Hurbinek expose the rightful appearance [*expose de droit*] of the purely human as such. Agamben suggests that in the coming community, the rightful taking–place of the human as such will be the matter subtending the *praxis* of law and human rights, surrounding it like a halo.

Notes

1. Agamben, *Homo Sacer,* 135.
2. Agamben, *Means without Ends,* page 20.
3. *Ibid.,* 20.
4. Aristotle, *Politics,* 1253a10–15.
5. Zizek, *Violence,* 66.
6. Zizek, *Violence,* 67.
7. Agamben, *Remnants of Auschwitz,* 133.
8. *Ibid.,* 117.
9. Agamben, *Remnants of Auschwitz.*
10. *Ibid.,* 63.
11. *Ibid.,* 76.
12. *Ibid.,* 156.
13. *Ibid.,* 104.
14. *Ibid.*
15. *Ibid.,* 107.
16. *Ibid.,* 113.
17. *Ibid.,* 115.
18. *Ibid.*
19. *Ibid.,* 116.
20. *Ibid.,* 138.
21. *Ibid.,* 145.
22. *Ibid.,* 116–117.
23. *Ibid.,* 122.
24. *Ibid.,* 123.
25. *Ibid.,* 125.
26. Anthelme, *The Human Race,* 5.
27. *Ibid.,* 129.
28. Agamben, *Potentialities,* 33.
29. *Ibid.,* 35.
30. *Ibid.,* 40.
31. *Ibid.,* 41.
32. *Ibid.,* 45.
33. *Ibid.,* 47.
34. *Ibid.,* 47.
35. *Ibid.,* 42.
36. *Ibid.*
37. *Ibid.,* 77.
38. *Ibid.,* 79.
39. Giorgio Agamben, *Potentialities,* 84, citing Kommerell's "Poetry in Free Verse and the God of the Poets" in his 1933 study, *Jean Paul.*
40. Agamben, *Means without Ends,* 57.
41. *Ibid.,* 56.
42. *Ibid.*
43. *Ibid.,* 91.
44. *Ibid.,* 92.
45. *Ibid.,* 98.

PART III

DIAGNOSING POWER, NONVIOLENCE, AND DISCOURSE

CHAPTER 10

VIOLENCE AND NONVIOLENCE

James Dodd

Here let mee warr; in these armes let me ly;
Here let me parle, batter, bleede an dy.

John Donne, "14. Elegie: Loves Warre"

Introduction

What can nonviolence tell us about violence? Critics of nonviolence are often dismayed at what they perceive to be naïveté on the part of the proponents of nonviolence, as if the perspective of the latter betrayed an almost complete lack of comprehension about both the nature and necessity of violence. This often comes to the fore when the example at hand is one of being attacked, as Malcolm X famously argued—can one meaningfully defend oneself with non-violence, when faced with the violence of another? For such critics there is something patently ridiculous about the gesture of walking away from what is clearly a fundamental necessity of human experience; however distasteful we may find violence, these critics say, human beings are dangerous creatures, and it is only willful blindness that leads one to argue otherwise. Yet, though it may repel some critics, this same purported lack of understanding is perhaps what makes nonviolence so attractive to others—there is something liberating about the idea of a world in which people not only fail to resort to violence in order to resolve conflicts, but perhaps simply do not understand what violence is in the first place. Is not the almost universal recognition of the irrationality of violence one step in the direction of just such a world?

But what if this presumption of incomprehension or blindness was mistaken, irrespective of whether or not one might be moved to praise or to condemn it? What if this assessment overlooks the possibility that nonviolence, whether conceived as a practice or a theoretical construct, in fact expresses an important insight about the essence of violence?

We can, and perhaps also must, ask the question the other way around: what can violence tell us about nonviolence? We must ask this question, if not simply to affirm, but also in order to submit to a clarifying critique what is suggested by the surface semantics of the term of "nonviolence," namely that it simply represents the absence of violence. The operating premise below will be that this is misleading, that nonviolence is something positive on its own terms. Yet if nonviolence is not violence, then what is it? And can we really comprehend what it is, if we do not fully understand what it is not, what it is being defined *against*?

Proponents of nonviolence often overlook the necessity of a sustained analysis of the nature of violence in order to understand the intellectual cogency, if not the political value, of their arguments to reject violence.[1] To reject recourse to violence, to suspend its possibility both practically and symbolically, has proven to be a powerful form of struggle,[2] but just what the nature of nonviolence amounts to clearly requires a precise understanding of violence itself. Perhaps we cannot really understand why it is that nonviolence is effective until we understand the violence that it negates or supersedes; perhaps, in other words, it is the case that the dynamics of the one cannot be understood without reference to those of the other.

Taken together, these two ways to pose the question of the relation between violence and nonviolence might suggest a possible dialectical structure. If nonviolence is an overcoming of violence, then perhaps this overcoming takes the form of a response to a specific problem or contradiction posed by violence as a form of action. Violence would, thus, be necessary to understanding nonviolence, to the extent that the latter must be understood as a response to something that has been set into motion by violence, namely, that contradiction that points forward to the rational necessity of its own being overcome. Likewise, nonviolence would then tell us something about violence, to the extent that its dialectic would require that it must affirm something about violence, some truth that defines its innermost essence, in order precisely to secure its overcoming.

If we think of political life as revolving around the question of recognition, then we might have a readily available basic structure within which to articulate such a dialectic. Namely, if violence reflects the inherent possibility of any demand to be refused, then the problem of violence might be how this possibility of refusal could mean something more than the arbitrary, irrational suspension of the demand for recognition as such—how, in other words, could a subject refuse a specific demand, while at the same time affirming the recognition of the general right to make demands? Nonviolence might then appear to be a solution, in that it can be seen as affirming the possibility of negation without being committed to the unidimensional negation of the conditions for recognition as a whole. A nonviolent protest, for example, emphasizes the necessity of recognizing the opposition as a participant in political life, a potential partner even in an open dialogue, while at the same time refusing to recognize the legitimacy of its unchecked claims to power. In this way, Mohandas Gandhi could conceive of nonviolence as a means for struggle against British imperialism, thus as an attempt to coerce Britain's withdrawal, but also as an appeal to the conscience of the British people; or Martin Luther King Jr. could affirm, in his "Letter From a Birmingham Jail," the foundational legitimacy of a legal system, the laws of which he endeavored to systematically break. Thus, in nonviolence, struggle seems to adopt the lucidity of recognition, suspending violence while at the same time raising it to a new form of legitimate coercion.

Matters are, however, not so simple. I will argue in this paper that the relation between violence and nonviolence is far more complex, and above all ambiguous, at least on a conceptual level, than might at first appear to be the case. This complexity will have to do with the ways in which both violence and nonviolence stand in tension with our attempts to fix them exclusively in terms of their *instrumentality*. That is, the relation between violence and nonviolence, I hope to show, becomes more and more problematic when we realize that instrumentality does not necessarily constitute an adequate understanding of the nature of violence or, by extension, nonviolence.

This discussion falls into three parts. The first outlines an account of the limits of instrumental violence; the second applies the notion of instrumentality to the relation between violence and nonviolence; and the third revisits the double question—what can nonviolence can tell us about violence, and violence about nonviolence—in light of an alternative manner of conceiving violence in excess of its instrumentality.

Instrumental Violence

From the beginning it should be stressed that the instrumentality of violence is *obvious*, to the point that to suggest that violence is not instrumental would be absurd. The point here will not be to claim that violence is not instrumental, but rather instead to argue that this face of violence, expressed with all-too-familiar concepts, only offers us a limited and misleading articulation of its nature.

Violence is not only incidentally instrumental; it is a highly developed instrument with which human beings are remarkably adept, and in a variety of different spheres. Whole ranges of human practices employ techniques for the concentration, manipulation, distribution, and escalation of force, from warfare to sporting events to the construction of mile–long atom smashers. All of these techniques, whatever their sphere of operation, are double-sided; they embody an understanding of how things are put together (the physiology of the soldier or the boxer, the physical composition of matter at the subatomic level), along with ability to discern how to approach the *disruption* of these structures. Due to this double-sided character, the techniques of violence can be seen to be inherently opportunistic, following the patterns of how things physical or social are put together in order to discover their potential fragility or vulnerability to disruption.

Sometimes such discoveries are quite by accident. Take for example the introduction of the Minié musket ball in the nineteenth century. The Minié ball was a conical bullet that expanded upon firing, hugging the rifle bore as it traveled through the barrel of the musket. This allowed for a rifled musket that was both easy to load compared to its predecessors (which were plagued by the difficulty of ramming the ball down the rifled barrel) and far more accurate than smooth bore muskets. Rapidity of fire and accuracy was the intended goal of the design; what was unexpected was the devastating effect that the Minié ball had on the human body as it entered tissue at high rates of velocity: made of soft lead, the ball often shattered against bone, the resulting fragments creating complex soft–tissue wounds that were very difficult to treat with the medical technology available at the time.

Such accidents are significant. If it is the case that the human capacity for violence develops along the lines of the understanding of the order of things physical and human, that the more we know about ourselves, the more we know how to destroy ourselves, it is also the case that the more we destroy ourselves, the more we gain an intimate knowledge of the dimensions of our fragility. Damage, destruction, and trauma are not static phenomena; we do not reach the same results with more and more sophisticated instruments, but different, more varied results that we are, nevertheless, immediately capable of experiencing. Our sense for what can be destroyed, what damage can be inflicted, always keeps pace with these accidental discoveries, or the concrete experience of the consequences of the development of weapons technology. Human beings have never encountered a potential weapon they had no idea how to use, for there seems to be no pre-set limit on our sense for destruc-tion—or, in general, on our ability to perceive how things can come apart.

Still, it is important to emphasize that violence does not circumscribe an infinitely expanding horizon of destruction, one that outstrips the given world; our understanding of destruction ultimately cleaves close to our understanding of how given things work. Violence in this sense is not something independent of given forms, even if the disruption of order it makes manifest has the value of the exceptional; it is not some mythical force of dissolution and disruption that threatens from without, but is always partially inscribed in things—above all in things *made*. For the human artifice, to use Hannah Arendt's expression, is intrinsically fragile; what we have put together posits, in its status as the establishment of a concretely human environment, the very possibility of its being destroyed. As Sartre points out in *Being and Nothingness*, "the original aim and meaning of war are contained in the smallest building of man."[3] Everything made by human beings—our cities, our artifacts, but also our alli-ances, our fictions, in short, our *worlds*—bears within itself the possibility of annihilation. The instrumentalization of violence thus follows the same consti-tutive patterns as does building; it draws on, inhabits, and reveals the same plasticity of things poignantly expressed by human making.

Reflecting on this close proximity of instrumental violence with the techni-cal comprehension of the world of *homo faber* allows us to better understand what we mean by *destruction*. To destroy something is not simply to rearrange its material components, though such a rearrangement is certainly entailed. A Minié ball crashing into the thigh of a soldier during the battle of Gettysburg is, of course, on one level the simple displacement of soft tissue and bone: fragments of bone are shifted from one place to another, reorganizing the arrangement of soft tissue in the thigh. That this displacement has the meaning of destruction has its origin in a specifically human awareness of the signifi-cance of the difference between the world in which the soldier is not wounded and the one in which he is; the "useless limb" as a structure of signification is founded on, but not reduced to, the rearrangement of matter. For in fact, the act, the violence, aims at this destruction, as a founded objectivity, and not on the simple reorganization of flesh and bone in the path of a Minié ball.

What are we aware of, when we are aware of this "object" called destruction; or what do we aim at, when we aim to wound? Both this awareness and this aim are on one level practical, and are articulated by an instrumental perspective. Thus, the tactical significance of the wound is expressed theoretically by the concept of a *casualty*, that is, the difference in meaning between a soldier who is able to act on the field effectively and one who is not. From a military perspective, "casualty" essentially means no longer operative, no longer a factor that needs to be calculated when taking stock of the force capabilities of the enemy, where the status of non-operative has been secured by violence. The captain leads the assault not simply to do damage, but to inflict casualties, that is, to render inoperative elements of the opposing force; the movement of the battle is grasped in terms of a practical landscape conceived in light of those exigencies defined in part by casualties inflicted, along with force concentrations, terrain impediments for movement, and so on.

This is in a sense both more and less than a full concept of destruction. It is more, in that the concept of casualty fits the factor of the wounded soldier into a more general description of the unfolding of a combat situation—storming the hill at Gettysburg, the soldier falls, the chances of the operation his unit has been charged with, thus, diminishing accordingly. But it is also less, in that it leaves unspoken the equally significant awareness of what we could call the existential dimension of destruction, and with that a more nuanced sense for what is at stake in violence—the wounding of a soldier, the shattering of bone and the collapse of his chances, illuminate for us a wider landscape of disrupted relations than what can be directly calculated in the tactical analysis of the battle.

Let us look closer at what this might mean. The point is not to emphasize that the significance of the wound is more profound than what is relevant from a military perspective, though that is also certainly the case. The thigh belongs to a man, the man to a life, the life to a world—family, community, and with that the promise of a future. Rather, there is more at stake in understanding the nature of the event of the battle itself. The idea is that we are aware of how violence can destabilize and throw into question a deeper order of events than what is evident in the tactical profile of a combat engagement or other physical conflict of whatever scale (say a boxing match). It does this because we have a sense for how violence can lend a fluidity to events by way of the affirmation of the possibility of rendering apparently inessential what would otherwise have a claim permanence. Violence is, thus, not simply limited to the quantity of disruptions of order, founded on easily identifiable physical patterns (the flesh wound on the battlefield or the knockout blow of the boxing match), but includes a fundamental qualitative dimension that modifies the operative sense of the relative permanence of things that defines the norm. Thus, violence is not only a destruction that must be given meaning from within the horizon of the world; it itself poses as a transformation of the manner in which events unfold as world. Again, violence is opportunistic, seizing upon the contingent in order to suspend the normal in favor of the exception, lending to the real a fluidity that seems to belie all the claims that process and pattern make on action. All of the concepts of tactic and strategy we have been alluding to are fundamentally limited as conceptions of this fluidity, which is just an intensified expression of the fundamental contingency to which any action is necessarily exposed—or better, the expression of the *risks* entailed by the contingent.

To be sure, the consequences of any action are never fully present to us, or ever adequately specified in advance; whenever we act, we always take aim at a future that is in fundamental respects opaque. This is even more the case in violence, and in a unique manner. It is more the case, in that violence effectively seeks to employ as a *means* the very obscurity of the contingent, and the future to which it relates: when the soldier opens fire on the enemy, he is part of a gamble that seeks to posit a future in which the other is absent, thus rendered effectively inessential in the moment. Likewise, when in a burst of passion I strike out at an interlocutor who is besting me in argument, I take part in a gamble for a future in which the conclusion that now seems inevitable does not, in fact, arrive—as if I could distort the world just enough to arrive at a result contrary to the one that would otherwise have a claim on my future. In both cases of violence, the only thing *actual*, the only thing *certain*, is that the normal connection between the present and the future has been suspended— not severed—in accordance with the logic of a violence that affirms only the uncertainty of the ultimate consequences of treating the exigencies of the given as inessential.

We might call this fluidity an expression of the *existential* dimension of vio- lence; but this is only in order to express the specific manner in which we inhabit a situation in which we have embraced violence. In other words, the sense in which we inhabit the horizon of the world through its virtual suspen- sion as an embrace of the contingent, as the basic truth that we need not accept anything as permanent, or given, that we may measure our path to the future through a distortion of the present.

If any full account of the nature of violence must take this fluidity of events through distortion as basic, then here we can begin to see the limit to a purely instrumental conception of violence. The concept of violence as a pure instru- ment constrains our intuition of the full scope of the implications of this affir- mation of the inessentiality of the normal, of the given, for it recognizes only obstacles (to an end) and procedures for their removal. *If* the enemy unit guarding the bridge is an obstacle, then *this* is the procedure for its removal: a series of actions that assumes a definite tactical morphology, as if we were simply conforming to a pattern already inscribed in things. And, to be sure, in some sense we are; but, nevertheless, the implied organization and structured action is shadowed by an equally significant risk, even necessity, of a *decompo- sition* that necessarily exerts a constant pressure on the shape of the unfolding action. For violence always unfolds by suppressing the sources of form, of organization and structure; its very employment takes aim at the weaknesses and vulnerabilities implied in a set of given conditions in order to attempt to impose a particular pattern on the future through the distortion of a present that excludes it. But the pattern is achieved only in that uncertain return from the state of exception imposed by violence; there is no guarantee or even promise as to how the order of things will reconstitute itself once we have entered into the state of violence.

The violent removal of protestors by the police may be an ordered affair, organized in accordance with the methodical application of pressure by making the costs of disobedience higher and higher as the action unfolds, but it is ultimately a gamble that the introduction of the disorder and decomposition inaugurated by violence itself will not undermine the coherence of the action. Violence in a basic sense is always a gamble of suspension, and there is no guarantee that the instigators will ultimately be in a beneficial position when the world recovers from its being torn asunder. This is why discipline is so important, since it insulates the police, or the army unit taking the bridge, from the forces of dissolution and distortion introduced by the violence they are employing; discipline extends the pretense of comprehensibility in a situation that is always on the verge of becoming incomprehensible. Discipline is, thus, not the mere consistency of application, but itself a kind of refusal, an insistence on being an insuperable obstacle to the negation of violence—even the violence that one is oneself exercising.

A perhaps surprising confirmation of this suspicion that the instrumental concept of violence is inherently incomplete can be found in the work of Carl von Clausewitz.[4] To be sure, for Clausewitz, war is explicitly understood to be an instrument; more, it is precisely the instrumentalization of violence that Clausewitz posits in his abstract definition of war. Thus, one might conclude that with Clausewitz we have a classic example of an instrumental conception of violence. Nevertheless, the whole point behind identifying war as an instrument of policy (*Politik*) in *On War*, is the recognition that the systematization of the techniques of mass violence—the tactics of the commander and the strategy of the general—represent an all too limited grasp of the full phenomenon of war as an existential event: the practice of war, in other words, cannot be reduced to a military science, or the explicit elaboration of the machinations of strategy, *à la* Antoine-Henri Jomini. Instead, Clausewitz argues that the conduct of any war requires the development of a complex political perspective on the unfolding of the situation at any given stage of operations in order to form appropriate judgments about what has and has not been achieved, and what aims have or have not become more or less feasible. War, as Clausewitz puts it, has its own grammar, elaborated in the tactical language of maneuver, defense, and attack; but it lacks its own logic, its own articulation of its full relation to purpose and end.[5] This is not limited, I would argue, to the mere positing of the goal of the war, or to developing convincing propaganda regarding the purpose or end the nation is "fighting for," but involves the ability of a political sovereign to move the situation effectively from a state of peace to a state of war and back again. One could argue that, for Clausewitz, it is the ability *to shape the peace* through the introduction of war and its suspension that is the ultimate test of sovereign power.

Clausewitz's perspective is instructive on a number of levels. For one, it points to the profound superficiality (but not simplicity) of instrumentalized violence, and the inevitable abstractness of any exclusive focus on such violence as a theoretical object. Yet, such a focus is perfectly rational, and clearly successful—to such an extent that it lends credibility to the argument that violence, to the extent to which we engage the topic within a theory of action, is "merely" instrumental. Again one should remember that it is obvious that violence is instrumental, whether as embodied in the weapons brandished by those who threaten its use, as Arendt expresses it in *On Violence*, or in the game-like strategy of the application of mass violence at the "decisive moment," as Jomini famously argues in *Traité*.[6] Once bound within the horizon of this rational superficiality, the question turns on understanding the limits of what one can achieve with such an instrument. Clausewitz is interesting as a military theorist because he recognizes that the horizon of war transcends the technical deployment of the instruments of violence, and with that resists being reduced to a system of warfare—one might say that the point is that war transcends warfare, thus pressing upon us the necessity to make decisions that the techniques of the strategist will always fall short in addressing. I would suggest that Clausewitz's insight is in fact about the essence of violence, namely that the existential phenomenon of violence transcends the limits of what is brought into view through its own instrumentalization. Violence, in other words, transcends its own inherent superficiality.

We can formulate the point more formally, in order to allow us to approach the question of nonviolence in the next section more systematically. Any instrument embodies an understanding of the potential for manipulating a given environment towards the realization of a certain set of definite possibilities. The structure, shape, and materiality of a chisel supports the articulation of how the stone both yields and gives way to the rigidity of metal backed by force, revealing the potential for shaping form; the printed word pre-articulates how the permanence of matter allows for the realization of an endurance of expression beyond the inherently temporary reality of verbal speech. As such, any instrument presupposes the conformity to laws, to those claims natural or human to put limits on the possible; all paths of manipulation are kept within defined boundaries of what is allowed. Nature only allows so much, and stands in the way of the rest; likewise, humans exist in confines mapped out by the intentions that constitute a world of interweaving projects of existence.

Violence institutes, unlike other instruments, at a *refusal* of such conformity; it is the refusal of the right of anything to stand in the way, to exercise the right of blocking the realization of a possibility; and it relates to what stands in the way not in the mode of a conformity to the given, but as a negation of the given. Thus, in a basic sense, violence is inherently *non-instrumental*, if we accept this element of conformity as basic to the being of instruments: it does not follow a course of manipulation circumscribed by a world, but suspends the very claim of the world, in the form of the given projects of others, to fix in advance the course of manipulation. A given complex of possibilities is suspended in violence, in the forcing of the realization of an end against a given predelineation of what is possible and not possible.

This possibility of refusal, of the denial of all process that would lead to a given result in favor of the brute insistence on the immediate result as such in the face of what does not allow, is what is "instrumentalized" in violence. But that means that a certain radical non-instrumentality is folded back, as it were, into an otherwise coherent instrumental complex in order to aim at a definite end—but now not through a process, but through *compulsion*. Yet, it is the compulsion of a distortion, not of law. Thus, when I suggested above that the instrumental conception of violence is limited, what I want to say is that this folding of a refusal of process back into instrumentality is not seamless, that violence retains its anti-instrumental character even in its very employment as a means. Violence is in this sense fundamentally *unstable*; its employment risks not only failure (this is true of any action or activity that aims at a goal), but also the *confusion* that results from this inherently distortive or decomposed attitude with respect to exigencies constitutive given world. Violence is never in a stable relationship with the ends towards which it is aimed as a means; thus, the question of nonviolence, one could say, will turn on how nonviolence relates to this inherent instability of violence.

Nonviolence

We should not lose sight of the fact that nonviolence is interesting as a category of action only if we conceive of it as an instrument of compulsion and force, thus as something that operates in essential ways within the orbit of violence. If all that is meant by "nonviolence" is the use of the arts of persuasion, or of symbolic protest, or of expressions of moral indignation to try to convince political opponents to change their behavior, then the entire phenomenon is *de facto* diluted, to the point that it hardly stands out as a distinctive factor within political and social life. This is not to say that persuasion, symbolism, and moral conscience are unimportant, which would be absurd; it is only that to emphasize their "nonviolent" character would at worst be trivial, or at best merely designate some aspect or other that may make them more desirable than war, torture, terrorism, or other practices of violence.

So, for example, persuasion may be morally preferable relative to torture in that it refuses to accept the destruction of others as the price for influence; or perhaps it represents a more practical alternative, if what is at stake is not important enough to justify physical and psychological suffering. But this does not get to the heart of the matter, after all, as there is nothing in the nature of persuasion, symbolism, and moral conscience that *excludes* violence. Often, the threat of violence is necessary to persuade, as any student of international diplomacy would recognize; likewise the symbolism of an act of violence can be an important catalyst for action, as the Spartan resistance at Thermopylae proved to be for the Greek alliance against the Persian invasion in 480 BCE. Even moral conscience often finds its voice in the willingness to fight or die for a principle. Nonviolence is, thus, a real issue only if it is recognized as a distinctive means for struggle, one that involves the ability to pressure and to shock—in short, nonviolence is an issue when it proves itself to be a recognizable pattern in which a *force* meets an *opposition*. Perhaps we can take for granted what it means to oppose, but what kind of force does nonviolence bring to bear on a given situation or struggle?

One of the factors that make nonviolence so difficult to fix theoretically (or even practically, for that matter) is the fact that it is always shadowed by the potential for violence. To be sure, the very concept of nonviolence posits the principle that struggle does not require actual violence, but this does not and cannot exclude possible violence, if we are to evade the charge of willful naïveté alluded to above. Whenever protestors confront the police, whenever one group refuses to submit to the limits imposed by another, the potential for violence becomes not merely an abstract but a concrete possibility.

This is, in fact, the source of a good deal of the symbolic effectiveness and potency of nonviolent action, that palpable sense in which individuals and groups assume the risk of being exposed to potential violence. Gandhi used to emphasize that nonviolence is a matter, ultimately, of courage—not simply the courage to stand for something, but the courage to expose oneself, to be a target for the potential violence that comes with any struggle in which someone has something to lose. Courage is, of course, a classical martial virtue; if it is relevant at all to nonviolent action, it is only because the landscape in which this action unfolds is essentially determined by the presence of possible violence.

If we accept the shadow of possible violence as a basic premise, we might have the basis from which to begin to describe the kind of force that nonviolence brings to bear in a struggle. For nonviolence can be seen to be an explicit relation assumed with respect precisely to possible violence: that is, nonviolent action expresses the claim that those who struggle have rejected violence, that the struggle will expressly check its own possibilities for violence. On one level, this takes the form of a kind of commitment, not a strict determination; the discipline needed for effective nonviolent action involves, among other things, fortitude in one's commitment not to resort to violence. But this is not simply the question of a moral resoluteness. It can also be part of a complex set of tactics that embrace nonviolence but prepare for violence—so for example the African National Congress during the struggle against apartheid never agreed to disarm its military wing, even if at the same time it continued to affirm its commitment to nonviolence. This is far from hypocrisy, which one might conclude from a purely moral point of view; nonviolence here stands in a definite conditional relation to potential violence, which itself remains a factor in the form of a *threat*. There is no logical reason why nonviolence should not simultaneously husband the threat of violence, and, in fact, one might argue that this has always been the case historically. Nelson Mandela, and Gandhi, as well, benefited from the threat of violence embodied in the simple fact that they represented the overwhelming majority of people in South Africa and India, respectively; likewise, the constant reminders of the presence of black rage during the 1960s and 1970s, thanks to groups such as the Black Panthers, were as much a part of the civil rights movement in the United States as were the nonviolent politics of Martin Luther King Jr. Everyone had a stick in these fights. Thus, nonviolence is often an engagement with a field of possible violence, one that succeeds, in part, by managing the force that the threats of violence can have in a particular political situation, whether explicit preparations for violence are held in reserve or not.

There is another modality of force characteristic of nonviolence, however, this time involving not the potential violence of the nonviolent, but the potential for reactive violence on the part of the other side. This, too, is something that is explicitly in view in many nonviolent actions. For nonviolence often involves a call on the opposition to abandon or forgo violence as a means; more, nonviolent action often acts as a catalyst that brings to a head the decision whether or not to respond violently. This is a key source of pressure, and is of great significance for any sustained reflection on the tactical dimension of nonviolent action. A mass protest, for example, potentially forces a political regime and its authorities into a very specific situation: if it does not simply succumb to the demands of the protestors, then it either chooses to respond with violence, or it seeks to pursue its struggle with other political means at its disposal. In order to succeed, the protestors must do everything they can to make the use of violence as costly as possible to the regime—there have to be consequences, such as loss of standing in public opinion, degraded relations with allies, or a schism within its own ranks. But this is equally true of the option of *not* resorting to violence—this, too, must be as costly as possible, for example in terms of the perceived integrity of governmental authority, or again schism within the ranks due to dissatisfaction with a perceived failure to act. The failure to respond effectively is a potentially valuable source of pressure for the protestors; long scenes of protests in the street, for example, can add to the sense that the government is not in control of the situation.

Formally, the tactical reality of nonviolence is, in this respect at least, identical with basic tenets of military strategy: maneuver the enemy into a situation in which either engagement or retreat is as costly as possible, thereby inflicting the most damage possible, whatever the decision. And here we should not be misled by the impression that nonviolence does not seek to inflict harm, to the extent that it represents the rejection of taking up arms and using, at least directly, either the threat or the actuality of damaged bodies or property to pursue its goals. In the end, this is only true in a limited sense. Nonviolence does not seek to harm, but it does seek to overcome; it does not seek to destroy life, but it embraces its cause by risking life. It is, to this extent, potentially "dangerous," to echo Mark Kurlansky, though perhaps not the spirit of his words.[7] The aim of any struggle is to be able to hold out in a situation that is as dangerous to the other as it is to oneself; if the action does not aim at being hazardous to the opponent, to putting something at risk that the other has refused to expose to regular modification, it is not a struggle. Nonviolence as a pattern of struggle is coherent only if it proceeds with open eyes, so to speak; and this means that it must seek, above all, to make the use of violence as costly as possible, so if violence does occur, the action is not simply routed. Many of Gandhi and King's actions, in fact, resulted in violence, sometimes terrible, and their political success rested in part on their ability to make their opponents suffer politically—and morally—for their attempts to shift the situation in their favor through violence. And the tragic results of the 1989 pro-democracy movement in China, resulting in the massacre at Tiananmen Square and the virtual eradication of the reform movement, is an example of the failure to do the same.

To be sure, one should avoid the cynical conclusion that nonviolence is just the use of the potential violence of the opposition against itself, or that nonviolent action is simply an instrument used to provoke a violent response that can in turn be used for propaganda purposes. That would be far too simplistic, reducing nonviolence to the familiar strategy of attempting to gain moral advantage in a conflict in which one tends, as aggressor, to be at some disadvantage. Rome, for example, would often befriend a state that it knew was about to be attacked, in order to cloak its designs against the aggressor with its purported defense of the victim. The issue here is not simply a moral one, or even a tactical point. One should not overlook the significance, and complexity, of the relation to potential violence, which is operative, I would argue, not only in the absence of actual violence, but also in a deeper, more constitutive sense than the attempt to trap an opponent in the consequences of his or her own actions. Our awareness of how any nonviolent struggle can degenerate into violence lends the action a weight and a seriousness that has nothing to do with provocation. It is, instead, an awareness of the general morphology of the task of suspending one state of things, of the world, in favor of shaping another—and the fundamental limits of what one can expect in our ability to navigate from the coast of one to that of the other without suffering complete collapse and disaster, however just the cause or likely the outcome.

Gandhi used to argue that "nonviolence" should be understood not simply in terms of not doing harm, as suggested by the word *ahisma*, but as a force, specifically a force for truth—and in this vein he suggested adopting the word *satyagraha*, "truth force."[8] This is often interpreted as a plea for a more active conception of nonviolence, in order to distinguish it from the passivity of an inactive pacifism, and, in fact, Gandhi seems to have understood it as a way of emphasizing the activist political nature of his movement. But the term has deeper resonance, I would argue; for it points not only to the task of exposing the lies and untruths of one's opponent, but the deeper sense that the field of action is itself a distorted reality—"truth" is a *force*, precisely to the extent that it can prove to be a factor of change in a world that is already shaped by our awareness of the possibility of embracing violence as a means. But, as Gandhi emphasized again and again, truth is only such a force once it is coupled with both courage and a capacity for *boundless suffering.*

However, if this understanding of the distorted character of our world and the role of violence as both origin and response is basic to nonviolence, then a certain ambiguity regarding the relation between violence and nonviolence seems to make itself felt, and in two respects. The first is the fact that violence shadows nonviolence, and in an important sense belies the very refusal of violence that lies at the heart of nonviolence, or at least complicates the finality of the commitment to nonviolence. The very decision to struggle, to stand against the exigencies of sharing political and social space with another, pulls our actions into the orbit of the realities of a world that requires that we reckon with the potential for violence.

But there is second source of ambiguity, as well. For nonviolent struggle is not simply the refusal of violence, but itself a complex instrumentalization of this refusal. We know what is at stake in violence, what is put at risk; we also know the potentialities for risking and putting at stake in nonviolence as a modality of exposure that, like violence, also folds back into the world of action in a distinctive manner. One could argue that nonviolence effectively folds back into an instrumental complex not the refusal of order and process, but the refusal of *that refusal that violence is,* which has on its part been made something concrete and established, a peculiar dimension of the world that stands in tension and conflict with the patterns of action and meaning that constitute its order. Nonviolence, one could say, thus directly confronts the distortions of violence, but in their having been normalized as a part of the order of things—that disorder within order that is a constant source of trans-formation and destruction.

From this perspective, it is perhaps not surprising that nonviolence received a powerful articulation and renewed energy in a century characterized by a radicalization of the scope and practices of violence. In a world that seemed addicted to violence, nonviolence seemed to represent a remarkable rupture with the global mobilizations of mass violence that had become the norm. One need only juxtapose the image of Russian troops storming a shattered Berlin at the close of the Second World War with that of the masses of demonstrators in 1989 demanding the dismantling of the Berlin Wall to believe that a turning point had been reached—each action hammered home a new political reality, changing the landscape of Europe against opposing bodies of interest, but the means utilized could not have appeared more different. Yet, despite these appearances, the fall of Berlin and the fall of the Wall share a common horizon, one that ultimately ties them together, despite all differences; for they both draw their potential from the same ontological fragility, the same potential for anything human to be brought to a state in which its continued existence is threatened, and from that threat to project another future.

Instrumentalized violence, as argued above, is intrinsically unstable, since it seeks to shape the movement towards the future through a radical distortion of the present. It represents an instrument that bears within itself a moment of the refusal of all instrumentality, all process of conformity to a pattern of given exigencies, folded back into the pursuit of an end that must nevertheless ultimately conform to unfolding reality. Violence is an effective instrument only if we understand how to pick up the pieces, so to speak. This, in part, means that the success of instrumentalized violence relies on a discipline that insulates the action from the potential dissolution of the sense of what one is attempting to achieve, or the consequences of the radical contingency introduced into the situation through the distortive negations of violence.

Is there a similar instability at the heart of nonviolence? It seems that this must be the case. Nonviolence, like violence, seeks to expose the fragility of an order in order to disrupt it; it seeks to overcome an obstacle by organizing the collapse of its resistance, from out of an outright refusal to conform to demands embodied in the given reality of that obstacle. Likewise, its success is dependent upon a similar combination of tactical intelligence and discipline. But, if that is true, then what is ultimately the difference between violence and nonviolence? If they seem to share so much, what keeps them distinct?

The Problem of Constitutive Violence

This question—what separates violence and nonviolence—is in all probability incorrectly posed, precisely on the grounds of what holds them within a fundamental, essential bond. Nonviolence is best defined as a refusal of violence; not its elimination, or an attempt to ignore the role of violence in human affairs, but a refusal to realize a possibility that is nevertheless a constitutive element of a concrete complex of potentialities that are inaugurated by any struggle. Nonviolence, thus, situates one's agency within the landscape of action in a very definite manner; it is, we can confirm, a definite *position*. But it is also more than this, since nonviolence is not simply the refusal of violence, but as a struggle it also exercises a refusal on a different register—namely, it takes the form of a refusal of a claim embodied in another's project, and the conditionality that project provides to the shape of the world. As struggle *against*, it is the refusal to allow something to stand, to continue to define the possible courses of behavior within the human fabric of relations. This refusal, like violence, takes the form of affirming the *inessentiality* of something, or its nothingness, in the form of illuminating its fragility and pursuing the orchestration of its collapse. Nonviolence refuses violence, but it is still grounded in an attitude that refuses to conform to a given claim, instead positing, in the modality of a distortion, the claim as a mute obstacle to be forced aside or *destroyed*. Nonviolence is not an *argument* against something, it is a *strike*, a blow that posits the opposition as a mute mass to be negated.

Thus, we can return to the questions that opened this discussion above: what does nonviolence reveal to us about violence, and vice versa? Nonviolence shows us that the possibilities of disrupting, checking, eliminating, and exposing being as susceptible to purely negating force are not limited to the possibilities we recognize as belonging to violence. More, it suggests that much of what we have come to understand about the fragility of things through our experience of violence, and which we conceive under the headings of conflict, struggle, force, and so on, are not limited to phenomena of explicit violence, but embrace a much wider range of examples. This is not just a matter of the aptness of metaphor, so for example the attractiveness of such phrases as the "war against poverty," as somehow evocative of the resoluteness we would otherwise only expect from warriors. For nonviolence is not simply evocative of metaphorical comparisons between certain general classes of actions, but is an explicit mode of *fighting*.

On one level, the recognition that the meaning of struggle is not limited to violence is not a particularly new idea; it has been recognized since antiquity, for example, that the martial virtue of courage expresses a moral disposition that is not limited to the explicit pursuit of warfare, even if it is not fully comprehensible outside of it. The fighting spirit that seeks to compel instead of to persuade, the courage to stand one's ground in the face of the threat of adversity, both assume distinctive forms outside of the horizon of violence; likewise the fortitude of conviction, and the mobilization of one's physical and spiritual resources to live a life in truth, have resonance far beyond the experience of the warrior, as is poignantly, if not always clearly, expressed by the Islamic concept of *jihad*.[9] This seems to suggest that, if our motivation to employ violence is to eliminate a threat, to struggle against an adversary, or to impose our will on the unwilling, then in an important sense when we adopt nonviolence *we lose nothing*—all the potential for compulsion, escalation, destruction, even risk of life and danger are still very much in play. Nonviolence reveals to us that the apparent claims to necessity embodied in the culture of violence—at least, claims to the necessity for a *serious life*—are limited, perhaps even ultimately illegitimate. Serious people "parle, batter, bleede and dy" nonviolently, even with love.

Yet, at the same time, we must also say that violence illuminates something essential about nonviolence, to the extent to which violence always remains an *issue* for nonviolence. This point, however, is more complicated, and obscured by our tendency to cast the issue in exclusively instrumental terms. Violence is not an issue for nonviolence in the limited form of an available if unused set of instruments for achieving a particular end; that would be more of a question of being an option than an issue. Instead violence, one could say, has in the end a fundamental claim on the *meaning* of nonviolence, both in terms of understanding what nonviolence is and is not.

This manner in which violence remains an issue for nonviolence is visible only if we bracket a purely instrumental conception of violence in favor of a broader sense of violence as something that is constitutive of its own sense or meaning. We are now perhaps in a better position to suggest what this could mean. As argued above, part of the difficulty of developing a concise conception of nonviolence is the fact that any nonviolent action is always shadowed by the potential for violence. What is the significance of this? The shadow of violence is not simply a factor that circumscribes the possibilities of a given course of action (for example, when one considers the alternatives open to the opposition at any given time in response to nonviolent action or struggle). Rather, the political calculation of nonviolence draws on our awareness of the fact that the world has already been shaped by violence, that both the nonviolent action and the potential violent response are significant precisely in this *given horizon* of violence.

I would suggest that the full significance of nonviolence, and with that of any given act of violence as such, can be grasped only if we adopt this broader perspective of a reflection on the legacies of violence, or on what Sartre would describe as the practico–inert reality of past violence as constitutive of the very fabric of the world. In fact, one could argue that it is the necessity to come to terms with this legacy that ultimately lies behind the distinctive moral posture of nonviolence, precisely as a departure from our addiction to violence as a means to achieve our ends; but it is also more than that. Nonviolence, as we have suggested above, follows those same furrows of potential dissolution already traced by violence; it seeks to capitalize on the same fragilities, the same weaknesses of the human condition—in short, nonviolence draws its sense from the fundamental reality of a world shaped by struggle, and more: the promise of struggle as the potential to shape a world through its dissolution in force.

Thus, in conclusion, we could perhaps argue that nonviolence is dependent on something that we have scarcely begun to understand about violence, at least theoretically; namely, a *constitutive dimension* of violence that is quickly obscured if we conceive of violence in purely instrumental terms. We all too often fall into the vagaries of opposing the cold instrumentality of violence with the humane morality of nonviolence, and fail to recognize their common root. Yet at the same time, the attempt to understand this dependency pushes us farther afield than the theme of violence alone—for the real foundation of the entire discussion, which has made itself felt time and again in our discussion above, has to do with the more complicated theme of the *world*. Or better: the question of what it means to change the world, or what it is about the human world that opens this possibility, and why refusal, struggle, and protest not only resonate with us so deeply, but seem to reveal how it is that our freedom has within it the potential for a new future. This, in the end, is why violence and its other represent a critical *philosophical* problem.

Notes

1. This is, of course, generalizing; the proponents of nonviolence are varied and numerous. For a sample of the available literature, see Ackerman and DuVall, *A Force More Powerful*; Hastings, *The Lessons of Nonviolence*; Hastings, *Theory and Practice in a World of Conflict*; and Sharp, *The Politics of Nonviolent Action*.

2. Especially in connection with democratization and social movements, as already argued by Clarence Case in 1923 (*Nonviolent Coercion*) and, of course, strikingly developed and embodied in Gandhi's nonviolent campaign against British rule in India. The theoretical development of the idea of nonviolent political action reaches its classical form in Sharp's 1973 *The Politics of Nonviolent Action*, and is still a vibrant and growing field of study today, so for example Schock's *Unarmed Insurrections*.

3. Sartre, *Being and Nothingness*, 40.

4. Clausewitz, *On War*.

5. *Ibid.*, 605–06.

6. Arendt, *On Violence*; Jomini, *Traité des grandes operations militaries*.

7. At least in part. Kurlansky blends in convincing way an appeal to nonviolence out of indignation at religious hypocrisy, such as one finds in Tolstoy, with an appreciation of the political potential for nonviolent action, embodied in the successes of Gandhi. See Kurlansky, *Nonviolence*.

8. See Gandhi, *Nonviolent Resistance (Satyagraha)*. Bharatan Kumarappa, ed.

9. For an interesting discussion of the concept of jihad relative to nonviolence, see Khan, *The True Jihad*.

Chapter 11

Lines of Fragility: A Foucaultian Critique of Violence

Johanna Oksala

We live in a world saturated with violence. Words such as "terror" and "terrorist" have become part of children's everyday vocabulary. Western democracies have recently allowed or actively participated in systematic torture, secret detention centers, and extraordinary rendition. Even without specifically focusing on the recent war on terror, we have already left behind a century in which, it is estimated, at least 100 million people died violently in world wars, the Holocaust, genocides, conflicts, and insurrections.[1] As Hannah Arendt[2] noted in the opening page of her now classic pamphlet *On Violence*, the twentieth century had become a century of wars and revolutions, hence a century of violence as their common denominator.

While the shear magnitude of these events alone forces us to acknowledge that the question of violence must be essential for understanding and diagnosing the present, the pervasiveness of violence should not be a reason for accepting political defeatism dressed as sober realism or as verbose analytics, however. Boldness in political thought should, rather, translate into radical attempts to imagine and bring about an alternative. Even if we did ultimately have to accept the permanent possibility of violence as something that is inherent in our bodily vulnerability, we are still left with the choice of working against its actuality. It is this choice that opens up the realm of the political: an enormous space for political imagination and action. We should accept violence as our predicament only to the extent that it commits us to the relentless exploration of this imaginative space, in philosophical thought and political action. A philosophical critique of violence is more imperative than ever.

A Foucaultian critique of violence must seem to many people like a totally deluded project. If it is tempting to think that any critique of violence is going to be naïve and hopeless, the attempt to undertake such a task with the help of Foucault's thought appears even more misguided. It seems that he simply does not offer us any grounds or tools for such a critique. If social critique consists not only of a diagnosis, but also of the articulation of its normative grounding, then this explicit grounding seems to be missing from Foucault's thought.[3] In terms of critically reflecting on violence, what seems to make matters worse is that he tends to equate violence with power and force instead of making clear distinctions between the notions. This means that if we accept his famous premise that power is everywhere—there are no pockets of society free from the effects of power—and then equate power with violence, we are left in a world completely pervaded by violence. It has therefore been suggested that Foucault's thought in fact marks the end of all critiques of violence.

I would agree that Foucault's thought does indeed mark the end of all those critiques of violence that are conducted within the humanist tradition of thought. The pacifist philosophies of such great twentieth-century figures as Martin Luther King Jr. or Mahatma Gandhi, for example, not only ground their hopes for a nonviolent world on the benevolence of a Higher Power, but they also appeal to the inherent goodness of human nature.[4] This same faith in the goodness of human nature also underlies some of the anarchist critiques of violence. The belief in the natural goodness of man is tied to the radical denial of state and government.[5] It is this optimism that Foucault clearly does not share.

I suggest that we inquire into the possibility of a Foucaultian, post–humanist critique of violence that suspends all assumptions concerning human nature—optimistic as well as pessimistic. One of Foucault's key methodological principles was to systematically question all anthropological universals:

> First (methodological choice) is a systematic scepticism with respect to all anthropological universals—which does not mean that they are rejected from the outset, only that nothing along those lines must be allowed if it is not rigorously indispensable. In the realm of our knowledge, everything presented to us as having universal validity, insofar as human nature or the categories that can be applied to the subject are concerned, has to be tested and analysed . . . The first methodological rule . . . is thus the following: to circumvent anthropological universals to the greatest extent possible, so as to interrogate them in their historical constitution.[6]

I suggest that we apply this principle to the issue of violence. We must question all views advocating that man is by nature evil or good, dangerous or violent: nothing along those lines must be allowed if it is not rigorously indispensable. Instead we must theorize political violence by analyzing the concrete, historical practices of violence and not assume any ahistorical foundation for it secured in human nature.

While such a critique would obviously still have to rely on the normative ideal of nonviolence, this ideal does not have to derive from religion nor from any natural order of things. Instead, it can be argued that it already forms part of the historically and politically constituted idea of a civil society—a political community devoid of violence. Richard Keane, for example, has argued that the striving for civil society as opposed to uncivil society—a type a social order torn apart by extreme forms of violence—has become encoded within our historical tradition to the extent that we mostly take it for granted.[7] Hence, I would argue that in the political debates revolving around questions of violence, what is contested is usually not the normative level of justification, but the analytic level of diagnosis: what counts as violence and whether or not it is unavoidable.

Against this background, I see two possible forms that a Foucaultian critique of violence could take. They should not be understood as two alternatives or options, but as two interrelated aspects of an analysis that radically historicizes political violence and analyses its specific forms and rationality.

First: The first could be characterized as ontological critique, although in Foucault's case, it must be understood as historical at the same time. The idea is simply that any critique of violence must presuppose that the form of violence in question is not necessary. In other words, for it to make robust sense and not only to be wishful thinking, it must establish as a preliminary move that political violence is ontologically contingent.

In making this ontological move, I suggest that Foucault can help us. The central aim of his thought, a philosophy understood as an ontology of the present, was exactly to question the ontological necessity of many of those phenomena that we take for granted. His genealogies aimed to critically question the ontological presuppositions upholding our practices, and one of his methodological principles was to suspend all ontologizing political claims by attempting to "historicize to the utmost."[8] A Foucaultian approach to violence would thus question the ontological necessity of it—for example all such views that violence is either an anthropological constant or an essential feature of human nature, human sociality, or the political. In his framework, violence cannot be thought in such terms, but must always be analyzed as contingent, historically specific, practices. And contingent practices can be criticized, and, moreover, changed. Foucault suggested that in thinking about power, one had to be a nominalist: "power is not an institution, and not a structure; neither is it a certain strength we are endowed with; it is the name we attribute to a complex strategical situation in a particular society."[9] I suggest that we should try to think of violence in similar terms, as historically constituted practices with context-dependent rationalities, ends and means. It is my contention that a consistently anti-essentialist approach to political thinking would mean understanding violence nominalistically, and not as a primordial, irreducible essence.

Second: A Foucaultian critique of violence does not restrict itself to specific practices of violence only for the purpose of denouncing them. Its task must, rather, be to uncover their implicit, or sometimes explicit, rationality. My claim is that Foucault's contribution is to show that there is no incompatibility between violence and rationality. He noted that while violence itself was no doubt horrible, what was, in fact, most dangerous about violence was its rationality.[10] His thought can, thus, alert us to analyze the dangers inherent in the historical triumph of rationality: violence in a modern civil society might have been eradicated from public sites and from open encounters between enemies only to reappear in the name of improvement in institutions of discipline, correction, and punishment.[11] We need to understand the specific ways in which modern governmental rationalities are interlinked with forms of political violence.

I will elaborate in more detail these two forms of a Foucaultian critique in the following two parts of this paper. I start by appropriating his lecture series *Society Must Be Defended*, delivered at Collège de France in 1976, for the question of the constancy of political violence. I demonstrate how these lectures challenge the ideas that political violence is a universal constant or an inevitable feature of the state of nature. Instead, Foucault radically historicizes political violence by connecting it with the historical events of war. The connections between physical violence and the political are understood as radically historical and contingent.

This initial move whereby political violence is rendered historical and contingent leads the way to the analysis of its rationality in the second section. It is my contention that exposing the rationality that produces and sustains various forms of political violence means being able to subject it to political debate. It also makes it possible to imagine concrete alternatives and to instigate change. While Foucault's thought effectively questions the acceptance of irreducible physical violence as an ontological constant, it attempts to analyze and expose its historically and empirically specific forms.

The Contingency of Political Violence

I argue that political violence should be understood in strictly historical terms—it refers to empirically specific and context-dependent practices aiming at intentional bodily harm. This approach provides a way of countering the arguments for the ineliminability of violence from the political which are based on excessively broad, ontological conceptions of it that are distinct from its conrete and physical meaning.

The permanence of political violence is often connected to the ineliminable violence of language. The hackneyed expression "violence of language" usually refers to the idea that language by necessity imposes a partial order: it simplifies experience by dividing it into manageable units through categories and common nouns, and artificially objectifies the referent by cutting it loose from its context. Several philosophers following Nietzsche, such as Heidegger, Foucault, and Derrida, have emphasised and explicated this fundamental violence of language. What remains less comprehensively theorised in many of the discussions on "the violence of language," however, is its relationship to physical violence.

While the ontological violence of language does, in significant ways, sustain, enable, and encourage physical violence, it is a serious mistake to conflate them: to unreflectively slide from the inevitability of violence understood as the violence of language—the way language always imposes a partial and contingent order—to ontological violence understood in a second and completely different sense as the fundamental hostility and aggression of human beings. It is my contention that such a slide characterizes many of the recent theoretical defenses of violence. Violence is understood to be ineliminable in the first sense, and this leads to its being treated as a fundamental constant in the second sense, too.

Slavoj Žižek, for example, discusses the violence of language in the sense delineated above in his recent book *Violence*.[12] He argues strongly against the idea that language is a medium of peaceful coexistence and insists that we should recognize that there is always "something violent in the very symbolization of a thing, which equals its mortification."[13] He concludes that we cannot, therefore, "wholly repudiate violence when struggle and aggression are part of life."[14] Chantal Mouffe makes a similar slide when she argues that violence is the inevitable precondition of any consensus. By refusing to recognize that violence is ineradicable, political theory has become incapable of grasping "the nature of the political in its dimension of hostility and antagonism."[15] While consensus is always a form of violence in the sense of being exclusive of some interpretations, the agonistic nature of the political does not imply the ineradicability of physical violence understood as the fundamental aggression of human beings. Sometimes, but not always, consensus is *also* the result of physical acts of violence: what are supposed to be free elections, for example, turn into a practice of organized violence and intimidation.

While the ontological violence of language and physical violence, thus, cannot be conflated, neither is there a necessary causal link between them. The linguistic stereotyping of Jews and blacks, for example, has undoubtedly justified and sustained anti-Semitic pogroms and lynching, but it does not, by necessity, cause them. While these historically specific practices of physical violence have, for the most part, fortunately disappeared, the offensive stereotyping has not. Conversely, no matter how sympathetically we name, describe, and characterize different groups of people, the ontological violence of language nevertheless remains. It is my contention that while the "violence of language" is precisely ontological and thereby a necessary and ineliminable feature of thought, physical violence is contingent, historically specific, and context-dependent.

This does not mean that ontology—understood as the historically changing framework of competing background beliefs about reality—is completely separate and free from physical violence. On the contrary, my aim in this section is to show the extent to which it is constituted by it. Following Foucault, I argue that we must historicize ontology too: ontology is the sedimentation of political practices—including horrendously violent practices, foremost among them war. The legacies of violence have sedimented into the structures and the meaning of our world. Reality as we know it reflects the outcome of past wars and is not an objective or politically neutral realm waiting to be truthfully described. My central claim is, however, that the investigation of the constitutive role of physical violence must be thoroughly historical and must not rely on any notion of originary violence as such.

Political theorists such as Hannah Arendt[16] have argued against the idea of constitutive violence by emphasizing the purely instrumental nature of violence: it can only be the means of politics and is devoid of any intrinsic meaning of its own. James Dodd[17] calls this "the stupidity of violence principle": in its barest form, it states that violence is and can only be a mere means. It remains trapped within the confines of a very narrow dimension of reality defined by the application of means. Violence as such is senseless; when taken for itself it is ultimately without direction. Dodd argues that such an understanding of violence is the counterpart and a rejection of another influential philosophical view on violence: violence as an originary source of meaning. In Carl Schmitt's thought, for example, pure violence must be understood as a radically constitutive event: existential violence defines a moment in which the political will of the nation as such comes into being.

My aim here is to argue that while violence is constitutive of meaning, its constitutive function must always be understood through concrete historical practices of violence, not in terms of pure or originary violence, as such. I turn to Foucault's lecture course *Society Must Be Defended* in my attempt to show how, alongside the political tradition that links the persistence and constancy of political violence to the primary state of war and the hostile and aggressive nature of man, runs another strand that also insists on a strong connection between politics and violence. This connection is historical rather than natural, and is crucially tied to the birth of the state.[18]

Foucault's lectures make an important contribution to this tradition of thought. They represent a major break with the Hobbesian legacy in political thought, while forming Foucault's most explicit engagement with the question of political violence. They expose the violent origins of states, which are covered over by theories of timeless war and legitimate contract. I argue that his engagement with Hobbes in these lectures has strong implications for the efforts to historicize political violence and to envisage agonistic conceptions of politics uncoupled from it. Foucault introduced his lecture course by noting that he would like to begin a series of investigations into whether war could provide a principle for the analysis of power relations. Rather than war being seen as a disruptive principle, he wants to treat it as a principle of intelligibility for understanding history, power, and society. He summed up his previous efforts to rethink power by noting that "until now, or for roughly the last five years, it has been disciplines," but for the next five years, it would be "war, struggle, the army."[19]

As we now know, this large-scale project never materialised.[20] It is my contention that while the war model was ultimately abandoned, what nevertheless remains significant in these lectures is that it was not abandoned in favor of an understanding of the political based on consensus or contract. In historicizing political violence and, thus, demonstrating its contingtency, Foucault is not thereby claiming that politics is a harmonious realm of rational consensus. The idea of power as the governing of conduct—a set of actions enacted upon actions—and the practice–based account of political rationality conveyed by the notion of governmentality and developed in the lecture series following *Society Must Be Defended* meant that political power was still understood as agonistic and strategic.[21] It is my contention that the agonism intrinsic to the political in his thought is derived not from the aggression and hostility of human nature, however, but from the inevitably exclusionary and power-laden nature of the constitution of reality. We live in an agonistic society because the social sphere is a hegemonic field of contestable interpretations and values, and not because it is irreducibly violent in the sense of being made up of violent individuals.

With the model of war, Foucault attempted to offer an alternative to what he called "the economic models of power": power should not be regarded as a right that can be possessed in the way that one possesses a commodity. It is not something that the individual can hold, and which he can surrender, either as a whole or in part so as to constitute a political sovereignty.[22] Rather than understanding political power in terms of contract, laws, and the establishment of sovereignty, we should understand it in terms of an unending and shifting struggle, a movement that makes some dominant over others. In the first lecture, he famously inverts Clausewitz's dictum that war is the continuation of politics by other means and chooses as his working hypothesis the claim that politics is the continuation of war.[23] He distinguishes this model from the juridical contract schema represented by Hobbes and his contractarian followers by claiming that the essential opposition is not between the legitimate and the illegitimate, but between struggle and submission[24].

This war is, thus, not the abstract Hobbesian war of every man against every man, but a concrete, historical struggle in which groups fight groups. Foucault argues that the tradition of Western political thought has been dominated by the contractarian discourse of political theory that has covered up the memory of real war that lay at the genesis of sovereignty. As he polemically formulates his aim, it is to show how the birth of states, their organization, and juridical structures are born and maintained in the blood and mud of battles.[25] Political violence is constitutive of reality in the concrete, historical, and political sense.

The task of unmasking the violent foundations of the state and the law attaches Foucault to a long lineage of thinkers, including such figures as Max Weber and Walter Benjamin. Similar to Benjamin in his famous essay *Critique of Violence*, Foucault attempts to reveal both the law-making as well as the law-preserving character of violence: the political order of the state, its laws and legal decrees are in their origin attended by violence and continue to be upheld by practices of violence.[26]

The way Foucault accomplishes this hackneyed task is strikingly original, however. His multilayered analysis moves through a complex and compressed set of historical material from sixteenth-century England to fascism. It is, thus, thoroughly historical, or to be more precise, genealogical. In these lectures he is not presenting an explicit philosophical theory of power, violence, or war, but a series of investigations into a historically specific discourse on power that emerged at the end of the sixteenth and the beginning of the seventeenth century in England and France. He names it the "historico–political discourse" and argues that although it took different forms, its central thesis always was that war, understood as concrete battle and organized violence, formed the ineradicable basis of all relations and institutions of state power. The historically specific facts of war found the order of the state and, thus, also the power relations as they function at present.

Foucault's lectures operate and attempt reversals on various levels. On the level of historiography, Foucault defends a practice of counter-history that is always perspectival, the discourse of a combat position rather than a supposedly neutral view from nowhere. He identifies the emergence of this historiographical counter-discourse and traces its developments in the truth games of historiography and its uses for political life. The new historical practice was characterized by the principle of heterogeneity: the history of some people was not the history of others. It revealed that history was in fact "a divisive light that illuminates one side of the social body but leaves the other side in shadows or casts it into the darkness."[27] He shows how historical knowledge has formed an important weapon in the political struggles since seventeenth century, how war is waged in history but also through history.

On a philosophical level, Foucault's historiographical arguments are supporting several theoretical insights. While the model of war clearly aims to unmask irreducible violence—violence that is foundational and indispensable for the functioning and existence of the state—it is important to note that this violence is not ontologized in Foucault's historico–political discourse. In challenging Hobbes's view, Foucault can be read to philosophically challenge the idea that violence is a universal constant, an inevitable feature of the state of nature. Instead, he moves the discourse on war and violence to a thoroughly historical level: the origin of states lies in a history of violence, and not in a natural state of war.

Foucault concedes that, at first glance, Hobbes appears to be the man who said that war is both the basis of power relations and the principle that explains them. Yet, more fundamentally, his thought in fact announced the beginning of a modern master discourse on law and sovereignty, which covered over the empirical realities of war and the violent facts of history. According to Foucault, the state of war that Hobbes propounded was not a direct confrontation of forces—marked by blood, battles, and corpses—but rather a certain state of representations that were played off against each other. The establishment of sovereignty was, ultimately, always the result of a contract, a calculation that made it possible to avoid war, and not of actual war.[28] Moving political violence to this ahistorical, representational realm strengthened the understanding of it as a foundational constant of politics, making it harder to criticize its historical and contingent forms and to attempt to eradicate them.

Foucault claims that Hobbes's theory was foremost an attempt to legitimize and defend the sovereignty of the state against the civil struggles that were tearing it apart in England at the time. By advocating a general and abstract discourse of contract and sovereignty, the historical fact that Hobbes was trying to cover over was the Norman Conquest. His discourse was directed against political historicism, its adversarial counter-discourse at the time, which could be heard in the discourse of the parliamentarians and in the more extreme positions of the Levellers and the Diggers. These groups contested the absolute power of the monarchy by evoking the historical knowledge of the Norman Conquest. They argued that the power of the monarchy was not the result of a legitimate contract, but an outcome of a violent conquest and, therefore, a state of non-right, where all laws and property relations were invalidated. It is in the analysis of this historical discourse on the juridical meaning of the Norman Conquest that Foucault recognizes the first implicit formulation of the war model as the analyzer of power.[29]

The Nietzschean formulation of power as a clash of forces in these lectures is also philosophically significant. The notion of force is, however, used in frustratingly elusive and even contradictory ways. Sometimes it is used as a noun: it is not an inert substance, but it is nevertheless something that can be used and possessed to empower. Henri de Boulainvilliers' counter-history (studying the historical and political development of the nation in order to undermine juridical power), for example, analyzed and interpreted the forces of the people and was also a force itself.[30] At times, Foucault restricts himself to the more relational formulation of "relations of force," but uses it in differing ways: sometimes it seems to be a synonym for "the play of power," sometimes power is "the play of relations of force."[31]

This means that the political ontology that Foucault lays out is not very clear, either. The political sphere is clearly understood as agonistic, it is an essentially open, even limitless field of shifting struggles or forces, but what exactly is the ontological status of these competing forces remains unclear. The substantive formulations suggest a vitalistic, Deleuzian ontology, while "relations of forces" echoes a Marxist conception in which politics is understood as a realm for the forces of history to play themselves out. The notion of force would, thus, seem to take Foucault back to advocating some form of essentialist political ontology, albeit a different one from the one he detects in Hobbes's thought—a position that I suggested his political historicism was intended to question.

We could also see the novelty of Foucault's notion of force as lying exactly in the fact that it accommodates the materiality of violent coercion, while not being reducible to it. He stated in his lectures that an army of the king could be a force, but so could the history of the people. With his notions of war and force, he could, thus, be read as breaking the ontological boundary between the discursive and the non-discursive: the hegemonic institution of meanings, identities, and systems of thought is intertwined with the violent inscription of bodies.[32] The political order is a crystallisation of power relations and an outcome of a concrete combat; objectivity is the result of a struggle between conflicting interpretations and is constituted through a silent "war," and importantly, the two are inseparable. As Beatrice Hanssen[33] formulates Foucault's aim, it was to show how the role of political power was perpetually to use a silent war to reinscribe the relationship of force established through concrete war in institutions, economic inequalities, and the identities of individuals. Politics sanctions and reproduces, through symbolic practices, the disequilibrium of forces manifested in war.

The model of war, as well as the notion of force, would, thus, articulate the intertwinement of the physical combat over life, with the interpretative combat over truth and objectivity. Our political history, as well as the present political order, reveals how the imposition of hegemonic meanings, identities and interpretations has been inseparable from physical violence—the historical facts of wars. Reality as we know it reflects the outcome of past wars and is not an objective or politically neutral realm waiting to be truthfully described.

I argue that Foucault must have come to see the dangers that the complete merging of these two meanings of force—physical and symbolic—would lead to, however, and he later abandoned the war model. If his intial question was: "To what extent can a relationship of domination boil down to or be reduced to the notion of a relationship of force,"[34] he later answered it unequivocally by denying that power could ever be completely reduced to force or violence.[35] The violent inscription of bodies fuses with the inscription of meanings in the functioning of modern political power, but these aspects cannot be completely superimposed without committing a fundamental ontological error.

Hence, my claim is that by putting forward the model of war as an analyzer of power relations Foucault was primarily arguing for an agonistic conception of the political and not advocating an ontology of violence. The agonism he argues for is not rooted in any kind of essentialist claims concerning violence. The fact that the social space is agonistic does not derive from a primal state of war or from the irreducible hostility of human beings. Rather, it derives from the ontological view that all political realities are contingent and contestable because they are constituted by historical practices incorporating power relations. The political space is understood as an unstable network of power relations which nevertheless constitutes such stable meanings and institutions as the "President of the United States" or the penal system. The existence of these political and institutional realities is, however, fragile in the sense that they are dependent on the continuous participation of people in the practices that alone can constitute them. The instability of the political realm is, thus, not due to a failure in the functioning of the political mechanisms or forms of knowledge. It is due to the nature of the political realm itself. While at times some practices and strategies prove to be victorious and, thus, reify momentarily into relatively stable structures, this incites counter struggles, ensuring that the power game moves on.

This agonistic political ontology of practices is also the reason why Foucault repeatedly refused to offer any overall political theory: resistances are formed of varying strategies in varying practices. They "cut societies on the diagonal" and aim at specific transformations.[36] While state power inevitably implicates us in violence by being both an individualizing and a totalizing form of power, Foucault does not envisage any radical overthrow of the state, no final or global liberation. Instead, the anarchistic struggles he promotes are specific, but immediate and transversal. They are struggles that primarily question the status of the individual by promoting new forms of subjectivity and by questioning the ways in which knowledge circulates and functions in its relations to power.[37]

This means that the resistance against violence can also only take the form of specific practices of nonviolence. It also means, importantly, that the significance of violence itself must be an object of struggle in our truth games—the historical and social practices productive of knowledge. This is the key idea of the second part of this essay. I argue that we cannot understand violence as purely instrumental and devoid of meaning, but as having a meaning and rationality that is always historically and culturally specific. It is precisely its meaning and rationality that is the crucial site for political contestation: we have to understand the specific and distinct rationality that practices of violence attain in different power networks in order to effectively criticize them.

The Rationality of Violence

Discussions on Foucault's view of violence often focus on his late essay "Subject and Power," an afterword to Hubert Dreyfus and Paul Rabinow's book *Michel Foucault: Beyond Structuralism and Hermeneutics* from 1982. In this essay, Foucault poses the same question as Arendt did in *On Violence*, namely whether violence is simply the ultimate form of power, "that which in the final analysis appears as its real nature when it is forced to throw aside its mask and to show itself as it really is."[38] He also follows Arendt in his negative reply and puts forward an oppositional view of the relationship between power and violence: they are opposites in the sense that where one rules absolutely, the other is absent. "Where the determining factors saturate the whole there is no relationship of power; slavery is not a power relationship when man is in chains."[39]

Foucault distinguishes power from violence by arguing that a power relationship is a mode of action that does not act directly and immediately on others, but rather it acts upon their actions: it is a set of actions upon other actions. This means, first, that the one over whom power is exercised is thoroughly recognized as a subject, as a person who acts. Second, he or she must be free, meaning here that when faced with a relationship of power, a whole field of possibilities—responses, reactions, results, and possible inventions—may open up and be realized. Violence, on the other hand, acts directly and immediately on the body. It is not an action upon an action of a subject, but an action upon a body or things.

This neat separation of power from violence no doubt restores the possibility of a critique of violence, as some of Foucault's commentators have aptly pointed out. Thomas Flynn,[40] for example, notes that for Foucault, all violence attaches to relations of power, but not all relations of power necessarily entail violence. It is rather the species of power that Foucault calls "domination" and which Flynn labels "negative" power, with which violence is necessarily associated.

In light of Foucault's earlier writings on power, the categorical distinction he makes between power and violence in this late text is in many ways perplexing, however. It seems as if there had been almost a complete reversal in his views. In his original and extensive work on modern forms of power such as disciplinary power, for example, Foucault seemed to have argued for exactly the opposite: any clear distinction between power and violence is untenable. He also used the model of war for analyzing the functioning of power relations, as shown in the first part of this essay, and argued for the superiority of this model in comparison to all contractual models of power.

Hanssen[41] interprets this shift by arguing that Foucault changed his mind. In the final stages of his scholarly development, he was willing to admit that his earlier model of power as struggle and war remained too elusive and that he gave up on it. Hanssen claims that under the mounting pressure from his friendly critics Dreyfus and Rabinow, demanding that he further explicate the category of power, Foucault turned squarely to the question as to how power was to be demarcated from violence, as, if, once and for all, he wanted to legislate the categorical difference between the two terms. The distinction expressed in this late essay thus represents his more mature and considered view on the topic.

It is my contention that while it is important to take seriously Foucault's late distinction between power and violence and its significance for critiques of violence, this is not the most original contribution that Foucault makes for critiques of violence. If Foucault's thinking on violence is reduced to a categorical distinction between consensual power and coercive violence, we lose sight of what is most original and important in it.[42] All definitions of violence, including the ones that Foucault himself provides, must be understood as political acts, and their extension and validity must be open to constant contestation. In my view, Foucault's most important legacy is not in providing us with a philosophically accurate distinction between power and violence, but rather in demonstrating how all definitions and social objectivities, including the meaning of violence, are constituted in power/knowledge networks, and are, therefore, matters of contestation and struggle.

In one of his final interviews conducted in January 1984, Foucault openly admitted that when he began to interest himself in the problem of power, he was not able to speak very clearly of it or to use the concepts needed, and that now he had a much clearer idea of it all. He then continues by distinguishing between three different levels in his analysis of power: (1) the strategic relationships between individuals, (2) states of domination, and (3) techniques of government. The strategic relationships refer to the ways that individuals try to determine the conduct of others, and domination refers to states where individuals are unable to overturn or alter these power relations. The third level, the analyses of governmental technologies, refers to comprehensive rationalities of power, such as bio-power. It is the analysis of this level that I claim is Foucault's most original contribution to the analysis of power. Indeed, he noted that this level of analysis was necessary because it was usually through the techniques of government that states of domination were established and maintained themselves.[43]

When we analyze power on the level of individual acts, it is possible to make fairly clear distinctions between acts of power and acts of violence. When we move to the third level and attempt to analyze the technologies of power, the distinction becomes more problematic, however. The practices and institutions of government, in the broad sense of the term, are always enabled, regulated, and justified by a specific form of reasoning or rationality that defines the ends and the appropriate means of achieving them. The analytics of power technologies concentrates not only on the actual mechanisms of power, but also on the rationality that is part of the practices of governing.[44]

If we, thus, think of power network as a practice or as a game, as Foucault has also suggested, then the analysis of the techniques of government would mean an analysis of both the implicit as well as the explicit rules to which this practice conforms.[45] On this level, it is difficult to start with a clear distinction between violence and power because the rules, to a large extent, determine what is understood as acts of power or as acts of violence in the specific game. Moreover, different rules or rationalities are compatible with different forms of violence.

Take the game of ice hockey, for example. To anyone not familiar with the rules and aims, it probably appears to be a succession of random acts of violence. It is only when one understands the rules and the aims that one is able to classify the actions of the individual players as either legitimate moves or punishable acts of violence. Similarly, we could take the example of domestic violence and argue that it is only in a certain cultural and historical context that it even exists. Forms of behavior that we now conceptualize as domestic violence have only very recently been understood as forms of violence at all.[46]

Jeff Hern,[47] for example, argues that in attempting to make sense of the connections between gender relations and violence it is important to consider the problem in a historical context. This applies in particular to understanding how men's violence against women has been accepted, condoned, normalized, and ignored by both individuals and institutions. It is only by considering the dismal historical context of men's violence to women that it becomes possible to understand the way in which men generally perceive and define violence in everyday contexts. As far as men who are violent to women are concerned, the construction of what is meant by violence is a major part of the problem. The naming and defining of violence is a social rather than a natural process, and attempts at all-inclusive definitions have to be treated with caution because they are located in gendered social processes. The process of contesting definitions of violence is, thus, an essential element of critiques and interventions related to it.[48]

Similarly, the recent critical analyses of terrorism have emphasized that various forms of violence are called "terror," not because there are valences of violence that can be distinguished from one another on objective grounds, but because the label functions as a way of characterizing violence waged by political entities deemed illegitimate by established states. Judith Butler,[49] for example, has argued, that to the extent that the Geneva Convention gives grounds for a distinction between legal and illegal combatants, it distinguishes between legitimate and illegitimate violence. The use of the term "terrorism" works to delegitimize certain forms of violence committed by non-state-centered political entities and, at the same time, sanctions a violent response by established states. In other words, terror does not describe a distinct type of violence, but a form of violence that is illegitimate. It is not a descriptive notion, but a prescriptive notion, the intelligibility of which depends on the normative claim that it makes. If violence is terrorism rather than political violence, this means that it is not only illegitimate but, more fundamentally, that it is unintelligible in the framework of accepted political rationality: it is conceived as an action with no rational political goal, an action that cannot be read politically.[50]

Hence, my claim is that, on the basis of Foucault's analytics of power, it is ultimately impossible to secure any categorical, context-free definition of violence. On the contrary, the implication is that we must be wary of all such definitions. We must be mindful of Nietszche's assertion that "only that which is without history can be defined."[51] Foucault's thought should be read as an attempt to uncover the underpinning rationality of specific practices of power and to study the extent to which this rationality implies and is compatible with specific forms of violence. To return to the example of domestic violence, on the basis of his thought, we could argue that what is most dangerous about gendered violence are those aspects of it that make it look like perfectly normal and rational behavior. Even though male domination and male violence against women should not be theoretically conflated, feminist analysis must study the extent to which rationalities upholding male domination and those supporting forms of male violence against women are interrelated, mutually supportive, or even identical. When a form of rationality according to which a husband's responsibility is to provide for but also to control his wife and children is coupled with the acceptance of physical force as a means of control, for example, the patterns of domestic violence are set. The rationalization of domestic violence is, thus, often not an attempt to legitimize violence as such, but is rather an attempt to legitimize men's hierarchical control of women.

The radicality of Foucault's method lies in showing how the meaning and the ontological order of things that we take for unquestioned reality is itself the outcome of a political struggle. His genealogies make visible the historical struggles over truth and objectivity; how our understanding of reality is constituted in a piece-meal fashion in historical practices that always incorporate power relations. The affirmation of agonism thus implies the ineliminability, not of war and violence, but of power relations. What the mechanisms for establishing, changing, regulating, limiting, and criticizing them should be are political questions *par excellence*.

To conclude, Foucault's vision of modernity is no doubt pessimistic, but it would be wrong to deduce that it relies on anthropological pessimism. Even if we had to accept that violence was so universally pervasive that it appeared as necessary for human nature or human societies, this observation itself, just like the positing of any social objectivity, can only be made as a historically perspectival and politically charged truth claim. If Foucault's critique is not really criticism in the usual sense of the word, then neither is his pessimism really pessimism, but rather a form of optimism:

> There is an optimism that consists in saying, "In any case, it couldn't be better." My optimism would consist rather in saying, "So many things can be changed, being as fragile as they are, tied more . . . to complex but transitory historical contingencies than to inevitable anthropological constants."[52]

Because human phenomena are radically contingent and exceptional, in the realm of the political there is always a limited space for hope. These "lines of fragility in the present" do not perhaps make space for utopias of a world free of violence, but they do imply that what is could be otherwise.[53] They force us to accept the profound contingency of the political realm and to recognize the structure of a promise implicit in the fact "that the human time does not take the form of evolution, but that of history."[54]

Notes

1. Santoni, *Sartre on Violence: Curiously Ambivalent*, 2003, ix.
2. Arendt, *On Violence*, 3.
3. Foucault's critics have repeatedly claimed that his thought makes all forms of critique impossible. Jürgen Habermas is perhaps the best-known critic of Foucault, and has accused him of a lack of normative grounding in his analyses. See Habermas, *The Philosophical Discourse of Modernity*, 1987.
4. King, *A Testament of Hope*, and Gandhi, *Non-Violent Resistance*, 1985.
5. The Tolstoyan anarcho–pacifist movement in Russia, for example, was built on the idea that the rejection of coercive authority necessarily implied absolute pacifism.
6. Foucault, *Cambridge Companion to Foucault*, 317.
7. Keane, *Violence and Democracy*, 2004.
8. Foucault, "An Historian of Culture," 99.
9. Foucault, *The History of Sexuality, Vol. 1, An Introduction*, 1978, 93.
10. Foucault "Foucault étudie la raison d'État," in *Dits et écrit II, 1976–1988*, 803.
11. Keane, 37.
12. Žižek, *Violence*, 2008.
13. *Ibid.*, 52.
14. *Ibid.*, 54.
15. Mouffe, *The Democratic Paradox*, 132.
16. Arendt, *On Violence*.
17. Dodd, *Violence and Phenomenology*, 11.
18. Max Weber gives a famous formulation of this idea in his lecture "Politics as Vocation," in which he defines the state as a human community that holds a monopoly over the legitimate use of violence. See Weber, "Politics."
19. Foucault, *Society Must Be Defended*, 23.
20. Hanssen, *Critique of Violence*, 148. Hanssen argues that the change of plan revealed Foucault's disenchantment with the unwieldy dimensions of what threatened to become an all-enveloping power/war matrix. Alessandro Fontana and Mauro Bertani argue that the lectures represent a transition between *Discipline and Punish* and *The History of Sexuality, vol.* I. From a concern with disciplinary power and

    sovereign power, Foucault gradually moved to a more pronounced interest in bio-power. See Fontana and Bertani, "Situating the Lectures."
21. Davidson, "Introduction," xvii–xviii. In his introduction to the English translation, Davidson argues that in studying the discourse of war in this course, Foucault formulated a strategic model of power. Although it is widely recognized that its articulation was one of his major achievements during this time, the full scope and significance of the model has not been fully appreciated.
22. Foucault, *Society Must Be Defended*,13.
23. Clausewitz, *On War*, 87.
24. Foucault, *Society Must Be Defended*, 17.
25. *Ibid.*, 50.
26. Benjamin, "Critique of Violence."
27. Foucault, *Society Must Be Defended*, 70.
28. *Ibid.*, 89.
29. *Ibid.*, 109.
30. *Ibid.*,168.
31. *Ibid.*, 169.
32. Foucault, "Nietzsche, Genealogy, History" in *The Foucault Reader*.
33. Hanssen, 15–16.
34. Foucault, *Society Must Be Defended*, 46.
35. Foucault "The Subject and Power", in *Michel Foucault. Beyond Structuralism and Hermeneutics*, 1982.
36. Foucault, "Polemics, Politics, and Problematizations: An Interview with Michel Foucault", in *The Foucault Reader*, 375–376.
37. Foucault "The Subject and Power", in *Michel Foucault. Beyond Structuralism and Hermeneutics*, 212.
38. Foucault "The Subject and Power", in *Michel Foucault. Beyond Structuralism and Hermeneutics*, 220.
39. Arendt, *On Violence*, and Foucault "The Subject and Power", in *Michel Foucault. Beyond Structuralism and Hermeneutics*, 221.
40. Flynn, *Sartre, Foucault, and Historical Reason*, 244–245, 250.
41. Hanssen, 148–149.
42. It is also essential to note that although both Foucault and Arendt emphasize that the relationship between power and violence is oppositional, they both claim that, nevertheless, they normally always appear together. Their oppositional relationship is always mutually limited and, thus, relative to the terms in the sense that as one increases the other decreases. The more passive and physically constrained the subjects are, the more clearly the relationship is one of violence and not of power. As the activity and the freedom of the subject increases, the relationship of violence is resolved into a relationship of power. Hence, what at first glance appears as a sharp distinction between power and violence, in fact, refers to the idea that power and violence are so intertwined that they always form a continuum and not a clear-cut dichotomy. See Arendt, *On Violence*, 1970, 46, Foucault "The Subject and Power", in *Michel Foucault. Beyond Structuralism and Hermeneutics*, 220.
43. See Foucault "The Ethics of the Concern for Self as a Practice of Freedom", in *Ethics, Subjectivity and Truth: Essential Works of Foucault 1954–1984*, 299.
44. Cf. Lemke, "Foucault, Governmentality, and Critique."
45. One of Foucault's favorite models for thinking about power was the notion of game. See, Davidson, "Structures and Strategies of Discourse," 4.
46. Indeed, the very term "domestic violence" is fairly recent, and has been deemed a highly problematic notion by many feminists The debate on the correct term is

ongoing. Stark and Flitcraft, for example, argue that domestic or family violence is a problematic notion because it implies that what is to be explained is a private event (Stark and Flitcraft, *Women at Risk*). "Violence against women," on the other hand, is problematic because it refers to a transhistorical phenomenon. They advocate the term "woman battering," and argue that it refers to "a historically specific constellation of structural, cultural, and psychodynamic forces."

47. Hern, "Men's Violence," 25.
48. *Ibid.*, 27–29.
49. Butler, *Undoing Gender*.
50. *Ibid.*, 87–88.
51. Nietzsche, *On the Genealogy of Morals*, 60.
52. Foucault "So Is It Important to Think?", in *Power: Essential Works of Foucault 1954–1984*, 458.
53. Flynn formulates Foucault's position on violence in these terms in his study on Foucault and Sartre. By distinguishing between violence and power, Foucault leaves open a space for limited hope, but not the utopian aspiration that Sartre associates with his notions of "socialism of abundance" and the "city of ends" (Flynn, *Sartre*).
54. Foucault "Is It Useless to Revolt" in *Foucault and the Iranian Revolution*, 266.

Chapter 12

The Logic of Violence: Foucault on How Power Kills

Peter DeAngelis

Today, we kill in the name of security. When we wage preemptive war, detain indefinitely, torture, assassinate, and clandestinely strike from predator drones, we do so to secure life itself. This means that violence today is biopolitical; it is made possible by and reinforces the political management of the life of populations. To forge a critical understanding of the violent practices of the contemporary world we thus need to understand what it means for politics to be biopolitics.

It is by charting the transformation of our politics into biopolitics and starting the investigation into what that transformation entails that Foucault becomes necessary to any attempt to critique violent practices today. Foucault's work starting in the 1970s examines the way in which power is exercised biopolitically, how political practices take the complex life processes of individuals and populations as an object to be rationally organized. It is not merely as legal subjects, but as beings that labor, exchange, consume, get sick, have sex, commit crimes, become mentally ill, fall into poverty, reproduce, and die that bio-power organizes the lives of its subjects. Foucault was haunted by the problem of how a form of power that takes the ordered maximization of life itself as its aim could sanction violent practices.

In a 1982 lecture, Foucault explains that "the coexistence in political structures of large destructive mechanisms and institutions oriented toward the care of individual life is . . . one of the central antimonics of our political reason."[1] The method with which he proposes to untangle this dilemma at the heart of modern political rationality is the historical analysis of the relationship between our thought and our practices. The novelty of the approach is perhaps lost in the following explanation's simplicity:

> . . . we are thinking beings. That means that even when we kill or are killed, even when we make war or when we ask for support as unemployed, even when we vote for or against a government that cuts social security expenses and increases defense spending, even in these cases, we are thinking beings, and we do these things not only on the ground of universal rules of behavior, but also on the specific ground of a historical rationality. It is this rationality, and the life and death game that takes place in it, that I'd like to investigate from a historical point of view.[2]

To historically analyze how forms of rationality are inscribed in the systems of political practices through which we organize our lives is, therefore, to lay bare the ways of thinking that provide violent practices with a credibility to not only those who govern, but those who are governed. It is only through such critical historical work that we can begin to understand how today it makes unassailable sense to kill in the name of life.

To show how Foucault lays the ground for such work, what follows is divided in two sections. In the first section, I highlight Foucault's central methodological innovations regarding the study of power. This includes rejecting the dominant tendency in Western political thought to think of power juridically, in terms of problems concerning the legitimate constitution and limits of sovereignty. Instead of a juridical approach to power, Foucault's method begins by asking *how* power is exercised. To interrogate power in this way means to treat power as a relation, more specifically a strategic relation, in which individuals and populations are governed. Asking how power is exercised not only turns critical attention to governing practices, but also to the level of reflection internal to all political practice, namely the forms of rationality that make possible and support the exercise of power. I argue that the questions we ask about violent practices are themselves shaped by the way we understand and critically examine power. Foucault's approach to investigating power thus opens up new critical questions to ask about violence, specifically what form of political rationality sanctions a specific violent practice and bestows upon it an inexorable logic. What I call the logic of violence includes not only the reasons that sanction violence (i.e., why it is done), but also the aura of obviousness that such reasons acquire when they become historically sedimented and taken for granted (i.e., why it is so easily and widely accepted).

In the second section, I show how this methodology makes possible Foucault's analysis of how power is exercised once politics becomes biopolitics. The form power takes when exercised biopolitically is what Foucault terms with the neologism governmentality. Governmentality refers to the ensemble of institutions, practices, and forms of reasoning that take the population as an object to be managed through a constellation of security mechanisms. By starting to forge an understanding of the modern biopolitical rationality that dictates our politics, Foucault accordingly begins the project of critically understanding how it has become a self-evident element of our politics to kill in the name of life itself.

Questioning Power and Violence

In this section, I argue that the way we question violence is determined by the understanding we have of power. What this means is that any attempt to critique violent practices must also engage in an interrogation of the exercise of power. In a 1979 lecture, Foucault already made this point clear:

> . . . those who resist or rebel against a form of power cannot merely be content to denounce violence . . . What has to be questioned is the form of rationality at stake . . . The question is: how are such relations of power rationalized? Asking it is the only way to avoid other institutions, with the same objectives and the same effects, from taking their stead.[3]

Politically effective opposition to violence thus requires that one not merely single out an isolated violent practice for condemnation, but rather interrogate the form of rationality that sanctions the more general regime of political practices, both violent and nonviolent, through which power is exercised. A critique of violence that fails to interrogate the form of power that makes violence possible is ultimately politically hopeless, because it leaves untouched the ways of thinking and political practices that make such violence imaginable. This also means that one's approach to violence must be grounded in a sophisticated understanding and analysis of power. Put differently, not only a refusal to question power, but a naïve understanding of it jeopardizes any critical attempts to question violence. Thus, in the remainder of this section, I set out Foucault's own approach to power and explain the critical space it opens up for the interrogation of violence.

Foucault rejects a juridical approach to the study of power.[4] This is because juridical theory reduces the investigation of power to problems concerning the legitimate constitution of sovereignty. Power on such a model is reduced to law; its exercise consists in nothing else but the legislation and enforcement of legal codes. All power relations are in turn modeled on the relationship between sovereign and subject. Foucault's claim is that juridical theory is not able to explain the way in which power is actually exercised once that exercise becomes biopolitical.[5]

Foucault stresses that the model of sovereignty does refer to an actual form of power, the way power was in fact once organized—feudal monarchy.[6] This is, however, only one historical form that has characterized the organization of Western political practice. As feudal mechanisms of power were slowly penetrated and supplanted by the new forms of power that would come to characterize modernity, the language of law and the model of sovereignty lost their explanatory power.[7] The complex political practices that constitute governmentality, its aims, and operational logic render the juridical "increasingly incapable of coding power."[8] The reason for this is that power exercised biopolitically takes a living being as its object, not a simple legal subject. Foucault's concern is simply that juridical thought cannot help us to understand a form of power that is exercised over living beings, not merely legal subjects, through extra-legal means.[9] To analyze the exercise of power in the political domain it is thus necessary to move past a juridical model of power. Or as Foucault famously puts it, in political thought we need to cut off the head of the king.[10]

I submit that juridical theory not only limits our approach to the investigation of power, but also of violence. Our criticisms of violence are plagued by the problem of sovereignty in two ways. First, it limits the questions we ask of violence to those concerning legal legitimation. For example, according to what legal power does the state claim the right to sentence one to death? Or, on what constitutional ground does the state derive its war powers? Before the issue of juridical legitimation is posed, however, there is the more significant question of why specific violent practices appear reasonable to us at all. One must first ask, for example, why waging war in general, but also in the ways and for the reasons we do, is assumed to be a perfectly rational means through which the securing of life can be achieved. It is only by setting violent practices in the context of the complex set of political practices and ways of thinking through which power is exercised that this type of question is asked. Moreover, it is only by placing questions concerning juridical legitimation against the same backdrop that such questions can be posed in a non-naïve manner; for example, by asking how law and sovereignty are organized and instrumentalized according to the necessities of biopolitical government.[11]

The second limitation imposed by the privileging of the problem of sovereignty on our attempts to critically understand violence is the temptation it induces to locate a sole agent as the source of all political violence. Because juridical theory is historically organized around the power of the king,[12] power is conceived as centralized in and emanating out from a single, all-powerful point. What this means is that every political practice, every relation and effect of power must be traced back to the transcendent sovereign. The dominance of the problem of sovereignty in turn tempts us to hold the sovereign alone responsible for all violent practices.[13] Violence can be understood, we believe, if we can only unlock the ruler's secret intentions, plots, and desires. Foucault, though, shows us the limits of this mode of critique:

> . . . I don't believe that this question of "who exercises power?" can be resolved unless that other question of "how does it happen?" is resolved at the same time. Of course we have to show who those in charge are, we know that we have to turn, let us say, to deputies, ministers, principal private secretaries, etc., etc. But this is not the important issue, for we know perfectly well that even if we reach the point of designating exactly all those people, all those "decision-makers," we will still not really know why and how the decision was made, how it came to be accepted by everybody, and how it is that it hurts a particular category of person, etc.[14]

It is the broad acceptability or consensus that exists around violent practices—that it is so easy to support the war, the torture, the predator drone assassinations—that forces us to acknowledge that the most politically significant form of reasoning is not that which is in the head of the sovereign decider, but rather that which is shared more broadly, the forms of rationality inscribed in the practices through which we organize political life.

To pursue the politically effective way of questioning violence to which I am gesturing here it is necessary to root that questioning of violence in a sophisticated understanding and analysis of power. Foucault provides such an approach to the investigation of power. His approach to the study of power begins by asking *how* power is exercised.[15] To ask this "how" question means that Foucault is agnostic on the problem of what power is in itself, proposing that we neither think of power as a property or thing that one might possess (i.e., official privilege, right, or wealth), nor as a brute capacity.[16] Rather to ask how power is exercised turns the object of analysis into the relation of power,[17] more specifically the "complex strategical situation,"[18] in which actors attempt to shape the actions of others.[19] Rehabilitating the broad meaning that government had in the sixteenth century, Foucault therefore understands power as a relationship of governing in which the "conduct" of individuals or groups is shaped and directed.[20]

The proper object of a Foucaultian analytic of power is not simply the complex of governing practices through which the lives of individuals and groups are managed, but rather the specific forms of rationality that are constantly at work within those practices.[21] At the start of his 1979 lectures at the Collège de France (*The Birth of Biopolitics*), he explains that his investigative concern is with "the level of reflection in the practice of government and on the practice of government . . . the way in which this practice that consists in governing was conceptualized both within and outside government."[22] What this means is that Foucault's concern with the analysis of networks of power/ knowledge in a text such as *Discipline and Punish*,[23] which treats of individualizing techniques of power, continues into his later investigations of the practices through which populations are governed.[24]

I stated above that it is through a historical analysis of the relationship between our thought and our practices that Foucault attempts to untangle the problem of how violence is sanctioned in our politics. What that method of analysis consists of is now coming into sharper focus. Foucault explains that what is at stake in an analysis of power is "how forms of rationality inscribe themselves in practices or systems of practices, and what role they play within them."[25] He explains the object of this work as follows:

> If I have studied "practices" like those of the sequestration of the insane, or clinical medicine, or the organization of the empirical sciences, or legal punishment, it was in order to study this interplay between a "code" which rules a way of doing things (how people are to be graded and examined, things and signs classified, individuals trained, etc.) and a production of true discourses which serve to found, justify and provided reasons and principles for these ways of doings things. To put the matter clearly: my problem is to see how men govern (themselves and others) by the production of truth.[26]

What the project of analyzing the relationship between our thought and our practices consists in is thus an investigation of the relation between the governing practices through which political life is managed and those forms of reasoning that make possible and sanction those particular ways of organizing and structuring the very fabric of our social and political lives.

It is not immediately clear why this way of interrogating power, which analyzes the relationship between political practices and forms of rationality, will help us in any way to forge a critical understanding of violent practices. This is especially so since Foucault in a number of places insists that the essential nature of power cannot be reduced to violence.[27] It would be misguided, however, to run from Foucault as if he cannot help us understand violence simply because he posits a conceptual distinction between power and violence.[28] To say that power is "something much more complex" than negative practices and effects (i.e., violence, repression, prohibition, etc.)[29] does not in any way entail the extra claim that power and violence have no relation to one another. To make a conceptual distinction between power and violence is by itself not necessarily problematic or original.[30] The problem is how we conceive of the relation between the two.

Regarding this relation, Foucault certainly affirms its existence, but does not necessarily clarify for us what it entails. He explains that power "does not exclude the use of violence" and that violence is one of power's "instruments."[31] Even more strongly, he insists that "power can never do without" violence and that one should not doubt the way in which power "can pile up the dead and shelter itself behind whatever threats it can imagine."[32] I suggest that we understand the relation Foucault is gesturing to as follows: (1) violence is always situated in a historically specific, complex, and strategic social situation, and it can only be understood by reference to that situation; and (2) violence is only one of the many practices through which individuals and groups are governed in that strategic field. What Foucault points us to in his refusal to reduce the nature of power to violence is the rather simple point that the way in which power is exercised includes a wide array of practices, both nonviolent and violent.[33] The task is to situate how violent practices operate within that more general regime of political practices through which power is exercised.

To close this section, I indicate two features that define questioning violence in this way. First, because in a Foucaultian account violent practices must be situated within a strategic field as one element of a complex regime of governing practices, they cannot be traced back to a single, all-powerful source that we fetishize as the font of all power and violence. Just as power is not locatable in any single institution nor possessed by any single leader or party, violence is similarly not the private work of any isolated political ruler or institution. Instead, violent practices must be understood as the product of sets of practices that extend beyond and are not created by or in the possession of any institution or sovereign leader. One must ask how violence results from the general forms of power that organize our lives.

The second feature of this method of questioning derives from Foucault's suggestion to understand power as "both intentional and nonsubjective."[34] He insists that "there is no power that is exercised without a series of aims and objectives," but he continues, "this does not mean that it results from the choice or decision of an individual subject."[35] He warns against the search "for the headquarters that presides over its rationality" and instead suggests that if we want to locate the "logic" and "aims" of power that we seek them in the rationality that is internal to the practices themselves.[36] I suggest that we also attempt to understand violence as intentional and nonsubjective. In this way, we cannot be content with seeking out the clandestine reasoning of the sovereign and his cabal who authorize this or that violent course of action. Rather, we must understand the rationality of violence as originating not in the head of any leader or bureaucrat, but rather as an extension of the forms of rationality that establish, justify and provide reasons and principles for the ways our political practices more generally structure our lives. The logic or intelligibility of violent practices—why they make good sense to us, governors and governed alike, as a course of political action—derives not from any single intentional agent who bestows meaning upon practices, but from ways of thinking that saturate political practices in general. Johanna Oksala argues in the previous chapter that Foucault's philosophy is an ontology of the present, the essential task of which is to use genealogical methods to demonstrate the contingency of our practices and the presuppositions upholding them. I submit here that asking the question "how does power kill?" is central to any interrogation of the present. Asking this question brings critical attention to the way in which the taken for granted practices and ways of thinking that structure our lives make possible the violence of our politics.

Biopolitical Violence: The Logic of Killing to Secure Life

It is now possible to turn to the question of how power kills today. To ask this question means to examine the reasons for which our form of politics sanctions violence. This examination requires investigating the relationship between historically specific forms of power and the violent practices they make possible. Foucault was concerned with this problem in the final lecture of his 1975–1976 course at the Collège de France (*Society Must Be Defended*) and the final section of *The History of Sexuality: Volume I* ("Right of Death and Power over Life"). In the March 17 lecture, Foucault asks:

> . . . how will the power to kill and the function of murder operate in this technology of power, which takes life as both its object and its objectives? How can a power such as this kill, if it is true that its basic function is to improve life, to prolong its duration, to improve its chances, to avoid accidents, and to compensate for failings?[37]

Corroborating the reading I pursued above, what this line of questioning suggests is that there is a "parallel shift"[38] in the way in which power is exercised and both the reasons for which violence is justifiable and the functions it serves in a regime of political practices. What demands investigation to understand violence today is the transformation in the way power kills,[39] when power no longer takes an exclusively juridical form, but is rather exercised biopolitically. Put differently, the problem is to make clear the differences between the violence of sovereignty and that of governmentality.

Sovereign power has an intimate relationship with violence. One of its characteristic privileges is the right to decide life and death.[40] Foucault claims that this right formally derives from the *patria potestas* granted to the father of the Roman family. This right to dispose of subjects, however, exists in a much diminished form as it is formulated by early modern political and juridical theorists.[41] The sovereign's power of life and death cannot be exercised in an absolute way, but only under specific conditions in which sovereignty itself is in jeopardy. When challenged by external enemies, the sovereign can legitimately wage war and require subjects to face death in defense of the state. When law is transgressed, which amounts to no less a challenge to sovereign right than that posed by external enemies, the sovereign can punish the offender and, in the extreme, take the offender's life.

The sovereign's power of life and death is dissymmetrical. It can only have an effect on life by exercising the right to kill or threatening to do so.[42] This is because sovereignty is a juridical form that refers "to a historical type of society in which power was exercised mainly as a means of deduction, a subtraction mechanism, a right to appropriate a portion of the wealth, a tax of products, goods and services, labor and blood, levied on the subjects."[43] In this way, the sovereign's violent practices are but one example of a feudal form of power that "was essentially a right of seizure."[44] Sovereign power seizes things: time and, in the end, life itself. For all of these practices, the end is consistently sovereignty itself. This means that "the end of sovereignty is circular":[45] sovereign violence is justifiable only in "the defense of the sovereign."[46]

Troubling as the self-referential logic of sovereign violence might be, it is no longer the logic of our violent practices. To understand the logic of our violent practices, we need to understand the way in which power is exercised today and how this differs from a sovereign model. Foucault identifies two reasons, the first practical and the second theoretical, for the development of a form of power that is not organized according to a sovereign schema. First, power organized on the model of sovereignty was unable politically and economically to govern a society undergoing both the demographic explosion and industrialization of modernity.[47] Political practices that were essentially means of seizure were supplanted by two types of practice: (1) technologies of observation, monitoring, judging and training with which individuals in local institutions (the factory, the military, the school, etc.) can by shaped into politically manageable and economically useful subjects;[48] and (2) regulatory controls and security mechanisms that adjust the large scale phenomena of the population (birth rate, morbidity, disease, productivity, consumption, environmental influences, accidents, criminality, etc.) to the exigencies of economic process.[49] These two forms of political practice, discipline and biopolitics, together constitute bio-power, which complemented and ultimately displaced sovereign power.[50]

The second and theoretical reason for the shift away from a form of power modeled on sovereignty is provided by classical political economy.[51] Foucault understands the liberal principle of *laissez-faire* as a revolution internal to the rationalization of governing practice. The problem posed by political economy for governing practice is no longer the juridical question of power's legitimacy, but the utilitarian question of its effectiveness.[52] Foucault sees Adam Smith's "invisible hand" as a solution to the technical question of power's utility. Smith puts forth a challenge to the theorists of *raison d'état* and police science [*Polizeiwissenschaft*], which together comprised the political practice of the administrative state of royal power,[53] by demonstrating the essential incapacity of the sovereign to govern economic processes through a totalizing cataloging and detailed control of all domains of life.[54] Central to this demonstration is the claim, which is seen throughout the traditions of British empiricism and utilitarianism, that the subject of interest [*homo œconomicus*] cannot be reduced to the subject of right [*homo juridicus*]. What this means is that liberal political economy, which Foucault understands as a mode of reflection on government, signals the disqualification of political practice and reason that is modeled on the problem of sovereignty. This is because political economy demonstrates that "juridical theory is unable to take on and resolve the question of how to govern in a space of sovereignty inhabited by economic subjects."[55] To solve the problem of how to govern a space that is occupied by not only juridical subjects, but also economic ones—for example, living beings that labor, exchange, consume, reproduce, get sick, fall into poverty, etc.— liberal political rationality carves out a new domain as the correlate of governing practice, namely civil society.[56] Instead of merely juridical beings, liberal political rationality turns the complex bio-economic[57] life of individuals and groups into the object of governing practice. This concrete living ensemble is civil society.

Foucault calls the form of power that takes the complex life processes of individuals and groups as its object governmentality. With this term, Foucault refers to "the ensemble formed by institutions, procedures, analyses and reflections, calculations, and tactics that allow the exercise of this very specific, albeit very complex, power that has population as its target, political economy as its major form of knowledge, and apparatuses of security as its essential technical instrument."[58] Foucault in no way is dedicated to the claim that juridical problems of sovereignty and law vanish with the emergence of governmentality. The three types of power that Foucault investigates in his work—legal mechanisms of sovereignty, disciplinary techniques and biopolitical security strategies—do not represent a historical schema.[59] Instead, as new governing practices develop, specific types of practice come to occupy a privileged position in the always-changing arrangements in the institutions and apparatuses of power. To understand how power is exercised today, what interests Foucault is the way in which juridical mechanisms (legal code, sovereignty) and disciplines (techniques of surveillance, diagnosis, classification, training, etc.) are reorganized to the needs of a form of power whose aim is the securing of the population's life—or governmentality.[60]

If liberal political rationality signals the final discrediting of the exercise of power exclusively modeled on sovereignty, the question remains of how the limitation of political power entailed by that critique (*laissez-faire*) is itself compatible with governmentality, which is a more robust form of power than sovereignty ever was. Nikolas Rose argues on this point that the demonstration by liberal discourse that there is a realm of bio-economic processes that rulers cannot govern through the mere exercise of sovereign will because they necessarily lack the requisite knowledge and capacities does not mean that governing practice is eliminated by liberalism, but only that it must be informed by a knowledge of that which is to be ruled.[61] It is expertise, authority resulting from claims to neutral and effective knowledge, that provides the solution to the need of government to guarantee political order and the wellbeing of the population, while also respecting the utilitarian restrictions placed on government by liberal political rationality.[62] It is in this way that the seemingly illiberal practices of bio-power, discipline and biopolitics, flourish as the very practices of liberal government. This is because liberal government becomes tied to:

> . . . the positive knowledges of human conduct developed within the social and human sciences. The activities of government becomes connected up to all manner of facts (the avalanche of printed numbers and other information . . .), theories (philosophies of progress, conceptualizations of epidemic disease . . .), diagrams (sanitary reform, child guidance . . .), techniques (double-entry book keeping, compulsory medical inspection of school children . . .), knowledgeable persons who can speak "in the name of society" (sociologists, statisticians, epidemiologists, social workers).[63]

By discrediting a form of power tied to the model of sovereignty, liberal reflection on government in turn creates an inextricable bond between the formal apparatuses of political rule and the authority of expertise provided by economics, statistics, sociology, medicine, biology, psychiatry and psychology, positive sciences that produce and disseminate truth.[64] It is in this space opened up by liberal governmental reflection[65] that biopower, which brings life into "knowledge's field of control and power's sphere of intervention," flourishes.[66]

Given this account, the relation between governmentality and violent practices becomes problematic. Sovereign power is essentially a right of seizure, which means that its violent exercise is but another extension of a juridical form of power whose only means for having an effect on the lives of its subjects is through negation: taxing goods, seizing land, killing subjects. The ultimate power that sovereignty holds over life is the threat of death. But this is not the case for governmentality. Foucault explains that the development of biopolitics means that "power would no longer be dealing simply with legal subjects over whom the ultimate dominion was death, but with living beings, and the mastery it would be able to exercise over them would have to be applied at the level of life itself."[67] What function does violence have within a form of power whose essential practice consists in the informed management of life? Put differently, how do we make sense of violence when society crosses what Foucault calls the "threshold of biological modernity," the point at which "the life of the species is wagered on its own political strategies"?[68]

Foucault does not understand political violence as an aberration that takes place outside the purview of governmentality, which perhaps results from a resurgent sovereignty. Insisting on the connection between biopolitics and the violence of modernity, he notes that "wars were never as bloody as they have been since the nineteenth century, and all things being equal, never before did regimes visit such holocausts on their populations."[69] "If genocide is indeed the dream of modern powers," he explains, "this is not because of a recent return of the ancient right to kill," but "because power is situated and exercised at the level of life, the species, the race, and the large-scale phenomena of population."[70] Instead of attributing violence to a resurrected sovereignty, which is itself a flawed thesis because sovereignty never went anywhere but was only reorganized to biopolitical exigency, Foucault is interested in how the development of biopolitical practice entails "a parallel shift in the right of death," a realignment with "the exigencies of a life-administering power."[71]

To understand how violent practices now serve the necessities of biopolitics, Foucault considers how war and the death penalty, the two historically privileged forms of state violence, function differently when not tied to sovereign power. Foucault argues that:

> . . . wars are no longer waged in the name of a sovereign who must be defended: they are waged on behalf of the existence of everyone; entire populations are mobilized for the purposes of wholesale slaughter in the name of life necessity: massacres have become vital.[72]

The transformation in question is not that war is no longer waged in the name of a single sovereign (i.e., the King), but rather in the name of a collectivized sovereign (i.e., the citizenry of a republican nation state). The problem is not one of number (monarchic versus collective sovereignty), but kind. Foucault argues that in war today "the existence in question is no longer the juridical existence of sovereignty; at stake is the biological existence of a population."[73] It is as "managers of life and survival," not the life and survival of a juridical sovereignty but a population of living beings, "that so many regimes have been able to wage so many wars, causing so many to be killed."[74] To say that war is now "vital" and waged in the name of "life necessity" is not mere rhetorical flourish that designates war's great urgency when waged with modern technologies, but it rather signifies that the violence of war is mobilized by governmentality only insofar as it also contributes to the management and ordering of life. It is not the simple sovereign maintenance of territorial integrity and legal right that motivates war, but rather the organization of a specific form of life and the elimination of threats to that life. In their analysis of how liberal governmentality entails its own unique way of war, Michael Dillon and Julian Reid argue that *"making life live"* is "the criterion against which the liberal way of rule and war must seek to say how much killing is enough" (italics added).[75] The idea that biopolitical violence "makes life live" means not only that violence secures populations from external danger, but also from threats that emerge from within life itself. Biopolitics wages war on life to secure it, not life in an unqualified sense, but in a way that is formed in a historically, politically, economically and culturally specific way.

Biopolitics reorganizes the rationale of the death penalty in a similar way. Foucault explains that "capital punishment could not be maintained except by invoking less the enormity of the crime itself than the monstrosity of the criminal, his incorrigibility, and the safeguard of society."[76] One can only kill those who represent "a kind of biological danger to others."[77] This means that power can no longer kill those who simply transgress legal code as is the case with sovereign power. Rather, the juridical institution that enforces the law is entangled in extra-legal apparatuses (medical, psychiatric, psychological, sociological, criminological, etc.) that condition and make possible its functioning.[78] It is here that Foucault's analysis of the emergence of the figure of "the dangerous individual" through the psychiatrization of criminal dangers is of grave importance.[79] Expert knowledges such as psychiatry introduce a rationality into penal practice that allows the punitive apparatus to not only ask what crime is being punished and how, but who is being punished and how. A whole set of techniques developed in the nineteenth century and continues to develop today for assessing, diagnosing, and normatively judging the criminal:[80] what kind of danger does he or she pose to society? Can he or she be reformed? And, if so, how? Or, is he or she "intrinsically dangerous?"[81] Does he or she pose an essential threat to society that cannot be tamed? It is no longer a simple juridical apparatus that authorizes the execution of the condemned, but a "scientifico–juridical complex"[82] consisting of an army of subsidiary authorities, experts and judges without whom the sentencing would be impossible. Not only the "decision-making" process, but also the "powers of decision"[83] over who lives and dies extend beyond the bare juridical apparatus to include extra-legal apparatuses of expert knowledge.

It is clear here that neither those who are killed, nor those who are safeguarded, nor even the mechanisms deciding on violent practice are understandable in simple juridical terms. What is safeguarded is not juridical sovereignty, collective or otherwise, but individuals and populations conceived as living beings. Even more strictly, what is secured is life itself. What life is secured against are "threats" and "dangers" that must be eliminated to safeguard a form of life that governmentality is tasked to order and manage.[84] These dangers are not of a juridical variety; they are not reducible to someone who merely transgresses legal code, nor a sovereign enemy who intrudes on a border, but are rather individuals whose very being represents an intrinsic danger to social welfare or groups whose form of life (whether that be political, social, economic, cultural) is itself a threat to a specific way of organizing and structuring life.[85] Finally, it is not a simple juridical apparatus that decides on what threats must be eliminated. Governmentality is an informed power, inextricably bound to the authority of expertise. A criminal is not executed without a series of expert judges attesting to the essential danger that the individual poses to society. Similarly, a war is not started if a consensus does not exist among a different army of experts (e.g., of international relations, military strategy, political economy, security studies, global and national development, etc.) who single out a specific nation, form of government or economy, or rogue leader (the list goes on) as posing a basic security challenge to a form of life that is to be protected.

It is now that we can make sense of Foucault's claim that when power is exercised governmentally:

> ... it is the discourse of truth that decides, at least in part; it conveys and propels effects of power. After all, we are judged, condemned, forced to perform tasks, and destined to live and die in certain ways by discourses that are true, and which bring with them specific power-effects.[86]

As I argued in the previous section, when questioning violence it is not the thought process of a single leader or bureaucrat with which we should be concerned, but rather the ways of thinking that saturate our political practices, violent and nonviolent alike. Or, as Foucault puts it, our concern must be the life and death game that takes place in forms of rationality. The preceding analysis of governmentality has revealed two levels of "ways of thinking" or "forms of rationality" that deserve attention. The first is political rationality, for example, liberalism, which cuts across state and local institutions and sets out the ends and means of rule, its reasons and justifications, the kind of problems with which it is concerned, and the limits of its exercise. The second are expert knowledges, which rationalize specific forms of experience (e.g., madness, illness, death, crime, sexuality, poverty, terrorism, etc.) turning them into sites that are at once intelligible and manageable. A Foucaultian critique of violence must operate on both levels by interrogating: (1) the schemes of security put forth by political rationality, both what is entailed by that project of security and the nature of the form of life that is secured; and (2) at the level of expert knowledges, the technologies for discerning and marking both individuals and groups as dangerous and the practices prescribed as means to eliminate those dangers.

The critical interrogation of the way in which the forms of reasoning operative at all levels of our political practice make violence possible requires a vigilance to all of power's claims that a particular individual or group is dangerous. This is because if governmentality sanctions killing to secure life, then what is killed is always the dangerous or whatever is designated so by a historically specific set of political practices and ways of thinking. The condition of a critique of violence, then, is a work on ourselves, specifically a transformation of the way we experience the dangers of our world. This is because, as Foucault indicates, the liberal project of managing security produces subjects that are "conditioned to experience their situation, their life, their present, and their future as containing danger."[87] Instead of the apocalyptic threats that characterized the political and cosmological imagination from the Middle Ages until the seventeenth century, with liberalism, "everyday dangers appear, emerge, and spread everywhere, perpetually being brought to life, reactualized, and circulated by what could be called the political culture of danger in the nineteenth century."[88] Although the specific objects of the nineteenth century's political culture of dangers are not all with us,[89] it is still true today that "the stimulation of the fear of dangers . . . is, as it were, the condition, the internal psychological and cultural correlative of liberalism."[90] If there is no liberalism without a culture of danger, this is because a form of power that is essentially concerned with the securitization of life itself can only function if the subjects and groups over which it is exercised are conditioned to experience their lives as replete with dangers, real and imagined. To critically focus on the ways in which individuals or entire groups are singled out as dangerous, threats to our way of life or life itself, requires challenging our very experience of those dangers. If power kills today through the marking of the dangerous, then the preconditions of that killing are not only the practices and forms of reasoning through which individuals and groups are marked as dangerous, but also our experience of those dangers. It is this marking and our experience of it that demands critical vigilance.

Notes

1. Foucault, "The Political Technology of Individuals", in *Michel Foucault: Power*, 405.
2. Foucault, "The Political Technology of Individuals", in *Michel Foucault: Power*, 405.
3. Foucault, "*Omnes et Singulatim*: Toward a Critique of Political Reason", in *Michel Foucault: Power*, 324.
4. Foucault, *The History of Sexuality: Volume I: An Introduction*, 85–91; Foucault, *Society Must Be Defended*, 23–40.
5. Foucault, *The History of Sexuality: Volume I: An Introduction*, 89.
6. Foucault, *The History of Sexuality: Volume I: An Introduction*, 86–89; Foucault, *Society Must Be Defended*, 34–35.
7. Foucault ascribes four historical functions to juridical theory. For that discussion, see Foucault, *Society Must Be Defended*, 34–37. For his discussion of how the mechanisms of sovereignty are penetrated and replaced by governmental or biopolitical practices, see Foucault, *The Birth of Biopolitics*, 3–22.
8. Foucault, *The History of Sexuality: Volume I: An Introduction*, 89.
9. Gordon, "Governmental Rationality," 7. Colin Gordon correctly notes that "Foucault does not say that legitimation theory is empty . . . but only that a theory of the legitimate basis of sovereignty cannot be relied upon as a means of describing the ways in which power is actually exercised under such a sovereignty."
10. Foucault, *The History of Sexuality: Volume I: An Introduction*, 89.
11. See, for example, Butler, *Precarious Life*, 50–100.
12. Foucault, *Society Must Be Defended*, 25–26.
13. The examples of this in the contemporary world are obvious. Bush himself, or perhaps with the help of a cabal of advisors, is seen as the sole source and responsible agent for the violent practices of the day. We even refer to a war as "Bush's War" or, now, "Obama's War" (the respective names of two PBS "Frontline" documentaries), thus showing how we tend to think that political violence emanates from a single point. The same methodological point holds for our diagnosis of the sources of terrorism and the tendency to trace it back to a single evil agent.
14. Foucault, "On Power", in *Michel Foucault: Politics, Philosophy, Culture, Interviews and Other Writings 1977–1984*, 104.
15. Foucault, "The Subject and Power", in *Michel Foucault: Power*, 336–339; Foucault, *Society Must Be Defended*, 24.

16. Foucault, *Discipline and Punish*, 26; Foucault, *Society Must Be Defended*, 13–14; Foucault, *The History of Sexuality: Volume I: An Introduction*, 94.
17. Foucault, "The Subject and Power", in *Michel Foucault: Power*, 339.
18. Foucault, *The History of Sexuality: Volume I: An Introduction*, 93.
19. Foucault, "The Subject and Power", in *Michel Foucault: Power*, 340.
20. Foucault, "The Subject and Power", in *Michel Foucault: Power*, 341.
21. Foucault, "*Omnes et Singulatim*: Toward a Critique of Political Reason", in *Michel Foucault: Power*, 324.
22. Foucault, *Birth of Biopolitics*, 2.
23. Foucault, *Discipline and Punishment*, 27. In *Discipline and Punish*, Foucault famously argues that "there is no power relation without the correlative constitution of a field of knowledge, nor any knowledge that does not presuppose and constitute at the same time power relations."
24. Gordon, "Governmental Rationality," 4. Gordon notes that "the same style of analysis . . . that had been used to study techniques and practices addressed to individual human subjects within particular, local institutions could also be addressed to techniques and practices for governing populations of subjects at the level of a political sovereignty over an entire society."
25. Foucault, "Questions of Method", in *The Foucault Effect: Studies in Governmentality*, 79.
26. Foucault, "Questions of Method", in *The Foucault Effect: Studies in Governmentality*, 79.
27. Foucault, "*Omnes et Singulatim*: Toward a Critique of Political Reason", in *Michel Foucault: Power*, 324; Foucault, "The Subject and Power", in *Michel Foucault: Power*, 340. In fact, the clear conceptual distinction that Foucault draws between power and violence in the late essay, "The Subject and Power," is not a new position as is often assumed, but is rather exhibited in his work of the 1970s, as well. In *Discipline and Punish*, for example, he studies disciplinary power by insisting on the "the positive effects" and "complex social function of these practices" (*Discipline and Punish*, 23–24). The positivity of power is pursued there not only in its production of "docile bodies" through complex regimes of disciplinary training, surveillance, supervision and judging (Foucault, *Discipline and Punish*, 125–169), but also in the correlative constitution of fields of knowledge (Foucault, *Discipline and Punish*, 27). The idea that power is productive of bodies and knowledges is seen again in *The History of Sexuality: Volume I*, where Foucault argues against what he calls the "repressive hypothesis," the common belief that sexuality in bourgeois society stands in a negative relation to power (i.e., it is censored, prohibited, etc.) (3–49).
28. See, for example, Deveaux, "Feminism and Empowerment," 222–226. Deveaux argues that Foucault's conceptual distinction between power and violence amounts to the claim that both power and violence are "inherently different and separable," for example, that they have no relation whatsoever, thus rendering his agonistic conception of power incapable of accounting for women's experiences of power and violence and, by extension, problematic for feminist theory and politics.
29. Foucault, "On Power", in *Michel Foucault: Politics, Philosophy, Culture, Interviews and Other Writings 1977–1984*, 102.
30. Arendt famously distinguishes between power and violence. See Arendt, *On Violence*.
31. Foucault, "The Subject and Power", in *Michel Foucault: Power*, 340–341.
32. Foucault, "The Subject and Power", in *Michel Foucault: Power*, 340–341.
33. Not only is it analytically incorrect to identify power and violence, but doing so makes it impossible to make any distinctions between which political practices are

violent and which are not. Collapsing the difference makes normative distinctions between types of political practice impossible.

34. Foucault, *The History of Sexuality: Volume I: An Introduction*, 94.
35. Foucault, *The History of Sexuality: Volume I: An Introduction*, 95.
36. Foucault, *The History of Sexuality: Volume I: An Introduction*, 95.
37. Foucault, *Society Must Be Defended*, 254.
38. Foucault, *The History of Sexuality: Volume I: An Introduction*, 136.
39. The operating definition of "killing" with which I have been working is borrowed from Foucault's rather broad definition, which he explains as follows: "When I say "killing," I obviously do not mean simply murder as such, but also every form of indirect murder: the fact of exposing someone to death, increasing the risk of death for some people, or, quite simply, political death expulsion, rejection, and so on" (Foucault, *Society Must be Defended*, 256). Although direct forms of violence (war, death penalty, holocaust, ethnic cleansing, genocide) are the obvious targets of a critique of violence and the ones on which I focus, the indirect violence that consists in exposing individuals and groups to preventable, life threatening danger also deserves critical attention. A complete investigation of how power kills must not only examine how the way in which we govern political, social and economic life results in direct violence, but also how it exposes select individuals and groups to daily living conditions that are permeated by violence.
40. Foucault, *The History of Sexuality: Volume I: An Introduction*, 135; Foucault, *Society Must Be Defended*, 240.
41. Foucault, *The History of Sexuality: Volume I: An Introduction*, 135–136; Foucault, *Society Must Be Defended*, 240–241.
42. Foucault, *The History of Sexuality: Volume I: An Introduction*, 136; Foucault, *Society Must Be Defended*, 240.
43. Foucault, *The History of Sexuality: Volume I: An Introduction*, 136.
44. Foucault, *The History of Sexuality: Volume I: An Introduction*, 136.
45. Foucault, *Security, Territory, Population*, 98.
46. Foucault, *The History of Sexuality: Volume I: An Introduction*, 136.
47. Foucault, *Society Must Be Defended*, 249.
48. Foucault, *Discipline and Punish*, 125–169.
49. Foucault, *The History of Sexuality: Volume I: An Introduction*, 140–141; Foucault, *Society Must Be Defended*, 242–248.
50. Foucault, *The History of Sexuality: Volume I: An Introduction*, 139.
51. Foucault, *The Birth of Biopolitics*, 10–22.
52. Foucault, *The Birth of Biopolitics*, 16, 40–47.
53. Foucault, *Security, Territory, Population*, 236–358. The royal administrative state from the sixteenth to the middle of the eighteenth century marks a significant transition in Foucault's genealogy of governmentality. For Foucault, *raison d'état* and police science, specifically mercantilism, are the first modes of governmental reflection and practice that take the population's life processes as the object of government. This form of governing reason and practice was still, however, expressed in a juridical framework. The problem of the population was reconfigured by political economy and statistics, which treat population as a set of natural processes with quantifiable regularities that have political and economic effects. Instead of being seen as contributing to the sovereign's strength as it is by mercantilism, population and its immanent processes are turned into the very end of government by political economy. See Foucault, *Security, Territory, Population*, 102–106; Foucault, *The Birth of Biopolitics*, 18.
54. Foucault, *The Birth of Biopolitics*, 281–286.

55. Foucault, *The Birth of Biopolitics*, 294.

56. Regarding "civil society," Foucault notes: (1) that by this time it has a fundamentally different sense than it had for Locke, for whom it retained a juridical structure; and (2) that the term quickly became synonymous with "society" and "nation." He claims that when Ferguson speaks of "civil society" (*An Essay on the History of Civil Society*) it has essentially the same meaning as when Smith speaks of the "nation" (*An Inquiry into the Nature and Cause of the Wealth of Nations*). See Foucault, *The Birth of Biopolitics*, 297–298.

57. Although Foucault describes the object of biopolitics to be living beings or the biological processes of the population, it is important to remember that the large-scale phenomena of population are of central concern to political economy. I use the term bio-economic to retain the wide scope of the object of governmentality. Foucault at least on one occasion refers to the object of biopolitics as "biosociological" (Foucault, *Society Must Be Defended*, 250), which captures what I attempt to here.

58. Foucault, *Security, Territory, Population*, 108.

59. Foucault, *Security, Territory, Population*, 8.

60. The problem of the relation between sovereignty and governmentality is in a way left unresolved by Foucault. The reason for this is that the relation between juridical discourse and the utilitarian rationality of governmentality is always in a historically specific, strategic relation and cannot be settled once and for all (Foucault, *The Birth of Biopolitics*, 39–47). Theorists who are unsatisfied with this resolution or who attempt to chart out this specific historical relationship include Judith Butler (*Precarious Life*, 50–100), Giorgio Agamben (*Homo Sacer* and *State of Exception*), and Roberto Esposito (*Bios: Biopolitics and Philosophy*).

61. Rose, "Governing," 44.

62. *Ibid.*, 39.

63. *Ibid.*, 45.

64. *Ibid.*, 39.

65. I formulate the point this way, because even though liberalism's revolution in governing practice marks for Foucault a definitive transformation through which the biological and economic complexity of living individuals and populations becomes the business of political power, there is no doubt that many decidedly nonliberal forms of politics have nonetheless been able to operate in that space, for example, the eugenic biopolitics of National Socialist Germany with which Foucault was greatly concerned (Foucault, *Society Must Be Defended*, 258–261).

66. Foucault, *The History of Sexuality: Volume I: An Introduction*, 142.

67. Foucault, *The History of Sexuality: Volume I: An Introduction*, 142–143.

68. Foucault, *The History of Sexuality: Volume I: An Introduction*, 143.

69. Foucault, *The History of Sexuality: Volume I: An Introduction*, 137.

70. Foucault, *The History of Sexuality: Volume I: An Introduction*, 137.

71. Foucault, *The History of Sexuality: Volume I: An Introduction*, 136.

72. Foucault, *The History of Sexuality: Volume I: An Introduction*, 137.

73. Foucault, *The History of Sexuality: Volume I: An Introduction*, 137. The issue of quantity is not completely irrelevant here, because it is only when biopolitics turns the living mass of populations into the stakes of politics that total war becomes possible. In this way, biopolitics removes war from the limited function it has in early modern theories of *raison d'état* and European competitive balance. See Foucault, *Security, Territory, Population*, 285–306; Foucault, *The Birth of Biopolitics*, 51–60.

74. Foucault, *The History of Sexuality: Volume I: An Introduction*, 137.

75. Dillon and Reid, *The Liberal Way of War*, 32.
76. Foucault, *The History of Sexuality: Volume I: An Introduction*, 138.
77. Foucault, *The History of Sexuality: Volume I: An Introduction*, 138.
78. Foucault, *The History of Sexuality: Volume I: An Introduction*, 144.
79. Foucault, "The Dangerous Individual", in *Michel Foucault: Politics, Philosophy, Culture, Interviews and Other Writings 1977–1984*.
80. Foucault, *Discipline and Punish*,16–22.
81. Foucault, "The Dangerous Individual", in *Michel Foucault: Politics, Philosophy, Culture, Interviews and Other Writings 1977–1984*, 149.
82. Foucault, *Discipline and Punish*, 19.
83. Foucault, *Discipline and Punish*, 21.
84. Foucault, *Society Must Be Defended*, 246–256.
85. It is for this reason that Foucault claims that racism, not understood as mere hate or prejudice, but as a complex political technology that separates groups out from a population or the species, is the condition of killing in biopolitics. Racial technologies introduce a break into the domain of life that is under power's control between what must live and what must die (Foucault, *Society Must Be Defended*, 254–260). In this way, what racial technologies are to groups, technologies that deem individuals dangerous are to individuals, i.e., mechanisms for selecting life that is killable.
86. Foucault, *Society Must Be Defended*, 25. Placing emphasis on Foucault's claim that it is discourse that decides on life and death puts him, if not in opposition to, at least in contrast with Giorgio Agamben, who is instead interested in Carl Schmitt's definition of the sovereign as "he who decides on the state of exception." See Agamben, *Homo Sacer*, and Agamben, *State of Exception*. What I have argued for here is not becoming preoccupied with the existential decision of the sovereign (nor any administrative or bureaucratic surrogates of sovereignty), but rather focusing on the way in which forms of rationality that extend beyond any sovereign individual decide on life and death.
87. Foucault, *The Birth of Biopolitics*, 66.
88. Foucault, *The Birth of Biopolitics*, 66.
89. Foucault's list of nineteenth-century dangers includes the appearance of detective fiction and the journalistic interest in crime; campaigns around disease and hygiene; fears concerning the degeneration of the individual, family, race and species due to sexual perversion; and campaigns for savings banks (Foucault, *The Birth of Biopolitics*, 66).
90. Foucault, *The Birth of Biopolitics*, 66–67.

Chapter 13

The Remainder: Between Symbolic and Material Violence

Ann V. Murphy

Many writing at the intersection of feminism and philosophy have—at one point or another—paused to wonder about the impact that distinctly theoretical labor might have on the lives of "real" women. Indeed, one of the more ubiquitous accusations confronting feminist theorists is that their own theoretical labor occurs at a problematic remove from the trials that mark the everyday lives of women. Of course, feminist philosophers are quick to remind their critics that an interrogation of the very category "woman" is requisite on both ethical and political grounds, and that there are myriad ways in which theory is essential in thinking through what is just and unjust in the most everyday and banal of circumstances. Still, this perceived rift—between a materialist politics that seeks to redress concrete instances of violence and oppression, and an allegedly more symbolic or theoretical approach, which seeks instead to interrogate the ways in which gender norms might enact a violence different in kind from ethical violence[1]—is an abiding one.

Nonetheless, from a feminist perspective, the implied breach here is potentially dangerous. It runs the risk of playing the violence of war, abuse, or torture against the violence of misrecognition or cultural abjection. It reifies the distinction between classically Marxist approaches—which privilege material inequity—and an allegedly more cultural or symbolic approach to violence. It also runs the risk of failing to adequately think the nuances of the relation between these various types of violence. Feminists must caution against an over-emphasis on the distinction between symbolic or normative violence and concrete and material forms of injustice. When one form of violence is presented as more "real" or urgently in need of redress, feminist theorists run the risk of obscuring the violence leveled against certain groups whose own vulnerability is somehow less intelligible or culturally legible. This risk is dangerous. While some feminists prefer to work for more sweeping social agendas, others are intent to focus on the very contingent and particular arrangements of power that govern certain cultural discourses on representation and recognition. To be sure, there are times when these two approaches very happily coincide, and others when a tension persists between the two.

To theorize any form of violence is to interrogate the vacillating boundaries of legitimacy that encourage the visibility of certain manifestations of violence and the invisibility of others. Bringing theory to bear on the issues of violence ushers certain dimensions of this problem into relief that may otherwise remain veiled, among them: who counts as a victim of violence, which individuals are "real" and valuable enough within the confines of our cultural imaginary to warrant attention, and what exactly constitutes violence. Despite the obvious lack of consensus on these matters, most would acknowledge that there is a difference between the discrete violence that threatens an individual physically, and the normative violence that renders certain individuals invisible or unintelligible, such that their own vulnerability to violence is obscured. It may be the case that the degradation of certain groups is so embedded in the cultural imagery that violence against them is not even recognized as such. There are images of rape, abuse, and torture that demand our attention and that urgently solicit both political and ethical response. And there is a different violence—no less cruel or destructive—involved in rendering certain individuals invisible such that their availability to violence does not even register within the purview of this economy of visibility. These images of suffering do not appear in the media, they are not privileged objects of analysis by academics, and they do not solicit cries of outrage. One of the greatest challenges currently confronting feminist philosophers is that of bridging this gap between material instances of violence and what is referred to as symbolic or normative violence, a violence embedded in the function of norms insofar as they govern who and what appears to be real and true. This normative violence structures a world in which sympathy, care, and moral worth are differentially allocated in accord with the cultural legibility and validation of one's identity.

The theme of normative violence has been a notable touchstone of Judith Butler's work for at least two decades, though it has assumed different forms over time. While her early work expressed a more explicitly feminist interest in the sexed body and its relation to gender, her concern has recently broadened to include an interrogation of the category of the human, and of what is at stake in this designation, particularly in those instances when it is withdrawn or denied to certain individuals and groups. There is a constitutive—which is to say ontological—availability to recognition (or the lack thereof) that defines a human life. In her more recent writings, Butler theorizes this availability to violence in terms of a constitutive vulnerability that humans evince, one that cannot be willed away, one that must be attended to in the elaboration of any ethics or politics. Corporeal vulnerability—as an ontological truism—marks the fact that we are capable of being undone in both good and bad ways. While our availability to each other may be realized in a sense of communion, as often as not it is actualized in more perilous scenes, marked by struggles for recognition, and the threat of abjection and social death. This availability to misrecognition, or to the complete denial of recognition (for these are surely not the same), is born of a vulnerability that all evince in the face of those norms that govern social discourse. In this scene, norms appear as violent to precisely the degree that they constrain and exclude in their very operation. Normative violence is, thus, requisite for the emergence of identity, and so marks a scene different from that of ethical or political violence as it is thought in the traditions of existential phenomenology or critical theory. This essay queries the relationship between symbolic (or normative) violence and material violence in Butler's work. I argue against a causal or analogical understanding of this relation, and instead for the claim that normative violence and material violence are not, and could never be, perfectly adequate to each other. They are co-constitutive, but irreducible to each other. More precisely, I argue that there is a *remainder* that marks the intersection of these discourses on violence, one that belies their conceptual parsing as much as it does their conflation. The problems of capturing this mechanism in language provide some testament to the evasive nature of materiality in reference to any discourse. Descriptions of the relationship between normative and material violence tend to (however inadvertently) construe normative violence as somehow prior to the types of violence that play out concretely; indeed, there are instances when the relationship is described in almost causal terms, where the normative violence that conditions the emergence of the subject is seen to somehow condition subsequent instances of material violence. In fact, Butler's elaboration of the relationship between normative and material violence implies that this interrelation cannot be adequately rendered in a narrative of causation or priority.

Butler shares this interest in normative violence with myriad other philosophers. Indeed, the motif of normative violence is one of the more expansive and amorphous themes in recent Continental philosophy. One hallmark of recent Continental thought is its evocation of a violence at play before or beyond linguistic or material violence. This violence is rendered as "symbolic," "normative," "transcendental," and "pre-ethical"—designations that collectively signal a distance from concrete, political instances of violence. But these constellations—"normative, "transcendental," and "pre-ethical" versus "concrete," "political," and "ethical" require some justification. It would be a mistake to read the terms in the former grouping as neat synonyms; they do not refer to the same thing. Whatever interchangeability they evince is uneasy at best. Nonetheless, all of them signal a violence that is operative in the very emergence of identity and requisite for the appearance of a socially intelligible subject. It is in this sense that normative violence is transcendental in a loose sense—that is it serves as the condition for the possibility of the emergence of a world and a subject. Jacques Derrida names a kind of "pre-ethical" violence in the essay "Violence and Metaphysics;" it warrants the name "pre-ethical" to precisely the degree that it is an "original, transcendental violence, previous to every ethical choice, even supposed by ethical nonviolence."[2] Derrida sometimes calls it the violence of "phenomenality itself." Importantly, this transcendental violence does not spring from any kind of ethical resolution or from the exercise of freedom; it signals no definitive way of encountering the other. Rather, it "originally institutes" the relationship with the other.[3] On this account, transcendental violence is conceived as both a gesture of discrimination and a claim to possession, and, so, accomplishes violence along two vectors, neither of them precisely ethical. The first is a kind of possessive violence of assimilation or totalization, of which transcendental idealism and (to a degree) phenomenology stand accused given their debatable prioritization of subjectivity and interiority. Various philosophers, Foucault and Levinas, for instance, have worried that the theory of knowledge that emerged from the phenomenological tradition enacted an effacement of alterity or exteriority, as knowledge was described as an intentional grasping of the world, or the other, by the subject, a model wherein there is a kind of assimilation at play that disrespects alterity and takes insufficient account of the other's difference from the self. Alongside this violence of assimilation there is the violence of discrimination, the violence whereby norms are employed in the service of a kind of social logic that mandates the visibility of some and the invisibility of others. In classical phenomenological analyses, of course, this discrimination and this possession are one, as consciousness must isolate its object in order to grasp it. Crucially, there is no model of thought, imagination, or intersubjectivity in contemporary philosophy that does not employ one or both of these manifestations of violence, with the result that we are left on theoretical terrain that more or less forbids the thinking of relationality *without* violence. The discrimination of the other is violent, as is any kind of thinking that involves the other in analogous relation to oneself. There are few renderings of knowledge, imagination, and intersubjectivity in recent French philosophy that do not entail one (usually both) of these gestures.

Butler's work bears an ambivalent relation to phenomenology, but to the extent that she is preoccupied with the various ways in which the other appears and is recognized, her project resonates with not only the phenomenological tradition, but also its critics. In this sense, when Butler describes normative violence, she refers to a kind of violence that is akin to the pre-ethical, transcendental violence that Derrida names in "Violence and Metaphysics." To the extent that norms function as the condition for the possibility of identity, they lay claim to a sort of transcendental status. Similarly, it would appear that normative violence is "pre-ethical" to the degree that it is said to somehow precede the kind of deliberative violence which one theorizes in the context of a normative ethics. Importantly, however, the two are not the same. Indeed, Butler has recently claimed that she is reluctant to ascribe a transcendental status to the violence of norms, a fact that implies that pre-ethical violence and normative violence are not the same, however intimate their relation. If Butler does not often write of pre-ethical violence, she does claim ethical violence as a significant designation in her more recent work. And if "ethical violence" is a meaningful category of analysis for Butler, then it would seem to be the case that there are other kinds of violence for which the designation "ethical" is not apt. What, precisely, is the relation between the various registers of violence in Butler's corpus?

Butler has advanced various claims regarding the mechanism that relates normative violence to material violence in particular. The relation is one that is hard to render, in which these types of violence are co-constitutive, but irreducible to each other. This implies the existence of a remainder and a lack of adequation that frustrates any attempt to think this relation as one of causation or analogy. I argue here that there is a tendency to understand normative violence as somehow—temporally or ontologically—prior to the violence that one confronts in the material realm. To afford normative violence this priority is mistaken, as it oversimplifies the relationship between normativity and materiality. The temptation to assign a causal narrative, or a narrative that grants priority to normative, symbolic, or pre-ethical violence, is understandable, not least because it seems implicit in the very designation "*pre*-ethical," but to endow either the normative or the material with priority is to deny the symbiotic complexity of this relationship in favor of the notion that ideal or symbolic violence somehow precedes material violence. Such a gesture repeats, and is complicit in, a denigration of the corporeal and the correlative favoring of idealism that is one of the hallmarks of Western philosophy. Stated otherwise, the parsing of normative and material violence repeats the Cartesian logic that separates mind and body.

What follows is not an attempt to exhaustively diagnose the myriad instances of violence to which Butler has turned her attention, nor is it meant as a critique of Butler's elaboration of the relationship between the normative and the material, at least not in any straightforward sense. This critical genealogy of Butler's work draws modestly on both the Kantian understanding of critique and the Foucauldian understanding of genealogy. It may be read as a critique in the Kantian sense to the degree that it is an exploration of the limits of normative violence, and an interrogation of the conditions under which one can coherently speak of a distinction between normative and material violence. Where and when does this analytical parsing run up against certain limits? What are the best ways to characterize the intersections of normativity and materiality such that one does not fall back into an idealist understanding of norms that allegedly impose themselves on brute matter? Specifically in relation to Butler's corpus, how has her rendering of this relation changed over time? In line with Foucault's descriptions of genealogy—particularly in the essay "Nietzsche, Genealogy, History"—this essay is an exploration of violence in Butler's work that refrains from trying to impose a causal narrative, and opposes the search for an "original" elaboration of violence in Butler's discourse that informs all subsequent accounts.[4]

Butler's interest in the exclusionary operation of norms is pervasive, and has informed much of her work since *Gender Trouble*, where Butler argued that a naturalized understanding of gender functioned as a preemptive and violent circumscription of reality.[5] In this sense, gender norms both establish and delimit an ontological field in which gendered embodiment is granted legitimate expression. In *Gender Trouble*, a performative model of gender was introduced, with the aim of querying the various ways in which norms dictated the performance of gender in such a way that conjured the illusion of an authentic or "natural" gendered self:

"Intelligible" genders are those which in some sense institute and maintain relations of coherence and continuity among sex, gender, sexual practice, and desire.

In other words, the specters of discontinuity and incoherence, themselves thinkable only in relation to existing norms of continuity and coherence, are constantly prohibited and produced by the very laws that seek to establish causal or
expressive lines of connection among biological sex, culturally constituted genders, and the "expression" or "effect" of both the manifestation of sexual desire
and sexual practice.[6]

Of course, Butler was preoccupied with the specifically constraining and limiting function of norms in this regard. More precisely, Butler's concern lay chiefly
with the foreclosure, expulsion, and abjection of those gendered bodies deemed
illegitimate, or rendered unintelligible, through normative violence. "Constraint
is thus built into what language constitutes as the imaginable domain of
gender."[7] If norms of necessity both constrain and permit the gendered subject's appearance as intelligible, the normative violence that is gestured to in
this early model is not one with which one could break in the name of any
straightforward critique. As Butler notes, the critique would be of something
we cannot do without, something essential for the appearance and persistence
of the social self.

In this scene, the violence of gendered norms is not only attributable to the
constraint and coercion that are mandated in the name of intelligibility, but
also to the idea that this constraint itself generates the ontological realm of
appearance. It is in this way that Butler's discussion of normative violence
resonates with Derrida's conception of the pre-ethical violence of phenomenality. Crucially, then, there is no way to critique normative violence from a position of exteriority, since this violence inaugurates and circumscribes the
possibility of critique itself. For Butler, all that one can hope for in a critique of
normative violence is "a critical genealogy of its own legitimating practices."[8]
Butler takes the more aspirational dimensions of this critical genealogy seriously; if norms rely on iteration, this iteration opens them—essentially—to the
possibility of unfaithful repetition, dispersion, and displacement. If the performative model of gender refuses the idea that gender is the manifestation of
essence and, instead, suggests that gender is the temporal effect of the repetition of certain norms, Butler resists the idea that the dynamic iterability of
norms could ever be said to be determined. Indeed, the iteration of norms is
irreducible to their uncritical replication, and vulnerable to the contingencies
of circumstance. This opens normative violence to reverberations both promis-
ing and pernicious, and for this reason normative violence is not in and of itself
ethical in any straightforward sense, though it opens the question of ethics
through its circumscription of the ontological realm of appearance.

Gender Trouble was subject to criticism insofar as certain critics read the
performative model of gender as favoring either an overtly volitional or a
problematically disembodied understanding of the subject. *Bodies that Matter*
responded to these criticisms via a discussion of the relationship between social
construction and the materiality of the body.[9] Following from the performative
ontology of *Gender Trouble* is the argument that bodies become intelligible
through their sculpting by various gender norms. In *Bodies that Matter*, Butler
aimed to clarify the relationship between discourse and materiality such that

the relationship no longer appeared to be one of absolute determination. Here, Butler insists that "to claim that sexual differences are indissociable from discursive demarcations is not the same as claiming that discourse causes sexual difference."[10] Yet, while she goes to great lengths to remind her readers that social constructionism does not deny the existence of the body so much as complicate the nature of our appeal to it, one of the more ubiquitous misinterpretations of Butler's early work remains the notion that the performative model of gender advanced therein is truly an idealist, immaterial determinism. In the face of this criticism, Butler has insisted, "To claim that discourse is formative is not to claim that it originates, causes, or exhaustively composes that which it concedes; rather, it is to claim that there is no reference to a pure body which is not at the same time a further formulation of that body."[11]

Bodies that Matter turns to the explicit theorization of the "domain of unintelligibility" or the "constitutive outside" that accompanies every realization of gender. Indeed, in this work, Butler privileges the language of abjection in her descriptions of gendered performance:

> In this sense, then, the subject is constituted through the force of exclusion and abjection, one which produces a constitutive outside to the subject, an abjected outside, which is, after all, "inside" the subject as its own founding repudiation . . . This is a repudiation which creates the valence of "abjection" and its status for the subject as a threatening spectre.[12]

If the normative construction of bodies serves as a constitutive constraint—that is, as one without which gendered identity cannot appear—then whatever normative violence marks this scene is also necessary for the emergence of gender itself. On her account, such an emergence is always enabled by the abjection of others, a purging that is requisite such that certain identities are permitted their own intelligibility and liberty. Among the more ubiquitous ploys operative in this dynamic would be the way in which certain identities assume their priority with reference to "nature" and "normalcy", an assumption that cannot help but occur at the expense of those who cannot or will not attempt such an approximation. Of interest here is the way in which the discussion of normative violence in *Bodies that Matter* relies on a kind of ambiguity in the structure of abjection, as abjection—in this text—marks a prohibition that is at once ontological *and* ethical:

> This delimitation, which often is enacted as an untheorized presupposition in any act of description, marks a boundary that includes and excludes, that decides, as it were, what will and will not be the stuff of the object to which we then refer. This marking off will have some normative force and, indeed, some violence, for it can construct only through erasing; it can bound a thing only through enforcing a certain criteria, a principle of selectivity.[13]

The scene that marks the emergence of the subject is a scene of prohibition and erasure and, for this reason, is similarly a scene of violence. To call the parsing of the unintelligible and the intelligible "violent" is justified with reference to the fact that this process is necessarily one of exclusion, foreclosure, and erasure in the domains of both ontology and ethics. In *Bodies that Matter*, it seems as though this scene is inaugural, that the "crafting" power of prohibition is one that importantly precedes the instance of physical violence. But, of course, this rendering of the relation between normative violence and materiality cannot be right, since Butler is here quite explicitly linking normative violence to the fact that one "comes to matter"—that is, appears as a body—at all. If abjection marks the scene of both an ontological and ethical expulsion, it would appear that even here one couldn't speak without complication of a causal relation between these domains. There is one sense in which that which is othered is matter itself, a material remainder that is not captured in discourse; there is another sense in which what is excluded is human lives that do not for whatever reason qualify as legible or intelligible.

Hence, the mechanism that enables the intelligibility of gender is the very same that threatens some individuals (and groups) with social denigration. The mechanism of abjection, thus, opens onto an ambivalent spectrum of ethical response spanning from validation to social death. Indeed, Butler explicitly claims some of her work in *Bodies That Matter* as a "politicization of abjection," one intent on affirming queerness as a site of resignificatory political promise. This promise is born of the fact that the norms that inform the construction of gender are animated in time, a fact that opens them to destabilization.

Of interest here is Butler's elaboration of the relationship between the violence of symbolic abjection—a normative operation at the level of the symbolic—and concrete instances of hate speech, homophobic hate crimes, etc. The tropes that Butler uses to describe this relation are many, and several seem to imply a kind of priority that Butler will later reject. For instance, in *Bodies that Matter*, Butler suggests:

> If the bounding, forming, and deforming of sexed bodies is animated by a set of founding prohibitions, a set of enforced criteria of intelligibility, then we are not merely considering how bodies appear from the vantage point of a theoretical position or epistemic location at a distance from bodies themselves. On the contrary, we are asking how the criteria of intelligible sex operates to constitute a field of bodies, and how precisely we might understand specific criteria to produce the bodies that they regulate.[14]

This rendering of the process of materialization is one in which a kind of normative violence comes to *animate* and *found* the appearance of the sexed body. Tropes such as these seem to assign a kind of priority to the power or violence that operates in normativity, without which bodies would not even appear, much less be subject to physical violence. But this is crucially not to claim that normative violence is *immaterial*. Indeed, Butler's point is the opposite. If norms govern which bodies come to matter at all, it is equally the case that the norms themselves exist only in and through this process of materialization; they do not exert their influence from afar, and in the end cannot be disentangled from the material life that they legislate. The concern is how to render in language a relationship that appears to be causal, but which cannot accurately be characterized as such. In the more recent text *Undoing Gender*,[15] Butler argues that while norms may be analytically separable from normative practices of materialization, they are wily in this regard, and not easily dissociated from instances of their own realization:

> A norm operates within social practices as the implicit standard of *normalization*. Although a norm may be analytically separable from the practices in which it is embedded, it may also prove to be recalcitrant to any effort to decontextualize its operation. Norms may or may not be explicit, and when they operate as the normalizing principle in social practice, they usually remain implicit, difficult to read, discernable most clearly and dramatically in the effects that they produce.[16]

This does not assign normative violence a priority in reference to material violence so much as call into question the legitimacy of the distinction between the two. Yet it remains clear that Butler is indeed invested in thinking through what she takes to be two (at least analytically) distinct kinds of social violence. The mechanism of animation seems to imply a kind of priority, but in the end this priority is undone in the co-constitutive mechanism that binds normative and material violence:

> As a norm that appears independent of the practices that it governs, its ideality is the reinstituted effect of those very practices. This suggests not only that the relation between practices and the idealizations under which they work is contingent, but that the very idealization can be brought into question and crisis, potentially undergoing deidealization and divesture.[17]

The above passage is remarkable for its emphasis on an under-represented dimension of Butler's discussion of materialization, namely the idea that it is not simply materialization that is constrained by norms—as is evinced in the discourse on social construction—but that the ideality of norms is itself an *effect* of those very practices. Hence, it can hardly be argued that norms constrain matter, so much as the normative constraint of matter creates the illusion of the ideality of the norm in the first place. Norms are not simply a kind of ideality that organizes the sphere of appearance. Their very ideality finds its genesis in the process of materialization. This fact is enough to belie the notion that normative violence is somehow prior to material violence, since material violence claims the ideality of norms as one of its effects. A tension remains in Butler's work, however, to the degree that the claim that norms are idealized in and through their concretization does not prevent Butler from frequently implying that normative violence is somehow prior (in the sense of founding or conditioning) to material violence. For instance, in *Undoing Gender* Butler thematizes the relationship in this way:

> To be oppressed means that you already exist as a subject of some kind, you are there as a visible and oppressed other for the master subject, as a possible or potential subject, but to be unreal is something else again. To be oppressed you must first become intelligible. To find that you are fundamentally unintelligible

(indeed that the laws of culture and of language find you to be an impossibility)
is to find that you have not yet achieved access to the human, to find yourself
speaking only and always as if you were human, but with the sense that you are
not, to find your language is hollow, that no recognition is forthcoming because
the norms by which recognition takes place are not in your favor.[18]

Speaking in reference to the norm of the human, Butler draws an important
distinction between the vulnerability one suffers as a member of a despised or
abject social group, and a violence that befalls those who fail altogether to
approximate the norms of recognition, those whose humanity is unintelligible.
Importantly, there is no claim here that normative violence *motivates* material
or linguistic violence, at least not in any straightforward sense. That there are
instances of this kind of causal relation is indubitable—indeed, Butler is
invested in thinking through such instances—but this does not mean that such
a causal account can legitimately be applied to all instances of the relationship
between symbolic and material violence. Rather, what is implied is a kind of
remainder, an existence on the margins, not misrecognition, or oppression, but
a profound denial of any recognition at all.

In spite of the abiding bond between normative violence and instances of
hate speech, hate crimes, and abuse, Butler insists that the normative process
that institutes the subject cannot be causally linked in a narrow sense to subsequent instances of physical abuse or neglect. Material violence and normative
violence are not adequate to each other. This is due to a certain instability that
all norms bear as a function of their existence in time, and this instability is one
that Butler has more recently chosen to describe in terms of a contingent relationship between normativity and power. No longer engaged in a debate about
social construction, Butler has more recently moved to different theoretical
terrain.

In a recent article, Butler argues that norms are constantly breaking with the
"contexts delimited as the 'conditions of production.' "[19] This is because the
context is iterability itself, and this makes the norms vulnerable to subversion
and alteration. Butler insists that this iterated "founding" gesture is not really
foundational, and that it does not belong to a scene of inauguration, wherein
norms that preexist the subject come to play in its institution.[20] In a sense, the
notion that norms—and, hence, normative violence—found or inaugurate the
subject would be a fantasy on par with the illusive ideality of norms. Butler
claims that materialization motivates the illusion of ideality and foundation,
even as these norms are implicated in the process of materialization itself. As
they are co-implicated, but radically irreducible to each other, normative and
material violence cannot be accurately rendered in a relation of analogy, causation, or adequation. Their interplay is marked by a dynamic remainder that
resists capture, a remainder that is requisite for the intelligibility of "matter"
and "norms" as legitimate referents of discourse.

Clearly, for Butler, the temporal life of norms forbids the assignment of a
foundational or inaugural priority to normative violence. Butler further suggests

that even *if* norms themselves are founded in violence, it would not necessarily follow that the norm is doomed to itself iterate the violence of its own genesis. Butler gestures towards a productive distinction between the violence at the origin of norms, and the "normative violence" that is born out in the norm's later instantiations. Catherine Mills has recently critiqued Butler on the grounds that her recent interest in a nonviolent ethics is importantly at odds with her elaboration of the relationship between normativity and subjectivity, to the degree that violence appears as a requisite moment of subjectivation.[21] Mills's argument is that if the norms that condition the emergence of the subject are inherently, constitutively violent, then this elaboration of the subject's emergence is importantly at odds with Butler's recent interest in elaborating a nonviolent ethics. The possibility of such an ethics would be compromised by the fact that there is a transcendental, ontological violence at play in the emergence of the subject, before and beyond the considerations of ethical violence that belong within the purview of moral philosophy.

In her response to Mills, Butler insists that it is illegitimate to ascribe violence to "normativity itself," but this claim seems perplexing in relation to much of what Butler has previously had to say about the transcendental status of normative violence.[22] Curiously, in her reply to Mills, Butler distances herself from the idea that normative or symbolic violence is transcendental, and instead insists that not all operations of a norm can be justifiably viewed as violent. But Butler has previously insisted that the operation of a norm is one of normalization, and so one which of necessity constrains and excludes. She did not hesitate to call this a "violent" circumscription of reality. It may be that Butler's early discourse on normativity was grounded in a specific examination of one particular norm, namely gender, and the specific kinds of violence that are manifest in gender regulation. Perhaps the norm of gender took on a more violent life in Butler's early work. Indeed, more recently, she has been apt to describe norms—and particularly the norm of gender—as "modes of dispossession," valences of vulnerability, which ethically speaking bear a profound ambiguity. If gender is but one way in which I am available to others—capable of being undone by others in ways both good and bad—then the dispossession that characterizes normative discourse may indeed refrain from violence, may indeed find an ethical life that is virtuous and not pernicious. Ever mindful of the specter of violence that haunts the operation of norms, Butler has more recently claimed that while the threat of this violence is omnipresent, its actualization is not.

In recent work, Butler is obviously reticent to subscribe to a scenario wherein ontology itself is necessarily violent by virtue of its normative constraints. Crucially, the parsing of violence and ontology is enabled by the segregation of power and violence in Butler's most contemporary writings. Power is understood as requisite for the production of the ontological realm, but Butler claims that power is not always exercised in violent ways.[23] Butler's recent resistance to ascribing a kind of transcendental status to normative violence culminates in her claim that "I would worry about any effort to ontologize violence, by which I mean an equation of any and all sorts of being with violence."[24] Further still:

> There are, to be sure, regimes of power that produce and constrain certain ways of being. But I am not at all clear about affirming or denying a transcendental thesis that would dismiss power from the equation and make violence essential to any and all ontologies. In my view, 'ontology' is an effect of power, and power operates in part through norms (though not exclusively.) So to speak of ontological violence is foreign to my way of thinking.[25]

But since her early work, Butler has insisted that norms circumscribe ontology with requisite violence, as norms can only do their work through a kind of erasure or exclusion. For this reason, her response to Mills is somewhat perplexing, to the degree that violence has indeed seemed "essential to any and all ontologies" in much of Butler's corpus. To be sure, the violence that circumscribes the ontological domain is not the same in kind as those instances of concrete abuse or injury. Nonetheless, Butler's rendering of normative violence is one that dictates that the emergence of a world, and a subject, is essentially enabled through some mechanism of parsing, exclusion, and delineation. By the lights of her earlier arguments, Butler's recent attempt to defend the possibility of an ontology *without* violence is interesting. What this may indicate is a move from a conception of norms as inherently violent to a more modest conception of the profound ethical ambiguity that norms evince in their temporal unfolding. It is certainly the case that these two conceptions of normativity are not mutually exclusive, but Butler's recent work is provocative in its attempt to critique the limits of violence in relation to power, in contrast to her earlier work, which called for an amplification in awareness regarding the violence of gendered norms, and the cruelty they were capable of enacting.

Notes

1. "Ethical violence" is the deliberate, intentional violence that one theorizes in the context of normative ethics. It can be either psychical or physical, though for the purposes of this essay, I will be referring chiefly to material (physical) violence.
2. Derrida, "Violence and Metaphysics," 125.
3. *Ibid.*, 128.
4. Foucault. "Nietzsche, Genealogy, History."
5. Butler, *Gender Trouble.*
6. *Ibid.*, 23.
7. *Ibid.*, 13.
8. *Ibid.*, 8.
9. Butler, *Bodies That Matter.*
10. *Ibid.*, 1.
11. *Ibid.*, 10.
12. *Ibid.*, 3.
13. *Ibid.*, 11.

14. *Ibid.*, 55.
15. Butler, *Undoing Gender*.
16. *Ibid.*, 41.
17. *Ibid.*, 48.
18. *Ibid.*, 30.
19. See Butler, "Reply from Judith Butler to Mills and Jenkins."
20. *Ibid.*, 183.
21. Mills, "Normative Violence, Vulnerability, and Responsibility."
22. "Transcendental" is used here in a modest sense, to connote the status of serving as "the condition for the possibility of."
23. Here, Butler echoes Arendt, who would claim that violence is always instrumental, while the exercise of power is not. See Arendt, *On Violence*.
24. Butler, "Reply," 185.
25. Butler, "Reply," 185.

BIBLIOGRAPHY

Ackerman, Peter. and Jack DuVall. *A Force More Powerful: A Century of Non-Violent Conflict*. New York: St. Martin's Press, 2000.

Aeschylus. *The Suppliant Maidens*. In *Aeschylus II: The Suppliant Maidens and The Persians, Seven against Thebes and Prometheus Bound (The Complete Greek Tragedies)*. Edited by David Grene and Richmond Lattimore. Translated by Seth G. Benardete. Chicago and London: University of Chicago Press, 1992.

Agamben, Giorgio. *Homo Sacer*. Translated by Daniel Heller-Roazen. Stanford: University of California Press, 1998.

———. *Potentialities*. Translated by Daniel Heller-Roazen. Stanford: University of California Press, 1999.

———. *Means Without Ends: Notes on Politics*. Translated by Vincenzo Binetti and Cesare Casarino. Minneapolis: University of Minnesota Press, 2000.

———. *Remnants of Auschwitz*. Translated by Daniel Heller-Roazen. New York: Zone Books, 2002.

———. *State of Exception*. Translated by K. Attell. Chicago and London: University of Chicago Press, 2005.

Améry, Jean. "On Torture." In *At the Mind's Limits*. Bloomington: Indiana University Press, 1998.

Anthelme, Robert. *The Human Race*. Translated by Jeffrey Haight and Annie Mahler. Evanston, IL: Northwestern University Press, 1992.

Arendt, Hannah. *The Human Condition*. Chicago and London: The University of Chicago Press, 1958.

———. *On Violence*. New York: Harcourt Brace & Company, 1970.

———. "Labor, Work, Action." In *Amor Mundi: Explorations in the Faith and Thought of Hannah Arendt*. Edited by James W. Bernauer, S.J. Boston: Martinus Nijoff Publishers, 1987.

Aristotle. *Politics*. Translated by Stephen Everson. New York: Cambridge University Press, 1988.

Bales, Kevin. *Disposable People: New Slavery in the Global Economy*. Berkeley, CA: University of California Press, 2004.

Bell, David A. *The First Total War. Napoleon's Empire and the Birth of Warfare as We Know It*. Boston: Houghton Mifflin, 2007.

Benjamin, Walter. "The Task of the Translator." In *Illuminations*. New York: Harcourt, 1973.

———. "Theses on the Philosophy of History." In *Illuminations*. Translated by H. Zohn. London: Fontana, 1973.

———. "Critique of Violence." In *Walter Benjamin. Selected Writings*. Edited by M. Bullock & M. Jennings. Cambridge, MA: Harvard University Press, 1996.

———. "Critique of Violence." In *Selected Writings, Vol.1*. Cambridge: Belknap/ Howard, 1999.

Benveniste, É. "Don et échange dans le vocabulaire indo-européen." In *Problèmes de linguistique générale*. Paris: Gallimard, 1972.

Bergdahl, Lovisa."Lost in Translation: On the Untranslatable and its Ethical Implications for Religious Pluralism." Unpublished paper read at the SCPR Conference at Gordon College, Massachussets, 2008,

Berman, Paul. *Terror and Liberalism*. New York: W. W. Norton, 2003.

Bernasconi, Robert. "The Ethics of Suspicion." *Research in Phenomenology* 20 (1990): 3–18.

————. "With What Must the Philosophy of World History Begin?" *Nineteenth Century Contexts* 22 (2000): 171–201.

————. "Who Invented the Concept of Race?" In *Race*. Edited by Robert Bernasconi. Oxford: Blackwell, 2001.

————. "Kant as an Unfamiliar Source of Racism." In *Philosophers on Race*. Edited by Julie K. Ward and Tommy L. Lott. Oxford: Blackwell, 2002.

————. "Will the Real Kant Please Stand Up?" *Radical Philosophy* 117 (2003): 10–19.

————. "Who Is My Neighbor? Who Is the Other? Questioning the Generosity of Western Thought." In *Emmanuel Levinas: Critical Assessments*. Edited by Claire Katz with Lara Trout. London: Routledge, 2005.

————. "Why Do the Happy Inhabitants of Tahiti Bother to Exist at All?" In *Genocide and Human Rights*. Edited by John K. Roth. New York: Palgrave Macmillan, 2005.

Bhaba, Homi. *The Location of Culture*. London: Routledge, 1994.

Borradori, Giovanna, Jacques Derrida, and Jürgen Habermas. *Philosophy in a Time of Terror: Dialogues with Jürgen Habermas and Jacques Derrida*. Chicago: University Of Chicago Press, 2003.

Branch, Taylor. "New Directions in American Philosophy." *The New York Times Magazine* August 14, 1977.

Brehl, M., and K. Platt, K., eds. *Feindschaft*. München: Fink, 2003.

Butler, Judith. *Bodies That Matter*. New York: Routledge, 1993.

————. *Gender Trouble*. New York: Routledge, 1999.

————. "Guantanamo Limbo." *The Nation*, April 1, 2002.

————. *Undoing Gender*. New York: Routledge, 2004.

————. "Critique, Coercion, and Sacred Life in Benjamin's 'Critique of Violence.' " In *Political Theologies. Public Religions in a Post-Secular World*. Edited by Hent de Vries and Lawrence Sullivan. Bronx NY: Fordham University Press, 2006.

————. *Precarious Life: The Power of Mourning and Violence*. London: Verso 2006.

————. "Reply from Judith Butler to Mills and Jenkins." In *Differences: A Journal of Feminist Cultural Studies* 18 (2007): 180–195.

Calasso, Roberto. *Literature and the Gods*. Translated by Tim Parks. New York: Knopf, 2001.

Camus, Albert. "The Myth of Sisyphus." In *Basic Writings in Existentialism*. Edited by Gordon Marino. New York: The Modern Library, 2004.

Case, Clarence. *Non-violent Coercion: A Study in Methods of Social Pressure*. New York: Garland, 1972.

Caygill, Howard. *Levinas and the Political*. London: Routledge, 2002.

Chickering, Roger. "Total War: The Use and Abuse of a Concept." In *Anticipating Total War*. Edited by Manfred F. Boemke, Roger Chickering, and Stig Förster. Cambridge: Cambridge University Press, 1999.

Cicura, Donatien M. *Identity and Historicity: Hermeneutics of Contemporary African Marginality*. Saarbrücken, Germany: VDM Verlag, 2009.

Clark, T.J. "Letter" *London Review of Books*, Vol 29 No 24, December 13, 2007.

Clarke, Richard A. "The Wrong Debate on Terrorism." *The New York Times*, April 25, 2004.

von Clausewitz, Carl. *On War*. Translated by Michael Howard and Peter Paret. Princeton: Princeton University Press, 1984.

Cornille, Catherine. *The Im-Possibility of Interreligious Dialogue*. Chestnut Ridge, NY: Crossroad Publishing, 2008.

Critchley, Simon. *Infinitely Demanding: Ethics of Commitment, Politics of Resistance*. London and New York: Verso, 2007.

————. "Anarchic Law." *Law and Humanities* 1 (2007): 248–255.

————. "Letter." *Harpers Magazine*, May 2008: 17–20.

Dabag, M.A., A. Kapust, and B. Waldenfels, eds. "Aporien der Gewalt." In *Gewalt*. München: Fink, 2000.

Daudet, Léon. *La guerre totale*. Paris: Nouvelle Libraire Nationale, 1918.

Davidson, Arnold. "Structures and Strategies of Discourse: Remarks Towards a History of Foucault's Philosophy of Language." In *Foucault and his Interlocutors*. Edited by A. Davidson. Chicago: The University of Chicago Press, 1997.

————. "Introduction." In Michel Foucault, *Society Must Be Defended: Lectures at the Collège de France 1975–76*. Edited by Mauro Bertani and Alessandro Fontana, translated by David Macey. Harmondswoth: Allen Lane, Penguin, 2003.

Deleuze, Gilles, and Felix Guattari. *A Thousand Plateaus: Capitalism and Schizophrenia*. Minneapolis and London: University of Minneapolis Press, 1987.

Derrida, Jacques. *Of Grammatology*. Baltimore and London: Johns Hopkins University Press, 1974.

————. "Violence and Metaphysics." In *Writing and Difference*. Translated by Alan Bass. Chicago: University of Chicago Press, 1978.

————. *The Ear of the Other. Otobiography, Transference, Translation*. New York: Schoken Books, 1985.

————. "The Force of Law." *Deconstruction and the Possibility of Justice. The Cardozo Law Review* 11 (1990).

————. *The Politics of Friendship*. Translated by George Colins. London: Verso, 1997.

————. "Force of Law." In *Acts of Religion*. Edited by Gil Anidjar, translated by Mary Quaintance. New York and London: Routledge, 2002.

————. *Rogues: Two Essays on Reason*. Translated by Pascale-Anne Brault and Michael Naas. Palo Alto: Stanford University Press, 2005.

Derrida, Jacques, and Jürgen Habermas. *Philosophy in a Time of Terror: Dialogues with Jürgen Habermas and Jacques Derrida*. Edited by Giovanna Borradori. Chicago: University of Chicago Press, 2003.

Deveaux, Monique. "Feminism and Empowerment: A Critical Reading of Foucault." In *Feminist Interpretations of Michel Foucault*. Edited by Susan J. Hekman. University Park, PA: Pennsylvania State University Press, 1996.

Dickson, Peter. *Kissinger and the Meaning of History*. Cambridge: Cambridge University Press, 1978.

Dietze, Anita and Walter, eds. *Ewiger Friede? Dokumente einer deutsche Diskussion um 1800*. Munich: C.H. Beck, 1989.

Dilke, Charles Wentworth. *Greater Britain: A Reward of Travel in English-speaking Countries during 1866 and 1867*. London: Macmillan, 1869.

Dillon, Michael, and Julian Reid. *The Liberal Way of War: Killing to Make Life Live*. New York: Routledge, 2009.

Dodd, James. *Violence and Phenomenology*. New York and London: Routledge, 2009.

Ebbinghaus, Julius. *Kants Lehre vom ewigen Frieden und die Kriegsschuldfrage*. Tübingen: J.C.B. Mohr, 1929.

Esposito, Roberto. *Bios: Biopolitics and Philosophy*. Translated by Timothy Campbell. Minneapolis: University of Minnesota Press, 2008.

Fackenheim, Emil. *Quest for Past and Future: Essays in Jewish Theology*. Boston: Beacon Press, 1970.

Ferguson, Adam. *An Essay on the History of Civil Society*. Piscataway: Transaction Publishers, 1980.

Flasch, Kurt. *Die geistige Mobilmachung*. Berlin: Alexander Fest, 2000.

Flynn, Thomas. *Sartre, Foucault, and Historical Reason. A Post–Structuralist Mapping of History*. Chicago: Chicago University Press, 2005.

Fontana, Alessandro, and Mauro Bertani. "Situating the Lectures." In Michel Foucault, *Society Must Be Defended: Lectures at the Collège de France 1975–76*. Edited by Mauro Bertani and Alessandro Fontana, translated by David Macey. Harmondswoth: Allen Lane, Penguin, 2003.

Förster, Stig. "Introduction." In *Great War, Total War. Combat and Mobilization on the Western Front, 1914–1918*. Edited by Roger Chickering and Stig Förster. Cambridge: Cambridge University Press, 2005.

Foucault, Michel. "Penser au dehors." In *Critique*, No 229, June, 1966: 523–46.

———. *The History of Sexuality: Volume I: An Introduction*. Translated by Robert Hurley. London: Penguin, 1978.

———. "The Subject and Power." In H. Dreyfus and P. Rabinow, *Michel Foucault. Beyond Structuralism and Hermeneutics*. Hemel Hempstead: The Harvester Press, 1982.

———. "Nietzsche, Genealogy, History." In *The Foucault Reader*. Edited by Paul Rabinow. New York: Pantheon Books, 1984.

———. "Polemics, Politics, and Problematizations: An Interview with Michel Foucault." In *The Foucault Reader*. Edited by Paul Rabinow, translated by J. Harari. Harmondswoth: Penguin, 1984.

———. "An Historian of Culture." In *Foucault Live, Collected Interviews, 1961–1984*. Edited by Sylvere Lothinger. New York: Seniotext(e), 1989.

———. "The Dangerous Individual." In *Michel Foucault: Politics, Philosophy, Culture, Interviews and Other Writings 1977–1984*. Edited by Lawrence D. Kritzman. New York: Routledge, 1990.

———. *The History of Sexuality: Volume I: An Introduction*. Translated by Robert Hurley. New York: Vintage, 1990.

———. "On Power." In *Michel Foucault: Politics, Philosophy, Culture, Interviews and Other Writings 1977–1984*. Edited by Lawrence D. Kritzman. New York: Routledge, 1990

———. "Questions of Method." In *The Foucault Effect: Studies in Governmentality*. Edited by Graham Burchell, Colin Gordon, and Peter Miller. Chicago: The University of Chicago Press, 1991.

———. "Foucault, Michel, 1926–." In *Cambridge Companion to Foucault*. Edited by Gary Gutting, translated by Catherine Porter. Cambridge: Cambridge University Press, 1994.

———. *Discipline & Punish: The Birth of the Prison*. Translated by Alan Sheridan. New York: Vintage, 1995.

———. "The Ethics of the Concern for Self as a Practice of Freedom." In *Ethics, Subjectivity and Truth: Essential Works of Foucault 1954–1984, vol. 1*. Edited by Paul Rabinow, series editor Paul Rabinow, translated by Robert Hurley and others. New York: New Press, 1997.

———. "*Omnes et Singulatim*: Toward a Critique of Political Reason." In *Michel Foucault: Power*. Edited by James D. Faubion. New York: The New Press, 2000.

———. "The Political Technology of Individuals", in *Michel Foucault: Power*. ed. James D. Faubion. New York: The New Press, 2000.

———. "So Is It Important to Think?" In *Power: Essential Works of Foucault 1954–1984, vol. 3*. Edited by James D. Faubion, series editor Paul Rabinow, translated by Robert Hurley and others. New York: New Press, 2000.

———. "The Subject and Power." In *Michel Foucault: Power*. Edited by James D. Faubion. New York: The New Press, 2000.

———. "Foucault étudie la raison d'État." *In Dits et écrit II, 1976–1988.* Edited by D. Defert and F. Ewald. Paris: Gallimard, 2001.

———. *Society Must Be Defended: Lectures at the Collège de France 1975–1976.* Translated by David Macey. New York: Picador, 2003.

———. "Is It Useless to Revolt." In *Foucault and the Iranian Revolution.* Edited by Janet Afary and Kevin B. Anderson. Chicago and London: Chicago University Press, 2005.

———. *Security, Territory, Population: Lectures at the Collège de France 1977–1978.* Translated by Graham Burchell. New York: Palgrave, 2007.

———. *The Birth of Biopolitics: Lectures at the Collège de France 1978–1979.* Translated by Graham Burchell. New York: Palgrave, 2008.

Freud. "On Narcissism: An Introduction." In *Freud's "On Narcissism: An Introduction".* Edited by Mr. Peter Fonagy, Dr. Ethel Person M.D., and Dr. Joseph Sandler. New Haven and London: Yale University Press, 1991.

Friedrich, Carl Joachim. *Inevitable Peace.* Cambridge, MA: Harvard University Press, 1948.

Fukuyama, Francis. *The End of History and the Last Man.* New York: Penguin, 2002.

Gentz, Friedrich. "Über der ewigen Frieden." In *Ewiger Friede.* Edited by Kurt von Raumer. Freiburg: Karl Alber, 1953.

Gandhi, Mohandis K. *Non-Violent Resistance (Satyagraha).* New York: Schocken Books, 1985.

———. *Non-Violent Resistance (Satyagraha).* Edited by Bharatan Kumarappa. New York: Dover, 2001.

Geertz, Clifford. "Description: Toward and Interpretive Theory of Culture," *The Interpretation of Culture.* New York: Basic Books, 1973.

Girard, René. *Violence and the Sacred.* Baltimore: John Hopkins, 1978.

———. *Things Hidden Since the Foundation of the World.* London: Athlone, 1987.

Gordon, Colin. "Governmental Rationality: An Introduction." In *The Foucault Effect: Studies in Governmentality.* Edited by Graham Burchell, Colin Gordon, and Peter Miller. Chicago: The University of Chicago Press, 1991.

Graeber, David. "Letter." In *London Review of Books.* Vol 30 No 1, January 3, 2008.

Graubard, Stephen R. *Kissinger, Portrait of a Mind.* New York: W. W. Norton, 1973.

Habermas, Jürgen. *Theorie des kommunikativen Handelns.* Frankfurt: Suhrkamp, 1982.

———. *The Philosophical Discourse of Modernity.* Cambridge: Polity Press, 1987.

———. *Die Einbeziehung des Anderen.* Frankfurt am Main: Suhrkamp, 1996.

———. "A Conversation about God and the World." In *Religion and Rationality: Essays on Reason, God and Modernity.* Edited by Eduardo Mendieta. Oxford: Blackwell, 2000.

———. *Between Naturalism and Religion.* Cambridge: Polity Press, 2006.

———. "Religion in the Public Sphere." *The European Journal of Philosophy,* 14 (2006):1–25.

Habermas, Jürgen, and Jacques Derrida. *Philosophy in a Time of Terror: Dialogues with Jürgen Habermas and Jacques Derrida.* Edited by Giovanna Borradori, (Chicago: University of Chicago Press, 2003).

Habermas, Jürgen, and Joseph Ratzinger. *The Dialectics of Secularisation.* San Francisco: Ignatius Press, 2006.

Hanssen, Beatrice. *Critique of Violence: Between Poststructuralism and Critical Theory.* London and New York: Routledge, 2000.

Hastings, Tom. *The Lessons of Nonviolence. Theory and Practice in a World of Conflict.* Jefferson: McFarland, 2006.

Hegel, G.W.F. *Phänomenologie des Geistes.* Frankfurt: Meiner Verlag, 1952.

———. *Grundlinien der Philosophie des Rechts*. Werke 7, Frankfurt: Suhrkamp, 1970.

———. *Werke*. Frankfurt: Suhrkamp Verlag, 1970.

———. *Lectures on the Philosophy of World History*. Translated by H. B. Nisbet. Cambridge: Cambridge University Press, 1975.

———. *Die Vernunft in der Geschichte*. Edited by J. Hoffmeister. Hamburg: Felix Meiner, 1980.

———. *Vorlesungen über Naturrecht und Staatswissenschaft*. Vorlesungen 1, Hamburg: Felix Meiner, 1983.

———. *Elements of the Philosophy of Right*. Translated by H. B. Nisbet. Cambridge: Cambridge University Press, 1991.

———. *Lectures on Natural Right and Political Science*. Translated by J. Michael Stewart and Peter C. Hodgson. Berkeley: University of California Press, 1995.

Heidegger, Martin. "Ursprung des Kunstwerkes." In *Holzwege*. Frankfurt: Klostermann Verlag, 1972.

———. *Die Selbstbehauptung der deutschen Universität* (*The Self-Affirmation of the German University*). Frankfurt A.M.: V. Klostermann, 1983.

———. *Gesamtausgabe*, Bd. 65. Frankfurt: Klostermann Verlag, 1989.

———. "Spiegel-Interview (1966)." In *Gesamtausgabe*, Bd. 16. Frankfurt: Klostermann Verlag, 2000.

Hern, Jeff. "Men's Violence to Known Women: Historical, Everyday and Theoretical Constructions by Men." In *Violence and Gender Relations. Theories and Interventions*. Edited by Barbara Fawcett, Brid Featherstone, Jeff Hern, and Christine Toft. London, Thousand Oaks, New Delhi: Sage Publications, 1996.

Herodotus. *Histories*. Translated by Robin Waterfield. Oxford: Oxford University Press, 1998.

Hill, Michael. "U. S. Pays Little Heed to Philosophy." *The Baltimore Sun*, January 12, 1999.

Hirsch, A. *Recht auf Gewalt?* München: Fink, 2004.

Hoeres, Peter. *Krieg der Philosophen*. Paderborn: Ferdinand Schöningh, 2004.

Hoffheimer, Michael H. "Hegel, Race, Genocide." *Southern Journal of Philosophy* 39 (2001):37–38.

Howard, Michael. *War in European History*. Oxford: Oxford University Press, 1992.

———. *War and the Liberal Conscience*. New Brunswick: Rutgers University Press, 1994.

———. *The Invention of Peace. Reflections on War and International Order*. New Haven: Yale University Press, 2000.

Hull, Isabel V. *Absolute Destruction. Military Culture and the Practices of War in Imperial Germany*. Ithaca: Cornell University Press, 2005.

Huntington, Samuel. *The Clash of Civilisations and the Remaking of World Order*. New York: Simon and Schuster, 2003.

———. *Who are We? The Challenge to America's National Identity*. New York: Simon and Schuster, 2004.

International Justice Mission. *Fact Sheet on Forced Labor Slavery*. Washington, DC, 2010.

———. *Fact Sheet on Illegal Detention*. Washington, DC, 2010.

———. *Fact Sheet on Sex Trafficking*. Washington, DC, 2010.

———. *Fact Sheet on Sexual Violence*. Washington, DC, 2010.

International Labour Organization. "International Labour Organization." http://www.ilo.org/global (accessed May 21, 2010).

Jomini, Antoine-Henri. *Traité des grandes operations militaries*. Paris, 1811.

Jünger, Ernst. "Die totale Mobilmachung." In *Krieg und Krieger*. Berlin: Junker und Dünnkaupt, 1930.

———. "Total Mobilization." In *The Heidegger Controversy*. Translated by Joel Golb and Richard Wolin, edited by Richard Wolin. Cambridge, MA: The MIT Press, 1993.

Kant, Immanuel. "Open Letter on Fichte's *Wissenschaftslehre*." In *Kant: Philosophical Correspondence 1759–1799*. Translated by Arnulf Zweig. Chicago: University of Chicago Press, 1967.

———. "Ideen zu einer allgemeinen Geschichte." *Gesammelte Schriften*, Akademie Ausgabe VIII, Berlin: de Gruyter, 1968.

———. *Critique of Judgment*. Translated by Werner S. Pluhar. Indianapolis, IN: Hackett, 1987.

———. "Über den Gebrauch teleologischer Principien in der Philosophie." *Gesammelte Schriften*. Akademie Ausgabe VIII., 1988.

———. "Idea for a Universal History with a Cosmopolitan Purpose." In *Kant. Political Writings*. Translated H. B. Nisbet. Cambridge: Cambridge University Press, 1995.

———. *Practical Philosophy*. Translated by Mary J. Gregor. Cambridge: Cambridge University Press, 1996.

———. "On the Use of Teleological Principles in Philosophy." In *Race*. Translated by Mark Mikkelsen, edited by Robert Bernasconi. Oxford: Blackwell, 2001.

Kapust, A. *Der Krieg und der Ausfall der Sprache*. München: Fink, 2004.

Keane, John. *Violence and Democracy*. Cambridge: Cambridge University Press, 2004.

Kearney, Richard. *Strangers, Gods and Monsters*. New York: Routledge, 2003.

Kearney, Richard and Eileen Rizo-Patron (eds). *Traversing the Heart: Journeys of the Inter-Religious Imagination*. Leiden, The Netherlands: Brill Academic Publishers, 2010.

Kearney, Richard and Mark Dooley (eds). *Questioning Ethics*. London: Routledge, 1999.

Kennedy, David. *Deterrence and Crime Prevention: Reconsidering the Prospect of Sanction*. New York: Routledge, 2008.

Khan, Maulana. *The True Jihad: The Concepts of Peace, Tolerance, and Non-Violence in Islam*. New Delhi: Goodword, 2002.

King Jr., Dr. Martin Luther. "Letter from a Birmingham Jail" (April 16, 1963): http://www.africa.upenn.edu/Articles_Gen/Letter_Birmgingham.html

———. *A Testament of Hope. The Essential Writings of Martin Luther King Jr*. Edited by James Melvin Washington. San Francisco: Harper and Row, 1986.

Kissinger, Henry. *A World Restored*. Boston: Houghton Mifflin, 1957.

Kleist, Heinrich von. *Über die allmähliche Verfertigung der Gedanken beim Reden* (*On the Gradual Construction of Thoughts While Speaking*). The essay first appeared in Paul Lindau, *Nord und Süd*, 1878. An English translation by Michael Hamburger appeared in *German Life and Letters*, Vol 5 No. 1, October, 1951: 42–46.

Knox, Robert. *The Races of Men*. London: Henry Renshaw, 1850.

Kohn, Hans. "The Permanent Mission. An Essay on Russia." *The Review of Politics* 10 (1948): 285.

Kommerell, Max. "Poetry in Free Verse and the God of the Poets." In *Jean Paul*. Frankfurt: Vittorio Klostermann, 4. Aufl edition, 1966 (1933).

Kurlansky, Mark. *Nonviolence: Twenty-Five Lessons From the History of a Dangerous Idea*. New York: Random House, 2006.

Lacan, Jacques. *The Other Side of Psychoanalysis*. Translated by R. Grigg. New York: Norton, 2007.

Lefort, Claude. "The Idea of Humanity and the Project of Universal Peace." In *Writing. The Political Test*. Durham: Duke University Press, 2000.

Lemke, Thomas. "Foucault, Governmentality, and Critique." *Rethinking Marxism* 14, 3, 2002.

Lenin, V.I. *The State and Revolution.* Translated by R. Service. London: Penguin, 1992.
Levinas, Emmanuel. *Totality and Infinity.* Translated by Alphonso Lingis. Pittsburgh: Duquesne University Press, 1969.
———. *Otherwise than Being or Beyond Essence.* Translated by A. Lingis. The Hague: Nijhoff, 1974.
———. *Totalité et Infini.* The Hague: Martinus Nijhoff, 1974.
———. *Du sacré au saint.* Paris: Minuit, 1977.
———. "Paix et proximité." In *Emmanuel Levinas, Les Cahiers de La nuit surveillé,* Paris: Verdier, 1984.
———. "Philosophy and the Idea of Infinity." In *Collected Philosophical Papers.* Pittsburgh: Duquesne University Press, 1987.
———. "Useless Suffering." In *The Provocation of Levinas.* Edited by Robert Bernasconi. London: Taylor & Francis, 1988.
———.*Nine Talmudic Readings.* Translated by Annette Aronowicz. Bloomington: Indiana University Press, 1990.
———. *Basic Philosophical Writings.* Edited by A. Peperzak, S. Critchley, and R. Bernasconi. Bloomington: Indiana University Press, 1996.
———. "Peace and Proximity." In *Basic Philosophical Writings.* Translated by Peter Atterton and Simon Critchley, edited by Adriaan Peperzak, Simon Critchley, and Robert Bernasconi. Bloomington: Indiana University Press, 1996.
———. "Levy-Bruhl and Contemporary Thought." In *Entre Nous.* New York: Columbia University Press, 2000.
———. "Useless Suffering." In *Entre Nous: On Thinking-of-the-Other.* Translated by Michael B. Smith and Barbara Harshav. New York, Columbia University Press, 2000.
Lincoln, Abraham. *Lincoln on Democracy.* Edited by Mario Cuomo and Harold Holzer. New York: Harper Collins, 1990.
Locke, John. *An Essay Concerning Human Understanding.* Oxford: Clarendon Press, 1975.
———. *The Second Treatise of Government.* Indianapolis: Hackett, 1980.
Loraux, Nicole. *The Invention of Athens: The Funeral Oration in the Classical City.* Translated by Alan Sheridan. Cambridge: Harvard University Press, 1986.
———. *The Divided City.* Translated by Corinne Pache and Jeff Fort. Cambridge: MIT Press, 2006.
Louden, Robert B. *Kant's Impure Ethics.* Oxford: Oxford University Press, 2000.
Ludendorff, General Erich. *Meine Kriegserinnerungen 1914–1918.* Berlin: Ernst Fiegfried Mittler, 1919.
———. *Der totale Krieg.* Munich: Ludendorffs Verlag, 1937.
———. *My War Memories 1914–1918.* Translation. London: Hutchinson, nd.
———. *The Nation at War.* Translated by A. S. Rappoport. London: Hutchinson, n.d.
Margolis, Joseph, Armen Marsoobian, and Tom Rockmore. *The Philosophical Challenge of September 11.* London: Wiley-Blackwell, 2005.
Martin, Laurence W. *Peace Without Victory.* Port Washington, New York: Kennikat Press, 1973.
McCumber, John. *Metaphysics and Oppression.* Bloomington, Indiana; Indiana University Press, 1999.
———. *Time in the Ditch.* Evanston: Northwestern University Press, 2000.
———. *Reshaping Reason.* Bloomington, Indiana: Indiana University Press, 2005.
Mills, Catherine. "Normative Violence, Vulnerability, and Responsibility." In *Differences: A Journal of Feminist Cultural Studies* 18 (2007):133–156.
Mouffe, Chantal. *The Democratic Paradox.* London and New York: Verso, 2000.
National Broadcasting Corporation (NBC). *Today,* February 19, 1998.

Natorp, Paul. *Kant über Krieg und Frieden*. Erlangen: Verlag der Philosophischen Akademie, 1924.

Niebuhr, Gustav. "A Nation Challenged: Placing Blame; Falwell Apologizes for Saying an Angry God Allowed Attacks." *The New York Times*, September 18, 2001.

Nietzsche, Friedrich. *On the Genealogy of Morals*. Translated by Douglas Smith. Oxford: Oxford University Press, 1996.

Nussbaum, Martha. *For Love of Country*. Boston: Beacon, 2002.

Pascal, Blaise. *Pensées* in *Oeuvres Complètes*. Edited by Gilberte Pascal Périer and Louis Lafuma. Paris: Éditions du Seuil, 1980.

Plato. *Menexenus. Republic*. Translated by G.M.A. Grube. Revised by C.D.C. Reeve. New York: Hacket Publishing, 1992.

———. *Statesman*. Edited by Julia Annas and Robin Waterfield. Translated by Robin Waterfield. Cambridge: Cambridge University Press, 1995.

———. In *Plato: Gorgias, Menexenus, Protagoras*. Edited by Malcolm Schofield. Translated by Tom Griffith. Cambridge: Cambridge University Press, 2009.

Platt, K., ed. *Reden von Gewalt*. München: Fink, 2002.

Plutarch, *Plutarch's Lives, vol. 4*. Translated by Dryden, edited by A.H. Clough. New York: A.L. Burt, 1932.

Ricoeur, Paul. "Entretien Hans Küng-Paul Ricoeur: Les Religions, La violence et la Paix. Pour une Ethique Planétaire." *Sens 5* (1998):211–230.

Roosevelt, George G., trans. "Rousseau's 'Critique' of the Abbé de Saint-Pierre's Project for Perpetual Peace." In *Reading Rousseau in the Nuclear Age*. Philadelphia: Temple University Press, 1990.

Rose, Nikolas. "Governing 'Advanced' Liberal Democracies." In *Foucault and Political Reason: Liberalism, Neo-liberalism and Rationalities of Government*. Edited by Andrew Barry, Thomas Osborne, and Nikolas Rose. Chicago: The University of Chicago Press, 1996.

Rousseau, Jean-Jacques. "Jugement sur la Paix perpétuelle." In *The Political Writings vol. 1*. Edited by C. E. Vaughan. Oxford: Basil Blackwell, 1962.

de Saint-Pierre, Abbé. *Projet pour rendre la paix perpétuelle en Europe*. Paris: Fayard, 1986.

Santoni. *Sartre on Violence: Curiously Ambivalent*. University Park: Pennsylvania State University Press, 2003.

Sartre, Jean-Paul. *Being and Nothingness*. Translated by Hazel Barnes. New York: Philosophical Library, 1956.

Scheler, Max. *The Nature of Sympathy*. Trans. Peter Heath. Piscataway, New Jersey: Transaction Publishers, 2009.

Schiller, Friedrich. "Resignation." In *Werke*; vol. 1 *Gedichte 1776–1799*. Edited by Julius Petersen and Friedrich Beissner. Weimar: Hermann Böhlaus, 1943.

Schmidt, Dennis. "Can Law Survive?" *Toledo Law Review* 26 (1994),147–158.

———. "Why Do the Happy Inhabitants of Tahiti Bother to Exist at All?" In *Genocide and Human Rights*. Edited by John K. Roth. New York: Palgrave Macmillan, 2005.

———. "What We Owe the Dead." In *Heidegger and the Greeks*. Edited by Drew Hyland and John Manoussakis. Bloomington: Indiana University Press, 2006.

Schmitt, Carl. *Theory of the Partisan*. Translated by G.L. Ulmen. New York: Telos Press, 2007.

Schock, Kurt. *Unarmed Insurrections: People Power Movements in Nondemocracies*. Minneapolis: University of Minnesota Press, 2005.

Schütz, Alfred. "Der Heimkehrer." In *Gesammelte Aufsätze, vol. 2*. Den Haag, 1971.

———. "Der Fremde und der Heimkehrer. Fremdheitsfiguren bei Alfred Schütz." In *Phänomenologie und soziale Wirklichkeit*. Edited by I. Srubar and St. Vaitkus. Opladen, 2003.

Seabrook, John. "Don't Shoot: A Radical Approach to the Problem of Gang Violence." *The New Yorker*, June 22, 2009.

Sen, Amartya. *Identity and Violence*. New York: Norton, 2007.

Sharp, Gene. *The Politics of Nonviolent Action. Part One: Power and Struggle*. Boston: Porter Sargent, 1973.

Simmel, Georg. "Gesamtausgabe." *Soziologie* 11 (1989);764–71.

Smith, Adam. *An Inquiry into the Nature and Cause of the Wealth of Nations*. Chestnut Hill: Adamant Media Corporation, 2000.

Smith, General Rupert. *The Utility Force. The Art of War in the Modern World*. New York: Alfred A. Knopf, 2007.

Speier, Hans. "Ludendorff: The German Concept of Total War" in *Makers of Modern Strategy*. Edited by Edward Mead Earle. Princeton: Princeton University Press, 1944.

Stark, Evan, and Anne Flitcraft. *Women at Risk. Domestic Violence and Women's Health*. Thousand Oaks, London, New Delhi: Sage Publications, 1996.

Stein, Edith. *On the Problem of Empathy*. Trans. Waltraut Stein. Washington, DC: ICS Publications, 1989.

Steinbock, Anthony. *Phenomenology and Mysticism: The Verticality of Religious Experience*. Indianapolis: Indiana University Press, 2007.

Strachan, Hew. "Clausewitz and the Dialectics of War." In *Clausewitz in the Twenty-First Century*. Edited by Hew Strachan and Andreas Herberg-Rothe. Oxford: Oxford University Press, 2007.

Stroud, Ronald S. "Theozotides and the Athenian Orphans." *Hesperia* 40 (1971): 283–299.

Süssmilch, Johann Peter. *Die göttliche Ordnung in den Veränderungen des Menschlichen Geschlechts*. Berlin: J. Spener, 1741.

Sywotek, Jutta. *Mobilmachung für den totalen Krieg*. Opladen: Westdeutscher, 1976.

Thucydides. *The Peloponnesian War, Book II*. Edited by S. Rusten. Cambridge: Cambridge University Press, 1989.

Todd, Emmanuel. *After the Empire*. Translated by C. Jon Delogu. New York: Columbia University Press, 2003.

U.S. Bureau of Democrcy, Human Rights, and Labor. *2009 Country Reports on Human Rights Practices*. http://www.state.gov/g/drl/rls/hrrpt/2009/index.htm (accessed May 21, 2010).

U.S. Department of State. *Second Periodic Report of the United States of America to the Committee Against Torture*. http://www.state.gov/g/drl/rls/45738.htm (accessed May 21, 2010).

Vorländer, Klaus. "Kant und Wilson." In *Kant und der Gedanke des Völkerbundes*. Leipzig: Felix Meiner, 1919.

de Vries, Hent, and L.E. Sullivan. *Political Theologies, Public Religions in a Post-Secular World*. New York: Fordham University Press, 2006.

Waldenfels, Bernhard. *Topographie des Fremden*. Frankfurt am Main: Suhrkamp, 1997.

———. "Das Phänomen des Fremden und seine Spuren in der klassischen griechischen Philosophie." In *Fremdes in fremden Sprachen*. Edited by B. Jostes and J. Trabant. München: W. Fink, 2001.

———. *Verfremdung der Moderne*. Göttingen: Wallstein, 2001.

———. *Bruchlinien der Erfahrung*. Frankfurt am Main: Suhrkamp, 2002.

———. *Fenomenologia dell'estraneità*. Neapel: Vivarium, 2002.

———. "Anderswo statt Überall." In *Idiome des Denkens. Deutsch-Französische Gedankengänge II*. Frankfurt am Main: Suhrkamp, 2005.

———. *Estraniazione della modernità*. Troina: Città aperta, 2005.

———. *Grundmotive einer Phänomenologie des Fremden*. Frankfurt am Main: Suhrkamp, 2006.

———. "Violence as Violation." In *The Question of the Other*. Hong Kong and Albany: The Chinese University of Hong Kong and State University of New York Press, 2007.

Weber, Max. "Politics as Vocation." In *The Vocation Lectures: Science As a Vocation, Politics As a Vocation*. Edited by David S. Owen, Tracy B. Strong, and Rodney Livingstone. Indianapolis: Hacket Publishing Company, 2004.

Weil, Simone. "Sketch of Contemporary Social Life." In *Simone Weil Reader*. Edited by George A. Panichas. New York: Moyer Bell Limited, 1977.

Wills, Garry. *Lincoln at Gettysburg*. New York: Simon and Schuster, 1992.

———. "The Day the Enlightenment Went Out." *The New York Times*, November 4, 2004.

Wilson, Woodrow. "Address to the United States Senate, January 22, 1917." In *The New Democracy*. Edited by Ray Stannard Baker and William E. Dodd. New York: Harper and Brothers, 1926.

———. "Address Opening the Campaign for the Fourth Liberty Loan Delivered in New York City, September 27, 1918." In *War and Peace*. New York: Harper and Brother, 1927.

———. "Four-Minute Address by the President, Read by Four-Minute Men, July 4, 1918." In *War and Peace*. New York: Harper and Brother, 1927.

———. "The Four-Point Speech, July 4, 1918." In *War and Peace*. New York: Harper and Brother, 1927.

———. "Memorial Address at Arlington National Cemetery, May 30, 1917." In *War and Peace*. New York: Harper and Brother, 1927.

Young, Iris. "Five Faces of Oppression." In *Oppression, Privilege, and Resistance: Theoretical Perspectives on Racism, Sexism, and Heterosexism*. Edited by Peg O'Connor and Lisa Heldke. Columbus, Ohio: McGraw-Hill Companies, 2004.

Žižek, Slavoj. *The Sublime Object of Ideology*. London and New York: Verso, 1989.

———. *The Parallax View*. Cambridge, MA: MIT Press, 2006.

———. "Resistance is Surrender." *London Review of Books*, 15 November 2007.

———. *In Defense of Lost Causes*. London and New York: Verso, 2008.

———. *Violence*. London: Profile Books, 2008.

———. *Violence*. New York: Picador, 2008.

Contributors

Robert Bernasconi is Edwin Erle Sparks Professor of Philosophy at Pennsylvania State University. He has written numerous articles on nineteenth- and twentieth-century continental philosophy, and on the critical philosophy of race. He is author of *How to Read Sartre* (2007), *Heidegger in Question: The Art of Existing* (1993), *The Question of Language in Heidegger's History of Being* (1985), and is co-editor of works such as *The Idea of Race* (2000), *Emmanuel Levinas: Basic Philosophical Writings* (1996), and *Re-Reading Levinas* (1991).

Peg Birmingham is Professor of Philosophy at DePaul University. She teaches and writes in the areas of political thought, ethics, and feminist theory, and is particularly interested in modern and contemporary political thought, emphasizing the texts of Hobbes, Rousseau, Arendt, Heidegger, Kristeva, and Foucault. She has published in journals such as *Research in Phenomenology*, *Hypatia*, and *The Graduate Faculty Philosophy Journal* on topics that include radical evil, human rights, and the temporality of the political. She is the author of *Hannah Arendt and Human Rights* (Indiana University Press, 2006) and is currently working on a manuscript tentatively titled *A Lying World Order: Deception as a Philosophical and Political Problem*.

Jeffrey Bloechl is Associate Professor of Philosophy and Director of Psychoanalytic Studies at Boston College. He teaches and publishes in the areas of phenomenology and psychoanalysis, as well as philosophy of religion and philosophical theology. He is author of *Liturgy of the Neighbor: Emannuel Levinas and the Religion of Responsibility* (2000), founding series editor of *Levinas Studies*, an annual review (2006–), and editor of *The Face of the Other and the Trace of God: Essays on the Philosophy of Emmanuel Levinas* (2000) and *Religious Experience and the End of Metaphysics* (2003).

Simon Critchley is Chair and Professor of Philosophy at The New School for Social Research. His work explores issues pertaining to Continental philosophy, phenomenology, philosophy and literature, psychoanalysis, and the ethical and political. His recent publications include *Der Katechismus des Bürgers* (2008), *On Heidegger's Being and Time* (2008), and *The Book of Dead Philosophers* (2008).

Peter DeAngelis is a PhD candidate in Philosophy at Villanova University. He received his M.A. in Philosophy from The University of Memphis. He specializes in the history of political philosophy and contemporary political theory. His current research is on just war theory and its history, liberalism and its critics.

James Dodd is Associate Professor of Philosophy at the New School for Social Research. Current research interests include classical phenomenology, philosophy of architecture, violence, the philosophy of Schelling, and the idea of a transcendental logic in Kant and Husserl. Recent publications include *Violence and Phenomenology* (Routledge, 2009) and *Crisis and Reflection: An Essay on Husserl's Crisis of the European Sciences* (Kluwer, 2004).

Richard Kearney holds the Charles H. Seelig Chair of Philosophy at Boston College and is visiting professor at University College Dublin. The author of two novels and a volume of poetry, his most recent works include *Anatheism: Returning to God After God*, and the trilogy *Philosophy at the Limits: Strangers, Gods, and Monsters: Ideas of Otherness*; *The God Who May Be: A Hermeneutics of Religion*; and *On Stories (Thinking Action)*.

John McCumber is Professor of Germanic Languages at UCLA. His teaching and research examines elements pertaining to the German philosophical tradition, including, but not limited to, the philosophy of language, temporality, questions of social and policitical ethics, and philosophical critiques of metaphysics. He is the author and editor of numerous books, and has published more than 70 articles and reviews. His *Reshaping Reason: Toward a New Philosophy* (2005) was winner of a Choice book award, as was his *Metaphysics and Oppression: Heidegger's Challenge to Western Philosophy* (1999).

Ann V. Murphy is Assistant Professor of Philosophy at Fordham University. Her interests lie in feminist theory, twentieth-century French philosophy, phenomenology, and political philosophy. She has recently completed a book manuscript entitled *Violence and the Philosophical Imaginary* (forthcoming with SUNY Press), which examines the images of violence that mark the thinking of the body in recent Continental philosophy.

Johanna Oksala is Senior Research Fellow in the Academy of Finland research project *Philosophy and Politics in Feminist Theory* at the University of Helsinki. She teaches and writes in the areas of twentieth-century European philosophy, political philosophy, feminist theory and phenomenology. She is the author of *Foucault on Freedom* (2005), *How to Read Foucault* (2007), and has published articles in journals such as *Continental Philosophy Review, Hypatia* and *Foucault Studies*. She has recently completed a book manuscript on the relationship between violence and the political.

Paul Ricœur (1913–2005), one of the twentieth century's most distinguished philosophers, was Professor Emeritus at the University of Paris X and at the University of Chicago. Ranging between existential phenomenology and philosophical hermeneutics, his work focused on the philosophy of the will, narrative theory, action and desire, memory and time, and philosophical anthropology. Among his many landmark texts are *From Text to Action* (1991), *Memory,*

History, Forgetting (2004), the three-volume *Time and Narrative* (1984–1988), and *Living Up to Death* (2009).

Dennis J. Schmidt is Liberal Arts Professor of Philosophy, Comparative Literature, and German at Pennsylvania State University. He is author of *Between Word and Image* (forthcoming, 2011), *Lyrical and Ethical Subjects* (2005), *On Germans and Other Greeks* (2001), and *The Ubiquity of the Finite* (1989). He is co-editor of *Difficulties of Ethical Life* (2008) and *Hermeneustische Wege* (2000), translator of Ernst Bloch's *Natural Law and Human Dignity* (1988), and published a revised translation and edition of Martin Heidegger's *Being and Time* (2010).

Bernhard Waldenfels is a Professor of Philosophy at the Ruhr University, Bochum, since 1976. He has been a Visiting Professor in Paris, New York, Stony Brook, Rome, Louvain-la-Neuve, San José, Prague, Vienna, and Hong Kong. Starting from issues including bodily behaviour, lifeworld, otherness, violence, technology, place, and attention, he develops a uniquely responsive phenomenology. His publications include *Order in the Twilight* (1996), *Grundmotive einer Phänomenologie des Fremden* (2006, English translation 2010), *Schattenrisse der Moral* (2006), *The Question of the Other, Hong Kong Lectures* (2007), *Ortsverschiebungen, Zeitverschiebungen* (2009), and *Sinne und Künste im Wechselspiel* (2010).

Editors

Christopher Yates is a PhD candidate in Philosophy at Boston College and received an M.A. in Philosophy from the University of Memphis. His areas of study include phenomenology, aesthetics, and ethics. His articles have appeared in publications such as *Philosophy and Social Criticism, Foucault Studies*, and *Religion and the Arts*.

Nathan Eckstrand is a PhD candidate in Philosophy at Duquesne University. He received his M.A. in Philosophy from Boston College and his B.A. from Earlham College. His research interests include social and political philosophy, contemporary continental philosophy, and fields within applied ethics.

CPSIA information can be obtained at www.ICGtesting.com
Printed in the USA
LVOW010226181212

312140LV00005B/44/P